What People Are

Calling Al

From Competition to Connection

"Sharon Cruse has written a comprehensive book for all women that will enable them to take charge of their lives through understanding their past and releasing any pain or trauma. This book will help them embrace their power, envision a life of possibilities, and set a course for achieving their passions and dreams. Through sharing her own journey, she will engage the reader with her humor, insight, and healing wisdom. Truly a gift to women of all ages."

—Julie Fisher Cummings
philanthropist and president/cofounder of
Lovelight Foundation

"A handbook to be referred to time and again. This guide speaks to transitioning women in a forthright, respectful, and honoring tone. On a variety of topics, Sharon Cruse shares her wisdom, strength, experience, and vulnerability and provides yet another avenue for women to connect with themselves and with others. I will recommend this book highly to family, friends, and clients."

—Jane H. deBrown, psychologist

"Let the truth be known. God has given Sharon the desire, courage, and imagination to never hide her talents under a bushel."

—The Rev. Dr. Sam Satkin

"This book is a gift to all women. It weaves a thread that binds women together in the experience of life. It is compassionately written with deep wisdom. A must read."

—Sandy Egan-McNiff,
psychologist, nurse, wife, and mother

"Sharon gleans the message of hope, faith, love, energy, passion, and optimism from the stories of the women she has encountered on her journey. Releasing the power that grows from the vulnerability of women, Sharon journeys again where the brave and the scared dare to go."

—**Carol Sexton,**
psychiatrist, wife, and mother

"Years ago, I read Sharon's book *Another Chance*. It changed my life. Now, I read this book and smile and notice again that she is having a huge impact on my life. In this new book, she shows us how to face our lives with courage, enthusiasm, dignity, and knowledge. She has helped me move from Maiden to Mover and now to Mystic. She has given me and my clients many things to think about, talk about, and most important, put into action. I love her advice and wisdom. I thoroughly recommend this book to all those who want richness in their lives."

—**Lorraine Wood**, executive director
of South Pacific Private,
Australia's leading treatment center

"A delightful book of wisdom emanating from experience, introspection, and mindfulness. Sharon Cruse speaks to women of all ages celebrating the feminine spirit and journey."

—**Claudia Black**, Ph.D., consultant and author

"This is a beautiful book about the subtlety of human interaction and relationship—what we often miss in the busyness of living. It is packed with wonderful wisdom and good orderly direction from a remarkable woman who has followed her own heart and brought hope and healing to so many."

—**Tian Dayton**, Ph.D.,
consultant, therapist, and author

CALLING ALL
WOMEN
FROM COMPETITION
TO CONNECTION

ADVICE AND INSPIRATION
FOR WOMEN OF ALL AGES

Sharon Wegscheider-Cruse

Health Communications, Inc.
Deerfield Beach, Florida

www.hcibooks.com

This book is dedicated to all the women
who have shared their stories, their laughter,
their tears, their wisdom, and their courage,
strength and hope over the years.
They have enriched my life in profound
and meaningful ways. I also dedicate this book to
my soulmate, Joe, who has supported and encouraged
my friendships and connection with all
my women friends and family.

Library of Congress Cataloging-in-Publication Data
is available through the Library of Congress.

©2009 Sharon Wegscheider-Cruse

ISBN-10: 0-7573-1420-1
ISBN-13: 978-0-7573-1420-9

Publisher: Health Communications, Inc.
      3201 S.W. 15th Street
      Deerfield Beach, FL 33442–8190

Cover design by Larissa Hise Henoch
Interior design and formatting by Lawna Patterson Oldfield

Contents

v

Acknowledgments

I WANT TO THANK all the people who have helped me bring this book into existence. First of all, there are the women I have worked with over many years who have trusted me with their lives and their experiences. I honor all of them. I thank Joe for giving me time, support, and space to work on drafts, then a manuscript, and finally a galley. My reader and supportive friend Gary Seidler encouraged me to move ahead on the project. Finally, Peter Vegso continues to support my visions and my work and has been there consistently for me as I try to bring new ideas to the forefront.

I want to thank Patrick Cotter, my personal editor, who painstakingly helped me to get my manuscript into presentation form. I thank Peggy Musegades for adding the creative artwork. Allison Janse (HCI) took the manuscript and has patiently gone the journey with me and I want to thank her for her efforts and dedication to bringing this manuscript to fruition.

It takes a team to get a project—like a book—from my computer to the bookstore and I have had the best of the best on the team. Thank you everyone.

Foreword

LONG AFTER MY FORMAL SCHOOLING had ended, I encountered the term *personal growth*. Until then, I had assumed that once I reached adulthood, I was finished growing and that was that. I was immediately fascinated by the implication that growth could continue. Those two little words—personal *growth*—carried hope. There would be no more dead ends. It was now possible to stretch, to discover, to become, and to experience wider horizons and beginnings.

Despite my eagerness to explore, it was difficult to find materials and teachers to help me on my journey. At the time, both books and seminars were written by men, for men. Apparently, women were either unteachable or uninterested. I decided to ignore the lack of attention to the female sex and adapt ideas and concepts from the existing material. Although I operated in secret, I came to think of myself as a card-carrying self-help junkie.

The real work was done in my day-to-day life, but the real work is never done. There's always another path to explore. As time went on, the notion of lifelong growth took root in my mind until I simply assumed it was something that would be part of my daily life. I came to see that the rewards of such a pursuit were greater than I'd realized. Actively pursuing personal development not only adds another dimension to life, it also might prolong one's life. "People don't grow old," says Deepak Chopra. "When we stop growing, we become old."

What does it take to keep yourself growing? One prerequisite for success is a willingness to change. I recently came across an article I had written about change. In it I pointed out that change comes in two different forms, and it's necessary to tell them apart. There's imposed change, which is the kind we can do nothing about. Taxes are raised, fashion designers stop making clothes in willow green, or road construction makes us take a detour. On the other hand, there's instigated change. That's the kind that we think of as improving our lives because we have chosen it. Best of all, we can instigate change anytime we want.

Occasionally, I think about how different my life would be if I hadn't had the good fortune to encounter a mentor who gently began suggesting books that he thought I'd find helpful. These were books like the one you're holding in your hands. There's a lovely old Eastern proverb: "When the student is ready, the teacher will appear."

You're in very good hands with Sharon Wegscheider-Cruse. Like me, she has used her own life as a laboratory, and she generously shares what she has discovered. She's a student, a parent, an entrepreneur, a therapist, a teacher, and an author. All these titles fit her and have shaped her, and, fortunately for us, she's not keeping her expertise to herself.

Every journey is enhanced by a guidebook, and the journey to the self is no exception. *Calling All Women: From Competition to Connection* is utterly brilliant in its concept. This could be your life-long handbook, and I'm guessing that it will become a favorite gift for mothers, aunts, and grandmothers to pass along to the younger women in their tribe.

Use *Calling All Women* to create your own growth curriculum. Make a list of old and new adventures not yet taken. Perhaps you'll want to focus on wellness first. Next month or next year, your relationships could be at the top of the list. Maybe the time has come to start your own business. Sharon Wegscheider-Cruse has insight and wisdom to share on these topics and on many more aspects of being a woman who is determined to live the fullest and best life possible.

One word of caution is in order. Most of us think of reading a book as zooming from its beginning to its end. This one is different. *Calling All Women* invites us to calm down and take a slower journey. The book's exercises are like rest stops along the way, allowing us to pause, reflect, and apply. Take your time.

Then follow the advice of Henry David Thoreau: "A truly good book teaches me better than to read it. I must soon lay it down, and commence living on its hint. What I began by reading, I must finish by acting."

—**Barbara Winter**
Author, *Making a Living Without a Job:*
Winning Ways for Creating Work That You Love
July 2009

Introduction

Sometime in your life, you will go on a journey.
It will be the longest journey you will have
ever taken. It is the journey to find yourself.

—KATHERINE SHARP

CALLING ALL WOMEN: *From Competition to Connection* grew out of my more than thirty years of experience in sharing with countless women the ways that they have lived in the world. Women walk through life in complex ways. Jean Shinoda Bolen writes about the goddess in every woman. Her writings awaken and highlight the beauty that is part of womankind. In addition, I believe that in every woman there is a little girl, a weathered and wise old woman, a fierce mother bear, a sensual kitten, a loyal dog, a powerhouse of strength, an executive, and a survivor. Being a woman is at once complex and fulfilling.

Young women deal with the anxiety and struggles of youth. There are issues of self-image, body image, and vulnerability. Early connections with friends and boyfriends are filled with excitement, angst, and fear. There are choices to make about sex, alcohol, and drugs. There are choices to be made about education and leaving home. We live in a fast-moving culture, and tension and expectations are high.

At the same time, young women in these years are beautiful, bright, and strong. They have a chance to bring their idealism and creativity to the foreground and take the women's movement forward another notch. They are interested in ecology, government, and the movement toward global consciousness. Among young women, there is a unity of spirit.

For adult women, there is attention to careers, partnerships, marriages, and motherhood. These bring a physical and an emotional intensity that preoccupies them in young adulthood. Learning to blend life with a partner or a spouse and become connected to another family is both a challenge and an opportunity.

Young adult women often modify personal goals and dreams when choosing to become a parent. Elizabeth Stone says it well: "Making the decision to have a child—it's momentous. It is to decide forever to have your heart go walking around outside your body." During these years, it's more difficult to find unity of spirit, simply because of time and energy pressures. However, through women's groups, vacation getaways, networks, and literature, the fire continues to burn among women.

Later in life, there are womanly changes that bring about a renewal of energy for many women. When most of the child-rearing and career years are finished, there can be a resurgence of energy, passion, and creativity. Using all her learning and experience, a woman can become renewed in her connection to life. One could say she becomes increasingly passionate and maybe even an activist. She has been many places, she has had many experiences, and her wisdom is deep and caring.

There is a natural flow for women from maiden to mover to mystic. Women take this journey seriously. By the time a woman reaches her later years, she has the opportunity and the possibility of becoming the core, leader, mystic, sage, or healer in her tribe. Tribes are units of people who are bound together by experience, time, love, and compassion. Sometimes they are blood families and sometimes they are families of choice. The blood is less important than the commitment and connection between people.

Men can also become cores, leaders, mystics, sages, and healers in their tribes. They have an energy all their own. In recent years, they have gathered with one another and found their own connections. They have become more interested in other men and have become willing to connect at a deeper inner level. Traditionally, male energy has been different from female energy. Men have often used sports, business, and competition to find ways to connect. Now there are many more men who are finding other ways to connect.

Nevertheless, this book is about female energy and wisdom. This energy is about inner connections between hearts and souls. Women know the value of feeling it all and feeling with intensity and gusto. When they are sad, they cry, and sometimes, in grief, they wail. When they laugh and feel joy, they giggle and belly-laugh. When women go into one of these moments of hilarity, they are willing to share embarrassment, triumphs, defeats, and victories.

There is nothing quite as healing as fun times together, yet women do not stop there. They know how to feel compassion. It has been said that compassion is the trembling of the soul in the presence of pain. Women are able to hurt with and for others. They can expand their love to include all children, their neighbors, their pets, and their friends. They become outraged when they see suffering. It is easy for women to become activists and do what they can to end suffering.

Women know how to *be* rather than just *do*. They know that when they are feathering their nest, cooking, cleaning, and paying bills, they are meditating, in their own way. They know the value of creating and furnishing a nest in which they and those they love are able to thrive, rest, and regroup.

I spend time at a wonderful center in Arizona that teaches mindfulness. My experience is that many women are mindful naturally. Whenever women hold something in their hearts and souls and think about it, they are meditating. I keep yellow notes on my prayer table that contain the names of those for whom I want to pray. Holding their names in my consciousness is my prayer.

To be a woman is to love and then be vulnerable. If we love, and then we lose someone we love, we suffer. Perhaps suffering is the sign of how much we have loved. All of life may be a matter of choosing love or choosing indifference or fear. These decisions shape what each woman becomes.

Women have needs and wants that are different at different stages of their lives. Little girls giggle and play together. They start early, with slumber parties and sleepovers. They connect by telling secrets, fixing each other's hair, and sharing fun. Teens get together for more slumber parties, shopping trips, boy talk, never-ending laughter, and sometimes tears. Adult women connect and share with other women over lunch, shopping, careers, and social groups. The laughter continues, and so do the tears. The sharing deepens and becomes increasingly valuable.

There are travel networks like Gutsy Women, magazines like *Girlfriend Getaways*, and spa programs for mothers and daughters. All these group gatherings add to the female energy that is life producing and sustaining. Later in life, the wise women, gutsy women, sages, and mentors find ways to help one another through the stages of life.

Calling All Women: From Competition to Connection is about finding more and helpful ways to be wise and connected. Women can connect through conferences, books, workshops, and the Internet. There are many hurdles and challenges in life when we can support each other. I wrote this book because I believe that in finding one another we can eliminate the myths that women are too introspective, too emotional, too sensitive, and too controlling. My intent in writing this book is to offer women clear, concise information and directions in areas of life that are familiar to us all.

The information is short and pithy to reflect the way we live today. Most women are too busy to read long books on each of the subjects in this book. My strategy for sharing is to give short, immediate direction and then guide the reader to more in-depth work should she want to find more information, counseling, or coaching.

This book is not meant to replace counseling. It is designed to address the normal transitions and circumstances in everyone's life. It may be all that a woman needs to make choices and changes in her life. Sometimes all we need to find resolution is information and direction.

If we make those choices and changes and still need help, it becomes necessary to seek objective input from a counselor, a coach, or a workshop. Life doesn't change; we change. Once we accept that it is our responsibility and opportunity to make these choices and changes, we will be well on our way to healing, satisfaction, and happiness in our lives.

Enjoy the journey!

Additional Reading

Bolen, Jean Shinoda. *Goddesses in Everywoman: Powerful Archetypes in Women's Lives.* New York: Harper, 2004.

Girlfriend Getaways magazine, www.girlgetaways.com

part one:

PERSONAL CHALLENGES

If you want the rainbow,
you gotta put up with the rain.

—*Dolly Parton*

one

Toxic People and Situations: They Wear Me Out

Surround yourself with people who
respect you and treat you well.

—CLAUDIA BLACK

MY PARTNER MEETS WITH some men once a month to share their creative talents. When their meeting is over and the men leave, he has a special smile and hums a lot. It's clear that these men have not only had a good time with each other, they have also enriched one another's lives with laughter, ideas, and support. They are nourishing friends.

Twice a week, I tap-dance with some wonderful energetic women. We laugh, struggle with the steps, enjoy great music, and share our lives with one another. These regular connections with caring women are nourishing for my body and my soul.

My partner and I share our lives with several people and relish the honesty and support we receive from them. We know about one another's lives, and we show interest in one another's needs and pleasures. Some of these times with our friends are over special dinners, others are filled with games and challenges, and others are just heartfelt visits.

On the other hand, we sometimes have people in our lives who are toxic to us. They are like a poison; they make us feel bad. Toxic people can be neighbors, coworkers, club members, classmates, or, worst of all, family members.

When we are with them, we feel bad, and when we leave them, the bad feelings linger. Whether it's a mediocre relationship or a close family member, this kind of less than satisfying situation is like being in a gray light, and we feel gloomy or worse. If the person is someone we do not have to be with, the solution is easy: separate and "detox" from him or her.

There have been a few such people in my life. One was a know-it-all in a class I attended. She always knew more and had experienced more, and she let everyone know it. Being around her aroused great feelings of inadequacy in me.

Another toxic person was in a social group to which I belonged. She had a rigid and demeaning attitude about both politics and religion. It was as though she had the right and only religion, the right and only politics, and the right and only way to think and believe. Being around her was difficult and tense.

Another toxic relationship I have experienced was a woman who had a bad relationship with her partner. She complained continuously. Our times together were primarily spent with her complaining about her relationship. Being around her was emotionally draining.

All these relationships were ones I could end, and I did. The relief that came with ending them and the energy that came back into my life was worth the difficulty of ending the relationship.

A more difficult situation occurs when the toxic relationship is with our past and our family. It would seem that we should always be connected to family, but that is an erroneous belief, and it has caused immense pain for some people. Our outworn and negative beliefs about family and past events or decisions can keep us from seeing ourselves in a brighter light. Our past can keep us in a prison if we let it. It's time to move on if you can see clearly and have a different vision for yourself. Just because you've been committed and devoted to your past doesn't mean that you have to continue being so if it is no longer good for you.

It might just be the time to step out of the gloom and shadows and find new situations and people to connect with in your life. Many years ago I felt trapped in some tough situations. When I changed my lifestyle completely in the 1970s, I was afraid that I would be isolated and lonely for the rest of my life. It was a sincere fear. Now, looking back, I am astonished by how many doors opened and how many people were out there waiting for me to connect with them.

Marilyn Ferguson, author of *The Aquarian Conspiracy*, says it this way:

> Our past is not our potential. In any hour with all the stubborn teachers and healers of history who called us to be our best selves, we can liberate the future. One by one, we can re-choose to awaken. To leave the prison of our conditioning, to love, to turn homeward. To conspire with and for one another. Awakening brings its own assignments, unique to each of us, chosen by each of us.

It is so easy to think that we always have to have the same friends, work at the same job, live in the same town or city, have the same hobbies, maintain the same interests, and keep the same connections, including all family relationships. The time has come to pay attention, evaluate, and eliminate. There are no prizes given out at the end of life for staying in toxic situations with toxic people. Think about it!

In his book *Actualizations*, Stewart Emery tells us about seeking out healthy relationships. He says the following:

In all my relationships, I consciously select people to relate to who will bring that part out in me, or support, encourage, inspire or awaken within me that part of me that needs to come out. . . . I choose to be with people who have a reality of abundance. I won't hang out with people who have a reality of scarcity. I won't hang out with people who have negative energy.

Facing and dealing with toxic people and situations is one of the most challenging tasks we have to deal with. Yet it is also one of the most freeing and healthy behavior changes we can make.

Additional Reading

Ackerman, Robert J., and Susan E. Pickering. *Before It's Too Late: Helping Women in Controlling or Abusive Relationships*. Deerfield Beach, FL: HCI, 1994.

Carnes, Patrick J. *The Betrayal Bond: Breaking Free of Exploitive Relationships*. Deerfield Beach, FL: HCI, 1997.

Emery, Stewart. *Actualizations: You Don't Have to Rehearse to Be Yourself*. New York: Doubleday, 1978.

Ferguson, Marilyn. *The Aquarian Conspiracy: Personal and Social Transformation in Our Time*. New York: J. P. Tarcher, 1987.

Lerner, Rokelle. *Living in the Comfort Zone: The Gift of Boundaries in Relationships*. Deerfield Beach, FL: HCI, 1995.

Miller, Joy. *Addictive Relationships: Reclaiming Your Boundaries*. Deerfield Beach, FL: HCI, 1989.

Palatnik, Lori, with Bob Burg. *Gossip: Ten Pathways to Eliminate It from Your Life and Transform Your Soul*. Deerfield Beach, FL: Simcha Press, 2002.

Whitfield, Charles L. *Boundaries and Relationships: Knowing, Protecting, and Enjoying the Self*. Deerfield Beach, FL: HCI, 1994.

two

I Feel Stuck:
How Do I Make a Decision?

I cannot expect my decisions to provide all the answers—
I only hope to keep asking the right questions.

—STELLA PERLMAN

MY PERSONAL STORY INCLUDES times in my life when I felt really stuck and powerless. The feelings of being overwhelmed and confused were overpowering. Indecision had paralyzed me.

One of my great teachers said to me that confusion is simply the result of not making choices. She urged me to make a decision. Any decision is better than no decision, she said.

Once a decision is made and things become clearer, celebrate that fact. If the decision is a bad one and things get worse, make another decision. My teacher's point was that indecision leads to further problems. Decisions are clarifying whether they are good ones or bad ones. If you don't like the result of one decision, keep making new decisions. It's important to take action.

Decisions provide answers.

Of course, I countered, saying, "That's hard to do when you are making big decisions." She acknowledged that this is true. However, even a big decision can be remedied if we make the wrong one. Very few decisions cannot be changed when we have more information and want to make a new decision.

We long for personal freedom and the right to make decisions. There are two forms of freedom in making choices: the freedom to leave something and the freedom to go after something. Both involve decision making.

When we start the decision-making process, we are usually choosing between something we do not want and something we do want. That's a decision between something bad and something good. This is the clearest and easiest type of decision we can make. If we make that decision and it turns out to be good, we are satisfied.

Then comes another phase of decision making: things are good, and we have the chance for something better. So now we have to choose between good and better. That is a little more difficult.

To get the best in life, we often have to give up some of our better parts. When we do, our life is the best. At this point, much to our surprise, some of the hardest kinds of decisions have to be made: choosing between better and the best.

Even if all our decisions are between better and the best, we nevertheless have limited time, resources, and energy. We cannot have everything for all time. We must learn to choose between the best and the best.

Workshop facilitator Mark Bryan asks this important question: "Tell me, what is it you plan to do with your one precious life?" In other words:

Who do you want to be?
What do you want to have in your life?

What do you plan to dream, to invent, and to enjoy?

Whom do you want in your life?

Where do you want to go in your life?

What do you want to make happen?

We all have the same amount of time. We get twenty-four hours each day, sixty minutes each hour, and sixty seconds each minute. For some it's not enough time; for others, it's way too much time. If we live to be seventy years old and sleep eight hours a night, we will have slept about twenty-three years. I never have enough time to read, enough time to hike, and enough time to study and learn. I do not see my family enough and I do not have all the time I want to see my friends. I could use a thirty-six-hour day. Yet all my daily choices must fit into twenty-four hours.

Whom I want in my life is another important decision I have to make. We have read about toxic people and toxic situations. It's difficult but necessary to clear one's life of toxic people and situations. We can't afford to let these people and situations drain us of our energy and serenity as we make our decisions.

Then there are ethical and moral dilemmas that require decisions. Sometimes, when I am so sure of the "right" thing to do, I encounter a situation that demands that I consider a shade of gray. The value that has shaped my ethics is challenged and has to be rethought. This is not a promotion of situational ethics, per se, but rather a plea for understanding all aspects of a situation before judging.

We must remember that we have ownership of ourselves from the day we are born. We have the right to share ourselves and our lives with only those whom we—and only we—choose. The musician Loudon Wainwright tells us the following:

Perhaps the best reason for having a calendar and for marking life in years is that the cycle itself offers hope. We need fresh starts and new chances, the conviction that beginnings remain available, no matter how many we have blown.

Here are five things to consider in making decisions:

1. *Try new behaviors.* Follow a hunch, take a class, take a trip, and eliminate nonessentials.
2. *Expose yourself to different people and different situations.* Learn from those differences. If you step out of your comfort zone, you just might find a whole new world out there.
3. *Be kind to yourself.* Put little stickers around your house that say the following:
   • I can make new decisions.
   • I can try new things.
   • I can take a class.
   • I can meet new people and make new friends.
   • I can learn, decide, and make changes.
4. *Make one decision at a time and work on it.* Leonardo da Vinci was one of the most creative and prolific masters of all times. He accomplished much of what he did because he focused completely on one thing at a time. That sort of discipline comes with practice and determination, and it's worth all the energy it takes to master it.
5. *Start.* Now.

It may seem easier and less risky to cling to the familiar patterns of old habits and interests, but without change and new decisions, you run a greater risk of missing the chance to become the person you would like to be.

There are people who resist decisions. They are resistant to change and avoid the possibility of vulnerability. They mask their fear by calling it boredom. They remain insulated from the richness of life. They miss a great deal. They are similar to, but not the same as, avoiders.

Avoiders have lots of thoughts about plans and ideas. They just simply do not get started. Perfectionism is a big part of avoidance, and it is a form of self-abuse. Perfectionism is measuring ourselves by some standard that has been set outside ourselves. It keeps us from trying something new; it frustrates us and keeps us from our creativity and our self-confidence. Perfectionism is a waste of time and effort.

Then there are the decision makers. These people sincerely want to grow personally and connect with others to find satisfaction, meaning, and happiness in life. They make decisions and do the following:

1. Try to learn new behaviors
2. Reexamine their lives
3. Leave behind toxic people, behaviors, habits, and attitudes
4. Take up new hobbies
5. Take some risks

When we have learned enough and hurt enough to know that we can't go back to the way things were, we are ready for some decision making. With that realization, we are likely to find our own inner wisdom. Then we can make the decisions, the choices, and the changes that will alter and improve our lives.

Additional Reading

Gregory, Danny. *The Creative License: Giving Yourself Permission to Be the Artist You Truly Are.* New York: Hyperion Books, 2005.

Moore, Thomas. *A Life at Work: The Joy of Discovering What You Were Born to Do.* New York: Broadway Books, 2009.

Pink, Daniel H. *A Whole New Mind: Why Right-Brainers Will Rule the Future.* New York: Riverhead Books, 2006.

Thomas, Marlo. *The Right Words at the Right Times.* New York: Atria Books, 2004.

Woods, John. *Leaving Microsoft to Change the World: An Entrepreneur's Odyssey to Educate the World's Childen.* New York: HarperCollins, 2007.

three

Regrets: What Do I Do with Them?

> *It is difficult to experience pleasure from reminiscing about things you haven't done.*
>
> —Ernie J. Zelinski

BEING OVERLY CAUTIOUS CAN lock you out of the richness and excitement of life. Can any of us forget the Cowardly Lion from *The Wizard of Oz*? For many years of my life, I was very shy and quiet. Growing up in a small town and lacking sophisticated experiences contributed to my holding back and feeling afraid a great deal of the time.

I guarded my heart and my feelings from hurt and embarrassment by limiting the number of risks I was willing to take, and I stayed in my own comfort zone. It felt safe, but it also felt lonely and self-defeating. When you lock people and adventure out, you lock yourself in.

Is it bad to be extremely cautious? That's a question we all have to answer for ourselves. It's not a pleasant thought to end up in life saying "I coulda, woulda, shoulda" had more fun, risked myself in love, taken that trip, changed that job, continued that hobby, bought that house, invested in that stock, or taken more time to smell the roses.

Sometimes our excessive cautiousness starts in childhood, when we find ourselves afraid to have a voice in our family. Strong and demanding parents have the ability to stifle the emerging and developing voice of a child by having too many rules, too many expectations, and no room for a difference of opinion or interest. Losing one's voice as a child is an early regret for someone who grew up in this kind of home. Many of my clients say, "I wish I could have stood up for myself. I regret that I wasn't strong enough to stand up for myself."

Regrets of the teen years may include too many parties and too little studying, or too much studying and not enough fun. There can also be some big regrets: early meaningless sex and sometimes a pregnancy or an abortion, or lots of experimentation with alcohol, drugs, and cigarettes. Some of these regrets can make us feel as if our teen years were wasted years.

In my work with families, there have also been many regrets from teens and young adults who felt a need for early achievement. They put such expectations on themselves that they stressed themselves out through both high school and college. They missed out on learning the rudiments of relationships and a balanced life.

The next series of regrets has to do with decisions that are made in early adulthood. Some women have focused on their careers, lost out on meaningful relationships, and let the clock run out for having children. All of a sudden their forties are here, there is no one special in their lives, and it's too late to have children. This kind of regret is permanent.

Other women have chosen early marriage and children. During the exciting time of engagement showers, the wedding, baby showers, and children, it's all wonderful. Then the reality of these responsibilities sets in. All of a sudden there are credit card bills, children with many needs, and responsibilities that weren't anticipated, and life begins to take a toll. There are few choices, and these young adults are strapped for money, energy, and a feeling of freedom. They are definitely at risk for having regrets.

Finally, there are the regrets that come later in life. Perhaps a woman has chosen a career that now isn't what she thought it would be, or she is in a marriage that isn't working, or money is tight, or disappointment occurs with her family and/or her children.

Sometimes people make life choices based on comfort, security, and fear. Options are seen as overwhelming and scary. Life, situations, and people cannot be controlled, and the sooner we recognize that there will always be some risk, change, and lack of security, the sooner we can give up our regrets for choosing to stay stuck.

Regardless of our age and time in life, it's possible to use our regrets to go forward. As people get older, they take into account the amount of time there is in life. Early regrets can be lessons that help us in adulthood. Adult regrets can help us later in life. We can adjust our goals and desires to make choices that will help us to find satisfaction and happiness. We can choose to use our regrets to propel us forward at any age.

It's important for us to realize that we do the best we can at any given time, given our experience and awareness. We can choose to change at any time. One of my dear friends spent many years following a career that his father wanted for him. By the time he was in his late forties, his marriage was crumbling, his children were in trouble, and he hated his job. When he assessed where he was, he realized that he could not go on with this life that he hadn't chosen for himself. He shared his raw feelings with his wife and his children and let them know that he would be there for them in the ways that mattered, but he was changing his career and they would all be affected.

There were many tough times, but his wife supported him. His children watched and learned and saw his determination to be true to himself. What they missed in material goods, they made up in learning how important passion is in life. Today, this man is doing work that satisfies him, he and his wife are a team in every sense of the word, and his children are pursuing their dreams.

Regret, at some level, is part of everyone's life. It is universal; it spans age and culture. For every choice we make, a number of options are left untried, each one an opportunity that offers different results. Those who study regrets say that there are six major areas of regrets that occur for people, and all are painful. They are as follows:

1. *Relationships:* marrying the wrong person or choosing the wrong partner; involvement in affairs; marriages that didn't work.
2. *Education:* not going to college or pursuing an advanced degree that would have opened more doors.
3. *Career:* choosing the wrong career altogether; not having the courage to leave an unfulfilling career.
4. *Family:* not wanting children until it's too late; sacrificing personal goals to take care of children; estrangement from parents and siblings.
5. *Self:* struggling with eating disorders, addictions, or workaholism; the depression that comes from realizing how much of one's life has been robbed by these problems. These are regrets that require professional care.
6. *Finances:* credit card debt and living way beyond one's means; workaholism that divides families; materialism that is found to be empty in the long run; children who have no concept of financial responsibility; having money yet producing children with a sense of entitlement and no financial wisdom.

Letting go of regrets is a process, not a one-time event. "Make the most out of your regrets," said Henry David Thoreau. "To regret deeply is to live afresh." One of the primary tasks of people between the ages of forty and sixty-five is to go through the process of looking at the past and reevaluating their lives. Dwelling on past mistakes or missed possibilities can detract from the present. Yet if we can make new decisions and behavior changes, we can minimize the power of regret. Regret is useful as a signal that it's time to make changes. It's a major part of healthy living and an indicator that our better selves are truly doing their best to guide us.

The young are more likely to regret things they did rather than things they missed. Older people are more inclined to regret things they haven't done. What is important is that we use regret to stir our current emotions, clarify our wants, and catapult us forward to make the necessary changes in our lives in ways that are satisfying and fulfilling.

I regretted not going to college after high school, and it pushed me to complete nine years of college later in life. I regretted an early marriage that was a painful relationship, so I left that marriage, even though it was very difficult to do so. Later I found my true partner and have had twenty-five years of joy and happiness in a meaningful relationship. Another regret was working for a company that was sexist and did not support my contributions. I left that job and started my own company, which became a very successful enterprise.

Not being with my children enough during my years of schooling and heavy workload was a major regret, so I made the decision to be with my grandchildren as much as possible and have done so. Traveling around the world in my later years has healed my regret of not having traveled in my earlier years. In many areas of my life, regret has been my friend, because it has helped me to make new decisions that have been good for me and have helped others. Having loosened my grip on the past, I became free to reach for the future.

Additional Reading

Gilbert, Elizabeth. *Eat, Pray, Love: One Woman's Search for Everything Across Italy, India, and Indonesia.* New York: Penguin, 2007.

James, John W., and Russell Friedman. *The Grief Recovery Handbook: The Action Program for Moving Beyond Death, Divorce and Other Losses.* New York: HarperCollins, 1998.

Sheehy, Gail. *New Passages. Mapping Your Life Across Time.* New York: Ballantine Books, 1996.

Wholey, Dennis. *Why Do I Keep Doing That? Breaking the Negative Patterns in Your Life.* Deerfield Beach, FL: HCI, 2007.

four

Middle Age:
Why Is It So Scary?

There are years that ask questions, and years that answer.

—Zora Neale Hurston

What exactly is middle age? Is it the end of all beginnings, the beginning of the end, or a moving target? Experts tell us that the average life span is seventy-seven years old. Some people will live longer, and some will die sooner.

Middle age is currently defined by the baby boomers, the generation that was born between 1946 and 1964. However, middle age is more a mind-set than a number. It's mostly a time when you begin to reexamine where you are, where you've been, and where you are going, says Gene Cohen, author of *The Mature Mind*. A simpler—and more amusing—way of defining middle age is that it's ten years older than whatever age you are now.

Part of the joy and satisfaction in life is coming to terms with who you have become. You may not be a movie star, an astronaut, or a dot-com billionaire, but you can find a way to live happily ever after with whatever you have become. One of the joys of youth is knowing that there is always a great deal more time. What happens, however, is that those chances become fewer and many of the things you hope to achieve might not happen.

Marsha M. Linehan, professor of psychology at the University of Washington in Seattle, offers us a way to look at our lives. She suggests that we learn from Buddhism a bit of radical acceptance. The term refers to a willingness to recognize and tolerate what is, rather than fighting it or judging it. It's a way to free ourselves from wanting something that we can't or won't have. It's a way of freeing ourselves to just be.

Maybe you wanted more financial freedom, yet you need to live frugally. Maybe you wanted children, but your childbearing years are gone. Maybe you wanted to be a dancer but became a nurse. How do you live with that kind of disappointment? Linehan suggests that life is a series of situations in which we don't always get what we want. There are really only five ways to look at solving a problem. They are as follows:

1. Solve the situation or problem, or leave it.
2. Change how you feel about the problem (reevaluate).
3. Radically accept the situation and live with the unhappiness. (Do not deny the pain, but rather accept it.)
4. Stay miserable.
5. Make the problem worse by focusing on it.

It's all a choice.

As we progress through our changes, there are many responses. Some people welcome change and some have a difficult time. The book *Who Moved My Cheese?* by Spencer Johnson is a testimony about either resisting change or embracing change. The fortunate people are those who can embrace change, because change is going to be part of everyone's life. Trying to avoid change is a surefire way to increase stress and discomfort.

Everyone ages in his or her own way, and this process starts the minute we are born. Nothing remains the same; every day of our lives, we are one day older. How we accept reality and live with it will determine many things about our health, energy, joy, decisions, and friendships.

One of the first challenges we deal with in life is going off to pre-school or kindergarten the first day. Some kids can't wait; they see all the excitement of going to school and making friends. Others hold back, cry, and hang onto their parents. By this age, there is already a tendency to be either an explorer or a resister. This choice is dependent on many events leading up to that first day of kindergarten.

In a family in which there are many different kinds of experiences, a child has already learned that newness can be exciting and bring rewards. There is a history of trust that has been built and a confidence that change will be a positive experience. In a family in which there is isolation or a level of wariness and fear, a child will be afraid to try new things, and going off to day care or school for the first time will be the first of many traumatic experiences.

Twelve Secrets to Being a Successful Baby Boomer

1. Ignore nonessential numbers like age and weight.
2. Keep only cheerful friends.
3. Keep learning: the computer, languages, sports, and anything else that interests you.
4. Find each day's gift.
5. Travel. Learn differences firsthand.
6. Accept that loss will occur. Cry and move on. Be alive while you are alive.
7. Surround yourself with everything you love, like family, pets, and music.

8. Cherish and protect your health.
9. Avoid guilt, shame, rage, and blame.
10. Tell the people you love that you love them as often as possible.
11. Stay active physically.
12. Learn and practice ways to reduce stress: yoga, dance, sports.

Once patterns are established, it's easy to fit all other experiences into this early conditioning. Some children become explorers and others become resisters. These patterns remain all through life unless they are recognized and challenged. As each milestone in the aging process presents itself, there will be resistance and discomfort.

On the other hand, some people become sages. A sage is a person who uses all of life's experiences to learn lessons and think in bigger and fuller terms. Almost every situation in life gives us an opportunity to learn one of life's lessons. A sage welcomes new opinions, learns new skills, and finds new hobbies and interests.

What happens when all of a sudden you look in the mirror and you look different: older, maybe heavier? You really are not sure who that is looking back. The book you planned to write, the trip to Tuscany you hoped to take, and the family you thought you would have by this time have not materialized. What happened, and what is happening?

Where did all your plans and ambition go? What can be done about this crisis? The best way to deal with this situation is through a "think tank": bring together some other women who might be asking the same questions. It makes for a thoughtful evening.

Invite several of your girlfriends. Pick some who work, some who are stay-at-home mothers, some who travel, and some who are nesters. Make sure the group is varied. Pour some glasses of wine, offer cheese and crackers, and discuss the following:

1. When you were graduating from high school, what did you think your future would look like? Is any of it close to where you are today?
2. Who gave you your best piece of advice when you graduated?
3. What was your biggest failure the first ten years after high school?
4. When did you start to feel financially on your own?
5. What was the biggest financial mistake you have ever made?
6. What are some of the biggest surprises you have had?
7. Share the best and worst things about being a woman.
8. What dream have you accomplished?
9. What dream do you still have?
10. Can you still chase that dream, and how?

In the book *The Success Principles*, Jack Canfield says that venture capitalists rarely invest in business start-ups, because so many of them fail. There is one exception: if the entrepreneur is fifty-five or older, the business's odds of success skyrocket. Canfield explains why:

> These older entrepreneurs have already learned from their mistakes. They're simply a better risk because through a lifetime of learning from their failures, they have developed a knowledge base, a skill set, and a self-confidence that better enables them to move through the obstacles to success.

It's quite possible that all of us have a little dream left in us.

There are advantages to being a seasoned and mature woman. My friend and mentor, the late Virginia Satir, a well-known family therapist, called mature women *juicy*. She said mature women can be sweet, tart, sparkling, mellow, playful, assured, scared, interested, interesting, sexy, competent, hesitant, and resourceful. A woman can be all those at different times of her life and at different times of the day.

A mature woman knows who she is, what she wants, and that it's up to her to get her needs met all through her life. She is less likely to lean on a man in her life to meet her needs. Because she is so independent, she brings a great deal to a man who is lucky enough to be in her life. It's a give-and-take relationship.

Women become "juicy" through time and experience. As the boomers mature, there is a new universe of passionate, accomplished, liberated women, both married and single. They are unwilling to settle for stereotypes of middle age and aging. They are open to learning new skills, traveling through the world, exploring their own spirituality, and celebrating who they are becoming. If married, they bring this energy to their mates; if mothers, they bring this energy to their children.

Five Tips for Active Aging

1. Be flexible in mind and body, learn to adapt to losses, and let go of thoughts and behaviors that no longer fit this time of life.
2. Get regular physical activity.
3. Discover all the benefits that come with growing older.
4. Use this time of life for spiritual renewal and growth.
5. Keep an ongoing record of the lessons that you learn and the wisdom you gain; share this with others.

Unless you are trying to do something beyond your boundaries and routine, you will not grow; rather, you will regress. Some people are very old at fifty, and others are very young at seventy-five. Negativity and passivity lead to depression, which leads to illness, and that leads to more negativity and passivity, in a vicious circle. The late comedian George Burns reminded us that you can't help getting older, but you don't have to get old.

Some great role models for growing older are the following:

1. Tiger Woods, who just keeps getting better and better at golf, the older he gets.
2. Ron Howard, who became a great movie director after being a child star on *The Andy Griffith Show*.
3. Lillian Carter, the mother of President Jimmy Carter, who joined the Peace Corps at age sixty-eight.
4. Mother Teresa, who won the Nobel Peace Prize at age sixty-nine for a lifetime of humanitarian work.
5. Helen Keller, blind and deaf from the age of nineteen months, who learned sign language and became a world-famous speaker, author, political activist, and advocate for people with disabilities.
6. Dick Clark, who hosted *American Bandstand* for thirty years
7. John Glenn, who at age forty became the first American to orbit Earth.
8. Ray Kroc, who at age fifty-two bought a hamburger stand and started McDonald's.
9. Walt Disney, who, after a long and successful career in animation, opened Disney World at age fifty-four.
10. Alex Haley, who at age fifty-six wrote *Roots*.
11. George Handel, whose most successful musical composition, *Messiah*, was written in twenty-four days and premiered when he was fifty-seven years old.
12. Betty Ford, who, after her own recovery from drug and alcohol addiction, founded the Betty Ford Center at age sixty-four.
13. Nelson Mandela, the anti-apartheid activist who, after being imprisoned for twenty-seven years and released at age seventy-two, became president of South Africa four years later.

14. Ruth Gordon, a successful actress *(Rosemary's Baby, Harold and Maude)*, screenwriter, and playwright who continued to work until she was ninety-one years old.
15. Jessica Tandy, another successful actress, who won her first Academy Award (for *Driving Miss Daisy*) at age eighty.
16. Benjamin Spock, the pediatrician whose revolutionary ideas about child rearing empowered mothers and focused on children's needs, who in his sixties became politically active, was arrested for his antiwar activities, and ran for president as the People's Party candidate with a platform that called for free medical care.

Six Essentials for Happy Middle and Older Age

1. Good health
2. Enough money
3. Friendship
4. Beautiful surroundings
5. Continued activity
6. Purpose

Maya Angelou was recently interviewed on her seventy-something birthday. She is a fascinating and interesting woman. She was asked what she thought of growing older, and she shared what she had learned in her seventy-plus years. She replied, "No matter what happens or how bad it seems today, life goes on and it will be a better day tomorrow."

Angelou noted that you can tell a lot about a person by the way that he or she handles three things: a rainy day, lost luggage, and tangled Christmas tree lights. She said that she has learned that regardless of your relationship with your parents, you will miss them when they are gone from your life. The audience cheered when she stated, "Making a living is different from making a life."

Angelou's final bit of wisdom was this: "I've learned that people will forget what you said, people will forget what you did, but people will never forget how you made them feel."

Additional Reading

Canfield, Jack, with Janet Switzer. *The Success Principles: How to Get from Where You Are to Where You Want to Be.* New York: HarperCollins, 2006.

Cohen, Gene. *The Mature Mind: The Positive Power of the Aging Brain.* New York: Basic Books, 2006.

Covey, Stephen R. *The 7 Habits of Highly Effective People: Powerful Lessons in Personal Change.* New York: Free Press, 1994.

Johnson, Spencer. *Who Moved My Cheese? An Amazing Way to Deal with Change in Your Work and in Your Life.* New York: G. P. Putnam's Sons, 1998.

Kabat-Zinn, Jon. *Full Catastrophe Living: Using the Wisdom of Your Body and Mind to Face Stress, Pain, and Illness.* New York: Delta, 1990.

Weil, Andrew. *Healthy Aging: A Lifelong Guide to Your Well-Being.* New York: Anchor Books, 2007.

five

I Feel Defeated, as If I'm Hitting My Head on a Brick Wall—Now What?

Brick walls are not there to keep you out, but rather to show you how much you want something.

—RANDY PAUSCH

CREATIVE PEOPLE OFTEN GIVE up before reaching the goals they have set for themselves or achieving what they have set out to accomplish. The quote above from Randy Pausch, a young man with a brilliant mind and terminal cancer who inspired America the year before he died with a speech he gave at Carnegie Mellon called "The Last Lecture," reminds us that obstacles can be a challenge rather than a hindrance.

Too often, disappointment leads to giving up. The stories of some of my clients will illustrate the effects of giving up.

Janet was a single woman who lived most of her life in a small town. She always wanted to travel but had been hesitant to take on the challenges of doing something new and different. She finally took an opportunity to travel to a foreign country with a coworker. The coworker turned out to be a difficult person to travel with, however, so as a result, Janet has never traveled again. Today she is experiencing many regrets about limiting her adventures, and she is depressed.

Daniel always wanted to publish a book. He worked day and night for almost six months writing his memoirs. His sacrifices were many, and he devoted much energy and time to put his book together. After receiving two rejections from publishers, he stopped sending queries. He packed away all his materials and began to see himself as a writing failure. He obviously hadn't heard about JK Rowling, who was nearly destitute and then became a multimillionaire after conceiving the Harry Potter book idea on a train ride.

Another thing Randy Pausch said in *The Last Lecture* was, "Experience is what you get when you don't get what you wanted." He urged us to take that experience, learn from it, and try again.

Peter Vegso, owner of Health Communications, Inc. (HCI), a successful publisher for more than thirty-five years, stresses that success is not an overnight accomplishment. In a recent presentation to Emory University's annual Home Depot Undergraduate Business School Leadership Conference, he listed the four pillars of success:

1. Successful habits
2. Excellent relationships
3. Unusual clarity
4. A focus on priorities

Vegso says that perseverance and learning to say no are important habits. People who care about what they do have touched Vegso deeply. He says, "Do what you love and love what you do. The rest will follow."

Peter's words mean a lot to me. When I was self-publishing small booklets and had a passion about getting information to the general public, my mission was clear and my priorities were to get the job done. I hired my teenage daughters to do bulk mailings for me. They put brown paper sacks all around our living room, marked them A to Z, and designed our home bulk mailing system. We got the job done and became quite successful in our self-publishing, self-distribution company, which was called Nurturing Networks.

Another inspiring person is Robert Stephens, the founder of the Geek Squad, which helps people at home with any technology problems. He tells us, "In the absence of capital, creativity flourishes." If you want to venture out and start a home business, if you want to change jobs, or if you want to move to another part of the country, do your homework and then try it.

Whether we are seeking meaning and satisfaction in relationships, business, goals, or life choices, we have to keep trying.

Donna spent twenty-five years in a marriage and became the mother of two children. When her daughter was twenty-three, she (the daughter) committed suicide. There had been no clues that Donna recognized, prior to this tragedy. She was devastated. She and her husband did their best to continue being a family with their son, but the pain was too great and blame became part of the family system. Their son, Mark, moved far away, seeking his own way of healing.

Donna was devastated again. Her marriage ended in a stressful divorce. Because of escalating stress in the family, Donna moved to a women's halfway house and stayed there until she had stabilized and had completed the divorce proceedings. She then got a job, went back to school, and trained to become a nurse. She is now caring for herself, communicating with her son, and, for the first time in a long time, dealing with the grief she has about her daughter by seeing a grief counselor. Donna has persevered and triumphed over devastating personal circumstances.

You may feel as if you are up against a brick wall, but there are some principles that will help you to start moving again. A universal law is that we are here to prosper in this life. There are four steps to take when you feel stuck:

1. Identify what you don't want in your life and plan to rid yourself of whatever is outdated for you.
2. Identify what you do want and plan to pursue it.
3. Start feeling as though these two actions will give you clarity and energy.
4. Expect, listen, become aware, and take steps toward your goals.

It's wake-up time, and we must make choices. Remembering that you deserve all good things will help you to move ahead. Give up all the cobwebs of doubt and every "if only," and take responsibility for yourself and your actions.

Additional Reading

Canfield, Jack, and Mark Victor Hansen. *Chicken Soup for the Soul: 101 Stories to Open the Heart and Rekindle the Spirit.* Deerfield Beach, FL: HCI, 2001.

Grabhorn, Lynn. *Excuse Me, Your Life Is Waiting: The Astonishing Power of Positive Feelings.* London: Hodder Mobius, 2005.

Lair, Jess. *I Ain't Much, Baby, but I'm All I Got.* New York: Fawcett Crest Publications, 1974.

Prosser, David C. *Peel Your Own Onion: How to Manage Your Life Like a Successful Small Business and Become Happier and More Productive.* New York: Everest House, 1979.

PART TWO:

BABY BOOMERS AND MONEY ISSUES

To me, money is . . . almost human.
If you treat it with real sympathy and
kindness . . . it will be a good servant . . .
and take care of you.

—*Katharine Butler Hathaway*

seven

Worried About Money:
Who Isn't?

*Taking responsibility for the part I play in the cause of my
problems frees me to do something about them.*

—STELLA MITCHELL

THROUGH TIMES OF ECONOMIC uncertainty, worries about money
abound. Home prices fall, credit gets tighter, and the stock market
is erratic. Net worth is decreasing, inflation is growing, and a reces-
sion is upon us.

The concern seems to be widespread, whether people are caring
for only themselves financially, have a family, or are living on a fixed
income. Money concerns those who used to feel safe with their savings and investments but are now finding that they simply do not
have enough money to live as they always have. It is becoming an era
of money changes and problems for many people.

The way to face money woes is to get a handle on what income
there is. That is relatively easy to do. We have earned income and
passive income. Then it gets murkier to look at where money goes.
There are standing expenses, such as housing (mortgage or rent),
mobility (an automobile and all that goes with it—gas, license,

insurance, repairs—or public transportation), food (at home or eating out), clothing, technology (phone, computer), and medical and dental care and keeping up with our with health insurance.

The list seems a little daunting. These standard expenses are necessary items. They cover the basics. It is only when we meet these needs that we can begin to explore our wants: gifts, entertainment, travel, education for ourselves and for our children, and a retirement plan.

It is pretty hard to expect earned income to meet all our needs and wants. This means that passive income becomes very important. There is only one way to ensure passive income, and that is to plan early and well to save money that can be invested. This decision requires very wise spending. Thus, we must go back to the basics and see what dollars can be saved and invested. It might mean the postponement of some of our wants until we feel comfortable that our money that produces passive income is growing.

These are hard decisions to make and even harder choices to implement. It's also a big problem when one partner wants to get ahead financially and the other partner wants to satisfy his or her wants immediately. These kinds of money issues are very serious and cause many relationships to struggle and some to end.

It is important to look at values. If a person is single, it's an easier task. If a person is married, then we must explore each spouse's values and find out which values are individual and which impact the couple.

One person might say that she values her savings account, yet the only account she puts a deposit in each week is in the bank of a coffee shop. The savings deposit is never made, but the daily coffee is a high priority. Another says that he values his child's education, but the only regular purchase he makes is the weekly beer run. Some people say that they value home ownership, but payments for a flat-screen TV, a snowmobile, and a new car come first.

The secret to learning to live well on less money is to figure out your priorities and put your money there first. You—and your partner, if you have one—need to have a very clear, single purpose for how you spend your money. Whether you want a trip around the world or you want to stay home with your children, once your priorities are set, you will find the resolve to walk past the coffee shop, look for a cheaper phone plan, or eat at home more often.

Along the way, you will find other alternatives. You can still eat out, but choose a less expensive restaurant, and you can still travel, but use economy hotels and less expensive destinations. You can still look really nice, but avoid expensive stores and shops. You can watch TV on a smaller screen and still see everything.

One of my clients, Cathy, is thirty-one years old and lives in Chicago. By the time she finished graduate school, she had $100,000 in student loans and debt. She had always tried to keep her expenses down but hadn't done a very good job. Then she met Steve. Steve knew about being frugal and started to help Cathy look at her spending habits.

She made some big changes. Instead of getting her daily coffee drink from a coffee shop, she started buying a bottled coffee drink at a discount store and cut her coffee expenditure in half. She then started paying attention to the other "under ten dollar purchases." She started using coupons. She and Steve decided to have just one car and use public transportation if they had a scheduling conflict with it. Their vacations became camping trips and visits to friends. They have now paid off all Cathy's debts and are working on their retirement plans. Little by little, they give themselves special treats and have just returned from the Greek Isles.

Janet has a degree from Harvard and a six-figure income. One would think that she has no problem with money, yet Janet is aware that as a single woman, she must plan for her future. She knows that she is dependent on only herself and her earned income, so the first thing she wanted to establish was an emergency plan. She has invested in better (and more expensive) insurance to make sure that she will have an income if something happens to her. Next she looked at her retirement plan. She wants to live in a warm climate, and she wants her dream house.

Janet therefore set out to save money. She started cooking; by preparing meals at home and limiting her outside eating, she cut her food costs in half. Instead of going out to fancy restaurants, she started to have potluck dinners with her friends. She also started looking for clothing bargains instead of following the latest trends. She found a good tailor who could make very simple clothes look tailored.

Janet decided to buy nothing that had to be dry cleaned, so there was no longer that expense. Even though she lives alone, she also began buying staple goods in bulk and storing what she wasn't using. Her true love is her dogs, so she spends what she has to spend to keep them healthy and cared for. What keeps her on track is her vision of the dream house in a warm climate.

One expense area to keep under control is technology. Be sure you are using everything you are paying for. Don't sign up for cable or phone programs that sound good but that you won't use. Keep only what you are using, and stay current on less expensive ways to get the same service.

Other saving tips include the following:

- Buy fewer books; use the library.
- See fewer movies in a theater; borrow DVDs from the library or subscribe to a DVD rental program.
- Eat dinner out twice a month instead of once a week.
- Carry lunch to work instead of eating out.

- Learn to do your own pedicures and splurge at the salon twice a year.
- Shop at discount stores rather than department stores.
- Have potluck dinners instead of meeting friends at expensive restaurants.
- Carry a thermos of your favorite coffee instead of going to expensive coffee shops.
- You will be surprised by how much money you can save by adopting even just one of these suggestions.

Additional Reading

Cameron, Julia, and Mark Bryan. *Money Drunk, Money Sober: 90 Days to Financial Freedom.* New York: Wellspring, 1999.

Mundis, Jerrold. *Earn What You Deserve: How to Stop Underearning and Start Thriving.* New York: Bantam Books, 1996.

Stanny, Barbara. *Overcoming Underearning: A Five-Step Plan to a Richer Life.* New York: HarperCollins, 2007.

_____. *Secrets of Six-Figure Women: Surprising Strategies to Up Your Earnings and Change Your Life.* New York: HarperCollins, 2004.

Williams, Nichole, with Cheri Hanson. *Earn What You Are Worth: A Wildly Sophisticated Approach to Investing in Your Career—and Yourself.* New York: Perigee Books, 2004.

Zimmerman, Stuart, and Jared Rosen. *Inner Security and Infinite Wealth: Merging Self Worth and Net Worth.* New York: Select Books, 2003.

Workshop

Healing Money Issues
Onsite Workshops
Cumberland Furnace, TN
www.onsiteworkshops.com
1-800-341-7432

Entrepreneurship: I Want to Work for Myself

No pessimist ever discovered the secret of the stars,
or sailed to an uncharted land, or opened
a new heaven to the human spirit.

—Helen Keller

ONE OF THE MOST wonderful and exciting women I have met in the last few years is Barbara Winter. She is full of ideas and inspiration for women who want to move from merely having a job to becoming entrepreneurs and self-starters.

In my life, there have been many jobs over the years, and some of them were very important jobs. Even though I did well and enjoyed the teamwork at several jobs, I struggled with a restlessness. It seemed that I was always exploding with ideas, wanting to do things differently. Finally after battling with a very sexist employer, I decided that the time had come to go out on my own.

At the time, I was director of a large department in an international training firm. An additional responsibility was to be on the management team of the entire company. It was a coveted position, and I had worked hard to secure it. My work took me to Europe,

Canada, and throughout the United States.

One day I was giving a presentation entitled "Thinking for Yourself" to about 300 people. About halfway through, the realization hit me that what I was saying was what I needed to hear. As I finished the presentation, my inner voice was saying, *I need to go back to my office and resign after this presentation.* That was exactly what I did. By that evening, my employment and grand career had ended (for the moment).

Someone once told me, "Entrepreneurs are born the moment they start challenging what is and begin to imagine what could be." That statement stayed in my mind and gave me comfort—even though, as I sat at the kitchen table that night, I felt much self-doubt and concern about the big decision I had made so quickly. Actually, it seemed like the decision was quick, but the nagging dissatisfaction had been there a long time. Guy Kawasaki, a venture capitalist, says, "*Entrepreneur* is not a job title. It is the state of mind of people who want to alter the future." That was me. The word comes from the French *entreprendre*, meaning to undertake or attempt.

My dream was to start a counseling center for families of alcoholics. There was no money available for this population, no path that had been paved for this in the counseling world, and not too many people interested in the subject. However, I had a dream and a vision.

Because I had very little money to work with, my first center was a rented H&R Block building. Knowing the owner of the building allowed me to rent very inexpensively. The only problem was that my program had to shut down between January and April, when the building was needed for preparing people's taxes, so we shut down for three months.

The woman who answered my phone was a volunteer. She had lived in an alcoholic situation for years, and her self-worth was pretty low. We had a phone with two buttons on it. If one line would ring, she would answer it professionally; if both lines rang at the same time, she would cry. She did a great deal of healing in this job, and we became great friends.

Because I couldn't afford to hire counseling staff, I trained volunteers. My staff came from the Junior League, schools, and churches. These were people who shared my mission and my vision.

Our clients got well and offered their own recovery and knowledge to future clients, so they were great successes. My belief was that people were in better shape than they thought. They just needed information, support, and a chance to better themselves and their lives. "I dwell in possibility," Emily Dickinson wrote.

One success followed another. In the early days, without money, great creativity was necessary just to be able to keep going. There was a church in my area with a house next to it that it was planning to sell so it could send the money to a mission somewhere. The people at the church read about my work and asked me to give several sermons. I did, and they liked them so much that they decided to give me the house for my mission of working with families of alcoholics.

A program was designed and implemented. The building became the House Counseling Center. Soon hundreds of people were going through some type of treatment or counseling there. We specialized in working with children and with entire families. A dreamer gets into situations, and miracles happen. I am a dreamer.

Oprah Winfrey says, "Own yourself in every way possible, so you never have to sell yourself short or be bought by anyone." Having my own center allowed me to be as creative as possible in finding ways to mend human hearts. There was very little time spent in excess paperwork, unnecessary staff meetings, or office politics. There were limited funds, and we wanted to make the program available to as many people as we could. We offered a sliding scale. The staff also had a mission philosophy, or the program wouldn't have worked. We were all following our dreams.

By paying attention to the vision and the dream, we developed a model for treatment that was successful. People could and did get well in our program. The staff gained confidence and experienced joy in the work it was doing. Everyone was amazed.

Later, the opportunity presented itself to bring this model to a bigger population. A larger, better-connected agency offered to buy our entire program, and it provided advertising and additional staff. More people kept getting well and changing their lives in important ways. There were also many changes in location throughout this process.

Finally, these years of work evolved into a center that, to date, has served more than 30,000 people directly. Because one person probably impacts at least nine other people (family and friends), we believe that we have served about 350,000 people indirectly. This is no small accomplishment. The program continues to this day at Onsite Workshops.

I share this with you to encourage you to follow your dreams. Maybe you want to write a book, start a business, develop a network, leave a job to start a career, or leave a career to have a fuller life. Whatever your dream or your mission is, there are some steps you can take to make those dreams come true. They are as follows:

1. *Subscribe to magazines that are in your passion zone.* Read about what other people are doing that supports your interest.
2. *Set up a home office.* My home office is filled with enough items from my past to keep me headed toward my future: photos, certificates, a lounge chair, my favorite pillows, all my collected treasures, a salt lamp, my collection of angels, fresh flowers (always), music, my collection of treasured books, my collection of butterflies, a picture of me as a child, a photo of my tribe, and all my scrapbooks. My home office is a place of nourishment, inspiration, and comfort.

3. *Find others who have stepped out on their own behalf, and become inspired by their successes.* There is a whole world of people who are self-starters and are enjoying themselves. One of the more creative ones I have met was a woman who started a business, called An Extra Pair of Hands, in a retirement community. She would come in and help single people, giving them an extra pair of hands around the house. Another was someone who loved flowers and so created a business shopping for containers (flowers and herbs) and planting them in a suburban neighborhood. She called her business Bloom Where You Are Planted.

4. *Carry a notebook.* Richard Branson, the founder of the airline Virgin America, carries a small notebook with him at all times. Hearing him talk about this prompted me to do the same. There are ideas everywhere.

In addition to taking the above steps, you should also watch out for the following pitfalls as you become your own boss:

1. *Don't act on every idea.* My biggest problem at first was thinking that I had to act on every good idea I had. I learned, however, that acting on everything kept me from getting started on any one focused project. It helped to have five boxes and prioritize my ideas one through five. Ones require immediate action, twos are tackled when the ones are finished, threes I do when I can, and fours and fives I throw away. Many ideas are therefore thrown out, but that leaves me time for the ideas I really want to act on.

2. *Notice when you spend more time planning and less time acting.* Acting is what makes things happen, so aim to spend 20 percent of your time planning and 80 percent acting.

3. *Beware of asking too many people for their opinions and advice before launching a project or creating a product or service.* Too many people

giving too much advice will slow you down, possibly confuse you, and definitely hamper your efforts. Do your best to create a project. Follow your dreams and do your research. Then get going. You might want to ask a few trusted people for feedback or advice, but do not weigh yourself down by soliciting too much advice or feedback. Trust yourself. And then get going.

Little did I know that my excitement, passion, and vision would grow into a million-dollar business—not bad for someone who started out renting an H&R building off-season!

I'd like to end this chapter with a poem I wrote to end another one of my books:

> *The soul is restless and will keep us restless*
> *Until we are fulfilled.*
> *I had absolutely nothing to*
> *Back me up except a*
> *Deeply rooted resolution and*
> *Belief. My belief was formed*
> *By my life and by my experience*
> *And a deep feeling within me.*
> *I listened to my inner self,*
> *My God, and many others and*
> *Did what I had to do.*
> *And it was good for me*
> *And good for others.*

Additional Reading

Blanchard, Ken, Don Hutson, and Ethan Willis. *The One Minute Entrepreneur: The Secret to Creating and Sustaining a Successful Business.* New York: Broadway Books, 2008.

Winter, Barbara J. *Making a Living Without a Job: Winning Ways for Creating Work That You Love,* rev. ed. 2009, New York: Bantam Books, 1993.

eight

Wealthy Parents: Gift or Handicap?

Inherited or sudden wealth can create a false sense of entitlement, a loss of future motivation, and an inability to delay gratification and tolerate frustration.

—Jessie H. O'Neill

Psychotherapist Tian Dayton explains that, "The child of wealth feels at once special and undeserving, chosen and like a hollow player in another person's dream, at once powerful and impotent." This echoes what I have heard from the countless trust-fund people I have worked with in my career. Money is a very transformational agent in our society, and it is seductive, troublesome, appreciated, and crippling. Money in itself is not the issue, however. The issue is the control, management, inadequacy, power, and mystery that surrounds great wealth.

We know what is positive and desirable. Living with money allows a sense of freedom and safety that people with limited recourses rarely find. It means not having to worry about necessities such as health insurance, dental care, the ability to travel, education, and living conditions.

Wealth, or affluence, could be defined as being able to maintain a lifestyle that our culture views as rich without having to work. Only a small percentage of the population fits this definition. In monetary terms, the definition might be a net worth of a few million dollars, an amount that would generate enough interest to provide a substantial income independent of the principal.

Money opens doors, seduces people to listen, and grants favors that others cannot reach. Many people who have come from "old" money and those who have come from sudden wealth have done wonderful things and have made life much better for themselves and their families. They have also made the world a better place through their philanthropy.

However, there are many problems that come with wealth and I want to highlight some of them, as follows:

1. Often, the person in the family who accumulated the wealth suffered from excess work that caused them to ignore their families and not be available physically and emotionally.

2. The children in workaholic families often feel inadequate, abandoned, and mistrustful of their parents.

3. There are many issues that children and spouses have to deal with in wealthy families. One is to learn to have a balance of power when the person of wealth is seen as all-powerful as he or she manages the wealth.

4. Although it is totally understandable in today's culture to have a prenuptial agreement (especially in the case of family wealth or remarriage), it also can cause mistrust, hurt, and fear in a new marriage.

5. The fortune maker in the family has a great deal of self-worth, almost to the point of feeling omnipotent. Children born into wealth do not have the opportunity to feel the same success,

especially if they are not in a situation that can bring about the same kind of wealth. They are always playing catch-up to their parents. Wealth shelters its heirs from many of the difficult and challenging tasks of life that produce self-worth.

The affluent family, although it has everything it needs, often has a pattern of personal deprivation that is similar to the pattern in poor families. Both rich and poor children suffer from having their parents absent much of the time. Rich parents might be traveling, working, and spending time with their peers. Poor parents might be working and spending their time trying to keep the household together. Either way, the children can be left behind and can suffer from low self-worth, loneliness, and emptiness. The result is a lack of intimacy and role models for the children.

When wealthy parents are emotionally unavailable to their children, they often try to give them things, activities, and people to fill in for them. There are nannies, teachers, trainers, hobbies, social activities, and lessons. Although these fill up time, they don't fill the hole in the soul.

My work has introduced me to thirty- and forty-year-old people who have extremely limited social skills and even less developed productive skills. Their wealthy parents continue to subsidize them even today. Some are rather tragic figures with new problems that they have created in their emotionally damaged lives. Others have developed a sense of entitlement that hurts their romantic relationships and friendships.

Children of wealthy parents are often set apart from their less affluent peers by going to special schools, by the cars they drive, and by the people they meet. During their youngest and most formative years, their role models were often away from home creating the family wealth. These children may have had little hands-on training for their own value and character development. They then stumble into adulthood with very little knowledge of how to make and maintain meaningful and honest relationships and very little ability to trust new people. The trust-fund young people I have worked with often ask if someone likes or loves them for their wealth or for themselves.

There is often a crippling type of preoccupation with what money can do that affects both the fortune builder and the children. There is pressure to be extremely aware of external appearances (clothes, cars, travel) and too little attention paid to nurturing oneself or maintaining mental, spiritual, or psychological health. The inner life is rarely nourished. People feel they must attend the "right" schools, get good grades, marry well, and do one's best to be thin, attractive, and powerful.

Studies tell us that there is a rapidly growing awareness that money solves many problems but also creates many problems. Resilience is a factor in the passing of wealth from one generation to another. The majority of wealth began with people of great intelligence and motivation. They were willing to sacrifice a great deal to amass their fortunes. This same genetic heritage is strong and can be used as a positive resource for those who want to use it constructively.

How people handle their wealth depends a great deal on how they learned about their wealth. The people that I have worked with do better when they share information about the family wealth with their children at a very early age. Giving clear, age-appropriate information takes some of the mystery and control out of the situation.

Parents can take their children into their confidence and give them early lessons about money. They can demonstrate to the children through role modeling how to handle, conserve, and spend the money. They can teach the children about giving money to philanthropy. The most important lesson the children can learn from the parents is that money does not define them or the parents. It is a tool, and one that requires training to use.

When wealthy people study their relationship with money, they can celebrate the fact that having money provides them with the time and the power to use that money wisely. When they spend their money wisely and invest in worthy situations and people, they will have the knowledge and satisfaction that they have been good stewards of good fortune. The happiest wealthy people are those who have found structure, motivation, purpose, and mission.

There are countless stories of people who sponsor children's camps, form foundations that bring hope and help to those in need, donate to worthy causes, give of their time and talent to communities, and make miracles happen. The people who find the greatest joy in their wealth are the ones who get personally involved in such causes.

Money understanding, independence, and acceptance is an experience of freedom on a psychological, emotional, and spiritual level.

Additional Reading

O'Neil, Jessie H. *The Golden Ghetto: The Psychology of Affluence.* Milwaukee, WI: Affluenza Project, 1997.

Robin, Vicki, and Joe Dominguez, with Monique Tilford. *Your Money or Your Life: 9 Steps to Transforming Your Relationship with Money and Achieving Financial Independence.* New York: Penguin, 2008.

Workshop

Healing Money Issues
Onsite Workshops
Cumberland Furnace, TN
www.onsiteworkshops.com
1-800-341-7432

nine

Money: Is Loving It Really the "Root of All Evil"?

Luck is a matter of preparation meeting opportunity.

—OPRAH WINFREY

IN MY WORKSHOPS WITH WOMEN, I have found that there are two subjects that are hard for women to talk about with one another. The second hardest subject is sex. The hardest subject is money. There seems to be much shame and inadequacy about money. These feelings are very different for different women, but the pain about the topic seems to stem from the following four sources:

1. *Not earning enough money to be debt-free and get ahead creates a sense of inadequacy.* There is a belief that there is something wrong with someone who can't get out of debt. This leads to envy and jealousy toward others. Feeling and being financially strapped is a great cause of lower self-worth. Worth is tied to wealth for many people, as illustrated by the common question "What is your net worth?"
2. *Shopping and acquiring to excess is strongly connected to salving our feelings with "stuff" and then comparing our stuff to others' stuff.*

This keeps us in debt and working harder so we can keep acquiring more stuff. This acquisition cycle is often what parents get into when they are making up to their children for the lack of time they spend with them. Many parents, for example, go into extreme debt with Christmas presents to make up for the rest of the year.

3. *Having too much money comes with its own set of problems.* There is often guilt when the money is inherited and not earned. Children from wealthy families often suffer a lack of motivation. When a parent is extremely successful financially, there is a one-down feeling that children develop from believing that they will never do as well as their parents.

4. *Being poor and feeling poor are two different things.* Being poor is not having enough food, no shelter, mobility, and too little health care. It means that our basic needs are not being met. Feeling poor is not having what we perceive the people around us have. It means not having everything we want.

Whether we have too little money or too much money, our money woes are tied to our money scripts. Family rules and expectations about money are a problem for people who have not taken the time or been willing to look at the historical and family messages about money that are still impacting life today.

Messages About Money That Can Affect Our Finances

- It's virtuous to be simple and not want too much.
- We should strive for intellectual achievement rather than financial gain.
- Always pay off your house, and you will have a place to live.
- Do not use credit; always pay cash.

- Credit cards can allow the good life, and payments can be made later.
- I deserve something for how hard I work, so buying _____ is good for me.
- Risking in the stock market or investments is not for me.
- The stock market and investments are the only way to make big money.
- Men should earn more than their wives.
- The man in the family should be the breadwinner.

The messages about money are actually endless. We must free ourselves from our own scripts to be skillful in evaluating our financial situation.

Assessing where you are is the best way to start. You may have inherited money, lost money in the stock market, suffered a trauma (such as illness, accident, or death in the family), discovered that your spouse had an affair, lost your job, or been in a depression about your finances. Anything that is overwhelming causes us to take stock of where we are.

Whatever problem you are currently facing, the following steps can help you to address it:

1. *Accept the problem.* Come to grips with the fact that there is a solution that is dependent on information, decision, and action. It's a waste of time and energy to blame someone else. Do not look back. Get ready to go forward.

2. *Lessen the burden.* Make a list of friends, family members, and contacts from whom you can draw support. Weed out any negative or toxic people. Step up the support by calling to ask for help, and say no to any negative family member or friend's advice.

3. *Take your financial temperature.* Decide what has to be done immediately and what can take a little longer. Gather information about your assets, insurance policies, debts, and liabilities. Get an accurate view of your financial standing.

4. *Take action.* Prepare and protect your home, car, health insurance, and tax liabilities. Postpone further purchases until you understand exactly where you are and what you can and cannot afford.

   Ask yourself if you use shopping as therapy. Some people refer to the constant need to be shopping as "retail therapy." It's one thing to need an item and go get it; it's quite another thing to go shopping "just to see what's out there" and to feel better. Eliminating these "fishing" trips can go a long way toward getting your spending under control.

5. *Get professional help.* Consult an accountant, a lawyer, or a financial planner.

Money Mistakes

There are five common mistakes that people make with money.

Postponing a Savings Plan

Unless you are at poverty level, you can save something. Keep track of your expenses for one month to see where your money goes. Then look for a way to save ten or twenty dollars each day. Then, every three months, invest that money. Get in the habit of saving, and your spending habits will become more clear.

Resisting Setting Goals

If you want to buy a car, take a vacation, go back to school, or retire, setting a long-term goal is necessary. This is a good time to look for someone who is doing well financially and find out how he or she did it. People are usually very willing to share their thoughts and ideas.

Thinking It's Too Late to Start Saving

Whether you are forty, fifty, or sixty years old (or even older), you have things you would like to do and have before you die. Start now. You might be saving money for an unexpected car problem or a trip around the world. Either way, you will be glad to have the money when you need it or want it.

Overspending on Family Because You Feel Guilty

If you ever find yourself in the trap of using material giving to make up for a lack of emotional giving, stop and reassess your thinking and priorities. Do you want to model this kind of behavior for your family? What a burden! Spend time and energy with your family instead of always buying and accumulating. Teach them by your behavior how you want them to think about themselves. If you always have to give a material gift to feel connected, that is the lesson you are teaching.

Paying Only the Minimum Monthly Amount on a High-Interest Credit Card

The average credit card balance carried in American households is about $7,000. However, even if it is less—for instance, $2,500—the consequences of making only the minimum monthly payment can be dire. If the bank's minimum monthly payment rate is 2 percent, you will be required to pay $50 a month. If your interest rate is 18 percent, it will take you thirty-four years to get out of debt, and you will have paid $6,430 in interest—more than twice your original principal. Make the decision to pay as much as you can each month. Make another decision not to charge another thing until the old debt is paid off.

Seven Ways to Improve Your Finances

1. Track your spending.
2. Read books about money.
3. Teach family members about the benefits of frugality.
4. Investigate Debtors Anonymous, which uses the twelve steps to solve problems with debt, spending, and earning.
5. Look for a telecommuting job. It saves on the costs of commuting, clothes, and eating out.
6. Save as much as possible using 401k and credit unions.
7. Reward yourself from time to time: take a trip, buy an outfit, or have a special meal.

Managing Your Money

There are two important aspects of managing money: how to protect what you earn and how to keep what you earn. In these hard economic times, one cannot afford to be lazy or complacent and hope that money concerns will take care of themselves. To be safe, we need to be constantly rethinking our financial plans and goals. Considerations include stock market fluctuations, changing tax laws, fluctuating interest rates, and volatile real estate values. For many, being a do-it-yourself investor has been enough. It's getting more difficult to be secure and be satisfied that way, however.

Wealth is the abundance of assets to live a more than comfortable life. The tricky word here is *comfortable*. One person's comfort level can be very different from another person's. A few years ago, a friend asked me, "Sharon, how much is enough financially?" I knew what was enough for me, but I hadn't really thought about putting it into words.

I have learned over the years that there are many kinds of wealth. The first, of course, has to do with money. The second kind is health and a feeling of well-being. The third form of wealth is having time to do the things one wants to do. The fourth, the most critical form of wealth for me, is the protection of one's relationships with the people one loves and who love one back. The fifth kind of wealth is what gives one pleasure, which for me is artistry and creativity. The sixth form of wealth is travel. I love to experience and learn. The seventh form of wealth is to make a spiritual contribution to the world.

Any one of these forms of wealth could be a full-time job. Thus, finding the balance among all of them became my goal. To reach all aspects of my goal meant that no one of them would consume my time, focus, and energy.

I need a comfortable home, a healthy diet, the ability to travel to see my family, a communication center (computer, phone, TV, books, music, pleasant office), exercise (walking, dancing, gardening), and an occasional learning trip. I belong to a few groups that make this world a better place. I am very clear about what I want and need, and it saves me a great deal of spending, acquiring, and hoarding. Finally, the answer to my friend's question became clear.

To me, wealth is the acquisition of assets to live a frugal, comfortable, and satisfying life. This sent me to Wikipedia to look up its definition of frugality. It is "The acquiring of and resourceful use of economic goals and services in order to achieve lasting and more fulfilling goals." That works for me.

Additional Reading

Cameron, Julia, and Mark Bryan. *Money Drunk, Money Sober: 90 Days to Financial Freedom.* New York: Wellspring, 1999.

Hayden, Ruth. *How to Turn Your Money Life Around: The Money Book for Women.* Deerfield Beach, FL: HCI, 1992.

Klontz, Ted, Rick Kahler, and Brad Klontz. *The Financial Wisdom of Ebenezer Scrooge: 5 Principles to Transform Your Relationship with Money.* Deerfield Beach, FL: HCI, 2008.

McCarthy, Susan. *The Value of Money: Uncover the Hidden Wisdom of Money.* New York: J. P. Tarcher, 2008.

Any book by Suze Orman.

Resource

Twelve-Step Work
Debtors Anonymous
www.debtorsanonymous.org

ten

Retirement: I'm Not Ready, But How Do I Plan?

*After all, it is those who have a deep and real inner life who
are best able to deal with the irritating details of outer life.*

—Evelyn Underhill

Have you ever had the following thoughts?

*I'm young, and retirement isn't in my near plans, but I want what
many retired people seem to have. What I will want is time, financial
security, and a zest for life. Many retired people I see have it. Others seem
to retire, feel limited, and age too soon. How can I best plan to have the
kind of wonderful retirement that I see so many have?*

Having enough money is only half the battle, but it is an important factor. How much money is enough for retirement? There are
countless books and workshops about the financial aspects of retirement, and at the end of this chapter there are several references that
contain information that should pertain to your particular situation.

Nowadays, retirement is about getting in touch with your inner
self, finding fulfillment in ways beyond playing golf and shooting
under par on the front nine. It has to do with staying healthy
because you plan to be around for a long time. Retirement must be

seen as a journey. Know thyself and look before you leap.

This chapter addresses the values and the emotional and psychological aspects of retirement. As I noted at the end of the previous chapter, when a friend asked me how much money was enough to retire, it took me awhile to formulate my thoughts, but then I came up with a list of needs. Once I had my needs in order, it became easier for me to estimate an amount of money that would ensure those values.

The next step was to find a good accountant or business manager who would help me put certain numbers to work and add inflation and incidentals. There will always be changes, both subtractions and additions, but I built a baseline that allowed me to move to the next step.

Activities are another important factor in retiring. Eric Sundstrom, a psychology professor at the University of Tennessee, says, "A little vacation sounds good and a long vacation sounds even better." He adds, however, "Golfing every day isn't a satisfying life. It's a common story: beach, mountains, or golf course for six months—and then boredom sets in."

That's also true about joining clubs, having hobbies, dancing, gardening, playing tennis, or doing any repetitive action. The lesson is that if you want a great retirement, think in terms of a redirection of your energies and interests and plan to be just as active as you were when you were working. If you don't have a diversified plan, it might be a disappointing transition.

Experts tell us that when people retire, they need a purpose, something they feel is both enjoyable and important. Retirees who become socially or politically involved and add to making the world a better place seem to have the most satisfying retirements. Eric Sundstrom's studies tell us that people who do not have a purpose in life do not live as long as those who do.

Some people find they want to mentor a young person; others volunteer at museums, become politically active, go back to school, or travel. Many do consulting or form meaningful groups. It's a great time to plan to do all the things you like to do and have never had the time for before. Sometimes it is easy, but for others it takes some real soul-searching.

Once you have an idea for what you might like to do, give it a trial run, suggests Maureen Mohyte, the director of corporate gerontology at Hartford Financial. Try it out one day a month and see if it is what you want to devote your time to doing. Be sure you have plenty of intellectual stimulation. That's very important as we grow older.

Regardless of what kind of career you have had, it has probably given you mental stimulation. This has to be redirected. You may want to learn to play a musical instrument or learn a new language. Just doing one or two things you enjoy during your years of retirement will not be enough. People who do not feed their minds with intellectual stimulation and new learning tend to become depressed and feel dissatisfied.

Building a social network is also extremely important, and it helps if this network is in place before your retirement. Being employed has been the central source of social connection for many people. When you leave work, you often leave that network behind, and it will be necessary to rebuild a new network.

Additional Reading

Cullinane, Jan, and Cathy Fitzgerald. *The New Retirement: The Ultimate Guide to the Rest of Your Life*. New York: Rodale Books, 2007.

Harrington, Judith R., and Stanley J. Steinberg. *The Everything Retirement Planning Book: A Complete Guide to Managing Your Investments, Securing Your Future, and Enjoying Life to the Fullest*. Avon, MA: Adams Media, 2007.

McCurdy, Diane. *How Much Is Enough? Balancing Today's Needs with Tomorrow's Retirement Goals.* Hoboken, NJ: John Wiley & Sons, 2005.

Warner, Ralph E. *Get a Life: You Don't Need a Million to Retire Well.* Berkeley, CA: Nolo, 2004.

Sundstrom, Eric, Randy Burnham, and Michael Burnham. *My Next Phase: The Personality-Based Guide to Your Best Retirement.* New York: Springboard Press, 2007.

Zelinski, Ernie J. *How to Retire Happy, Wild, and Free: Retirement Wisdom That You Won't Get from Your Financial Advisor.* Berkeley, CA: Ten Speed Press, 2004.

part three:

RELATIONSHIPS

By maintaining an attitude of love
and regard for every soul, you create a
life filled with dignity and purpose

—*Brahma Kumaris*

eleven

Mothers and Daughters

*The truth is that when one woman gives birth
to another, to someone who is like her, they are
linked together for life in a special way.*

—Nancy Friday

WHEN I READ THE statement by Dr. Christine Northrup that "Every daughter contains her mother and all the women who came before her," I was startled. In her book *Mother-Daughter Wisdom*, she also says that every woman who heals herself helps to heal all the women who came before her and all those who will come after her. Through Northrup's writing, I came to see myself as a link in a chain.

My mother and my grandmothers have all passed away, and I am the oldest living link. My two daughters and my three granddaughters come after me. With that realization, my life took on added meaning. I realized that only I can bring the past alive and teach them about their foremothers. There are never perfect people or perfect relatives. I know both the strengths and the weaknesses of the special women who preceded me, and it is my pleasure to share this knowledge with my daughters and granddaughters.

As I remember my relationship with my own mother, I am reminded of the statement of D. H. Lawrence, "Down the flood of remembrance, I weep like a child for the past." What I wouldn't give for one more day with my mom to tell her how much I, as an adult, understand and appreciate so many things I did not know as a child or as a young woman.

In my childhood, my mom was always there. I watched her care for our home, work alongside my dad, and make sure that everyone was cared for. That was just normal; that's what moms did. My energy and my focus were often outside the home. My secrets and fears were shared with my friends or kept to myself. It didn't really occur to me to make my mom my friend. She had many needs because of circumstances in our family, and sometimes I felt like her mom, trying to help her. Our relationship was more about what needed to be done rather than sharing our thoughts and feelings.

Today, as an adult, I understand her circumstances better than ever before. I am aware of the memories I hold in my heart: the special Christmases, the little box in which she kept money for when any of us needed something special, her laughter, her love of playing cards, and her pride in her cooking. Today I would say the following to my mother, and I invite any woman to say it to hers:

Mom, I understand and appreciate you. Perhaps it's the sadness of every generation that these lost feelings and this gratitude come too late. As an adult, I know that no one in life ever loves you as much as your mother does. A mother's love is strong, pure, unconditional, everlasting, and fierce.

There are several mothering types, and each comes with opportunities and handicaps.

The stay-at-home mom is the traditional mother type. She is often referred to as *earth mother*. Being with her children is her most fulfilling and happiest activity. Her focus is on the needs of her children, the home she creates, and the activities in which her children are involved.

These mothers love the process of being pregnant, nursing their children, and being with them most of the time. The opportunity in this kind of mothering is that a woman bonds with her children strongly when they are young. This often prevents problems as the children grow up, because they have a deep sense of belonging and of being loved.

This kind of mother sometimes goes through stages of loss as her children grow up and move away. The tendency to hold on to her children can be strong, and it takes strength and courage to let them grow away emotionally and physically.

The nontraditional mom has financial, educational, or career issues that take her away from mothering. She may have to see to other issues in the family, and although she protects and cares for her children, it grows increasingly difficult for her to juggle many responsibilities. This often happens with single mothers. Circumstances pull them outside the family more than they would choose if things were different.

The mom who tries to do both works outside the home and wants to spend as much time with her children as possible. She may compromise many of her own needs during the child-rearing years. Her days are very full, and she may adjust her career or even postpone some advancement to do both jobs.

All these situations cause many feelings between mothers and children, and especially between mothers and daughters. All the time that a woman is mothering, her daughter is looking to her to be a role model. When the mother makes a choice or behaves in a way that doesn't fit the daughter's beliefs, conflict arises.

Some therapists believe that the mother-daughter relationship is the most difficult one to navigate. There are many factors to consider in a mother-daughter relationship. There is the history of the mother. The analyst Carl Jung said, "The greatest unconscious force in the lives of children is the unfulfilled dreams of their parents." Then there are the expectations and style of the daughter and the culture in which she lives. Both women are impacted by friendships, belief systems, and personal hopes and dreams.

In my work with mothers and daughters, I have found that there are countless situations and issues to be addressed. After listening and observing, I have found that the following set of ideas works the best to heal wounds and increase closeness. It's important for both people to do the following:

1. *Ask.* Instead of assuming, judging, or waiting, ask when you want to know something. Be direct. Asking can be framed in

such a way that it does not seem to be prying or threatening. Let the other person know that you are asking because you care and want to understand.

2. *Listen.* Listen to each other with an open mind and an open heart. Put yourself in the place of the other person. Listen carefully and quietly to both the words said and the feelings behind the words.

3. *Try to understand.* It's not always easy to understand someone else's position, but do your best. Thinking it through over time may help.

4. *Accept.* Once you have heard what the other person has to say and why it is important to her, accept the reality (whether you understand completely or not).

5. *Love and support.* These steps are the meaning of unconditional love. Using this plan over and over will bring about greater understanding and create more closeness in the relationship.

One of my adult daughters went on a spa experience with me. We were looking forward to spending some special bonding and fun time together. In my understanding and opinion, we were lucky to be able to have the time and experience in a beautiful setting. However, for my daughter, it turned out to be a painful experience. It is her experience, so I won't attempt to explain what happened to her at the spa.

The result, however, was that she realized that she had old hurts and feelings of abandonment from the years that my career took me away from the family with great frequency. Fortunately, she asked me to listen to her. I stopped what I was doing and listened. I tried to understand her old feelings and fears, and she tried to understand my circumstances at that time. We both accepted what had happened and made plans to love and support each other in the future.

We also felt certain that we could continue to bond through her children, my grandchildren, and this is happening. In the beginning, we both worked hard to build the positive parts of our relationship. We are growing together with each day, and it isn't work anymore. It has become a way of life together. Today, we work together in a mother-daughter workshop.

This experience raised a concern about my relationship with my other daughter. Her memories and her feelings are different from those of my first daughter. Letters and e-mails have gone back and forth, and our relationship, too, is continuing to grow. She has five children, and we also connect through my grandchildren. Loving my daughters unconditionally helps me to understand their relationships with their daughters and their sons.

Every mother-daughter relationship is different. Just because you have more than one daughter does not mean that your relationship to each of them is the same. Because of the time in which they were born and the circumstances in which they grew up, each one will have a different relationship with you.

My plan is to keep communicating with my daughters by e-mail, letters, phone calls, and greeting cards, especially when I know they are busy and hassled. I can also offer them support and love. You see, it doesn't matter how you maintain the mother-daughter bond; it just matters that you do. A daughter needs a mom to teach her that you can't start life over, but you can change the way it ends. The mother-daughter relationship is one of the most intimate and rewarding relationships that we will ever have, and it is often one of the most complicated.

Stories can give wonderful messages. The following parable, written by Temple Bailey in 1933, illustrates a mother's experience as she moves through life:

A young mother started out on the path of life. She asked her teacher, "Is this the way?" The teacher replied, "Yes, and the way is challenging and difficult. You will grow old on your search."

So the young mother went on, birthed and raised her children, loved them, and felt that nothing would be better than this time. Storms and struggles came, and her path became dark. The children were afraid and clung to their mother. They said, "Mother, we are not afraid, for you are near and nothing can hurt us."

The next day came and there were many hills. The mother climbed, and the children climbed, and everyone was tired. The mother said, "I will hold your hand, and you can do it." The children responded, "Mother, stay with us and we will make it."

Next came difficult times. People were cruel to each other, they hurt each other, and the children were confused by hate and indifference. The mother said, "Look to God and accept and love." The mother had shown her children courage and strength and had introduced them to God.

Time went on: days, months, and years. The mother grew old and tired. Her children were tall and strong and walked with courage. When times were hard for her, they carried her. Finally, the mother said, "I have reached the end of my journey, but it is all right because my children can walk alone, and so can their children after them."

The children answered, "You will always be with us, Mother, even after you are gone. Even when we can no longer see you, you will be with us. You are more than a memory. You are a living presence in each of us."

If you want your daughter to be healthy and happy, your job is to be healthy and happy yourself so you can be her role model. It's not your job to think only of what makes her happy. It is your responsibility to make yourself happy and let her watch how you do it. Ignoring your own wants and needs can only serve to teach her to do the same. Christine Northrup shares this insight: "Dimming your own light to make another's appear brighter makes the whole world darker."

Later in life, the mother-daughter roles often change. As the years go by and the daughter makes her own way in the world, the mother must come to grips with the fact that her daughter has her own life. The mother is then responsible for her own life, her own choices, and her own happiness. This doesn't mean that the mother and the daughter will disengage. It means that they will now have a friendship, and each will enjoy her own life on her own terms. The relationship moves from mother and daughter to friends. Adrienne Rich calls it "the knowledge flowing between two alike bodies, one of which has spent nine months inside the other."

The final role change is sometimes a reversal. It happens when the mother becomes weakened, ill, or incapable of caring for herself. Then another kind of bonding can take place. It is another time that it's very important to use the model of ask, listen, and so forth described above. Compromise and understanding is very necessary at this time. The mother is not used to losing some of her independence and health, and the daughter may be at the busiest time of her life.

This is an opportunity for another type of letting go. At some point, daughters have to let go of their mothers, and this is much like the time that the mothers had to let go of their daughters. Regardless of how the relationship has gone in life, the aging and pending death of the mother is another opportunity to heal both people. It can be a time of reflection, gratitude, and forgiveness on the part of both people for the lack of a job that has not been done perfectly.

Forgiveness is the key to letting go of another person. It releases you from the past and from your perceived losses and gives you power and serenity in your life. Forgiveness creates an inner peace when you take responsibility for your own feelings and give up wanting someone to fill all your wants and needs. When we are willing to each take responsibility for our own lives and our own happiness, we can forgive others for what they didn't give us.

With a deep and true forgiveness of our mothers and our daughters, we will find that our world opens up. There is a great deal of pain for everyone when mothers and daughters each expect the other to have been or continue to be perfect. It is not the other's job to make an adult child or her mother happy. It is each person's own job and a gift to the other. When this is realized, both people are set free to find the clearest and most powerful happiness available.

Additional Reading

Chapman, Annie. *10 Things I Want My Daughter to Know: Getting Her Ready for Life.* Eugene, OR: Harvest House Publishers, 2002.

Firman, Julie, and Dorothy Firman. *Daughters and Mothers: Making It Work.* Deerfield Beach, FL: HCI, 2003.

Northrup, Christine. *Mother-Daughter Wisdom: Understanding the Crucial Link Between Mothers, Daughters, and Health.* New York: Bantam Books, 2006.

Rich, Adrienne. *Of Woman Born: Motherhood as Experience and Institution.* New York: W. W. Norton & Company, 1995.

twelve

Do I Want a Divorce or Am I Just Bored and Angry?

Every relationship is a teacher. If I don't learn the lesson, the teacher will come back.

—EMILY MASON

HAVE YOU EVER HAD the following thoughts? *Today I want a divorce. I am angry and hurt. Yesterday I was afraid to even think about a divorce, and all I could do was see the best parts of my marriage. Today, however, I want to be free of the heaviness that is in my marriage. I can no longer stand feeling wrong, misunderstood, and taken for granted. Yesterday I couldn't imagine giving up the feeling of being part of a couple and facing this world alone. I want out, I want to stay in. I am so confused and afraid. It is easier to just avoid how I feel. How can I know what I really want?*

There are important criteria for staying in a marriage. The marriages that have the best chance of working toward a meaningful relationship are those in which the following are true:

1. Both partners are able to honestly talk about the status of the marriage.
2. Both partners still like and respect each other.
3. Both partners share similar values and dreams.
4. Both partners are faithful to the relationship.
5. Both partners are willing to seek outside help for the relationship.

Even relationships that have to deal with betrayal on the part of one partner or both partners have a good chance of healing and strengthening if the five above-mentioned criteria are met.

The future looks bleak for couples who have already experienced a spiritual divorce. This means that they have gone through all the steps to end a relationship without actually leaving each other physically. A spiritual divorce occurs when a couple remains living together, keeping up a facade of harmony and a pretense of mutual satisfaction with the relationship.

They live in the same house and relate to their children, yet the relationship is void of any direct emotional energy with each other.

They rarely fight because they rarely share themselves with each other. A great deal of their communication has to do with tasks, and they often communicate with each other through their children or through their friends.

They get so in the habit of masquerading before others that they soon appear disguised before their family and their friends. This is spiritual divorce. The couple itself might even come to believe the pretense and may make strenuous efforts to perpetuate the myth of still being in love.

Such marriages take a lot out of each partner, and the children get caught up in the relationship and undergo pain and devastation. In my work, I feel pain and sadness whenever I hear a couple admit, "We are staying together for the sake of the children." By the time the couple makes this statement, the children have usually felt the emptiness and phoniness of the marriage for a very long time. Children carry this type of felt stress in their own lives.

All couples go through hard times, passive times, doubtful times, and hurt times, but these times are usually transitory and short-lived. The pain is only periodic, then it is resolved. The relationship remains secure. When these conditions become chronic, it's a sure sign that spiritual divorce has set in.

If these conditions sound familiar, a spiritual divorce may have already taken place, and the important thing to do is for both people to admit and accept that divorce may be the best decision. Couples often know when this time has come. When there is respect and acceptance, they can move toward a divorce on good terms.

Twelve Symptoms of Spiritual Divorce

1. Chronic sadness between partners
2. Chronic boredom and emptiness, manifested in overeating, TV or computer addiction, or compulsive outside activities and relationships

3. Indifference to each other's problems; a cooling of mutual interests
4. Habitual sexual coldness
5. A lack of small courtesies and tenderness
6. A climate of insincerity and mutual mistrust
7. Superficial communication
8. A feeling of being alone and misunderstood
9. An atmosphere of chronic tension and stress
10. Sarcasm, insults, and pervasive rudeness
11. A relationship permeated by the silent treatment
12. Loss of the capacity for surprise and wonder with each other

---

Sometimes one person comes to this realization much sooner than the other, and there is a great deal of discomfort and discord. Divorce in this situation is much more difficult. One person will file for divorce, and the other person will try to block the divorce or make it very difficult. It is always better to have a cooperative divorce, if possible. There is a network of professionals (accountants, family therapists, and lawyers) who can work with a couple that is seeking a collaborative divorce. See the information at the end of this chapter.

However, if only a few symptoms of spiritual divorce are evident, there may be time to work toward mending and healing the relationship. If two people can talk about what is going on and commit to making changes, perhaps the relationship can be saved. Some of the ways this can happen are the following:

1. The partners make a commitment to each other that they will do their best to understand what each person needs, and they begin to make the changes to meet those needs.
2. Each person takes the responsibility to make a separate life and to find ways to fulfill individual needs without expecting the partner to fill all of his or her needs. Each person hears what the

other is asking, and if it does not interfere with either's well-being, each will offer a way to fulfill the request. Neither will stand in the way of the other's development. One of the important tools my partner and I have used is keeping a file on our disagreements. Some of them solve themselves in time; others get bigger. If a problem gets too big or we have too many disagreements in our files, we seek counseling and make some decisions that help both of us.

3. Each person commits to sharing as honestly as possible what his or her hopes and dreams are. The other listens and finds a way to help make those dreams come true. Each person has to be willing to bend a little to offer help to the other person.

4. Each day the partners find some time for each other and come together, enjoying each other's company. They are not embarrassed to come together like children at play and be there for each other. There is a sense of warmth and trust.

There is nothing as painful as feeling alone in a relationship and nothing as powerful as feeling connected to someone you love.

Whether you are in a predivorce situation or have already decided on divorce, you can get help.

Additional Reading

Tesler, Pauline H., and Peggy Thompson. *Collaborative Divorce: The Revolutionary New Way to Restructure Your Family, Resolve Issues, and Move On with Your Life.* New York: HarperCollins, 2007.

Wegscheider-Cruse, Sharon. *Coupleship: How to Build a Relationship.* Deerfield Beach, FL: HCI, 1988.

Wegscheider-Cruse, Sharon. *Life After Divorce: Create a New Beginning.* Deerfield Beach, FL: HCI, 1994.

Workshops

Coupleship
Couples Intensive
Both programs available at:
Onsite Workshops
Cumberland Furnace, TN
www.onsiteworkshops.com
1-800-341-7432

Resource

International Academy of Collaborative Professionals
www.collaborativepractice.com

thirteen

Affairs: Betrayal Is One of the Deepest Hurts

A crisis is a turning point.

—ANN LINDTHORST

WEBSTER'S DICTIONARY CALLS AN affair an "amorous episode." Oh, the temptation! It can start so easily. Sometimes it's a friendship that simply grows into something more. It might be the shared interest of a job, Little League moms and dads meeting at the games, business colleagues on a travel assignment, two people with a mutual interest, or simply next door neighbors. If a friendship adds sexual tension, it's an easy step to an affair.

It feels good to be noticed, to be touched, and to be understood. Affairs have the luxury and emotional charge of secrecy, which adds energy to the situation. If no one knows about it, no one can interfere or interrupt. How often does that happen for the average married couple? There are countless interruptions from phone calls, family, friends, work, and appointments. Affairs are protected because they have to be planned to be secret, detached, and a matter of focus. This intensity adds a great deal of emotional charge to the togetherness.

There is something that has drawn these two people together. There is some bonding that feels intimate. It might be a sport or a hobby, it might be a career goal, or it might be music or art.

Affairs bring about an ideal situation sexually. Our sensuality and sexuality is dependent on passion. Passion means "full of emotion." To plan, conceal, and actualize an affair, there are many emotions involved: excitement, guilt, happiness, lust, loneliness, curiosity, and fear. With all the feelings that affairs require, there is a great deal of arousal, which feeds sexual passion.

In the beginning, most affairs are full of hope and excitement. This arrangement may go on for some time. However, most affairs come from a place of brokenness or lack in one partner or both partners. People who are full and whole feel deserving of a full committed relationship and are not as vulnerable to getting caught up in an affair. By full and whole, I mean having the self-esteem and confidence that they can have a total relationship and not settle for only part of a relationship.

The term *affair* implies that at least one of the partners is attached to someone else. This someone else has claims on the person who is having the affair: a claim of time, a claim of money, a legal claim, and a claim of connectedness. The claim of connectedness is much more complicated if there are children involved.

Every person in an affair knows what it is like to spend holidays alone, to know that there is a tug from someone else on the time, emotions, and energy of the lover. Ultimately, this decreases self-worth, and a tension grows in the relationship. New feelings of anger, disappointment, and hurt arise, and there is seldom anywhere to go for support for these feelings. (Remember the secrecy.)

My counseling practice introduced me to several young women who continued to believe that their lovers would leave their wives and keep the affair going, yet they themselves were making most of the sacrifices. Depression would set in when they realized that they had let their biological clock run out and had cheated themselves out of a full family life and children of their own.

Many of the men I saw in my practice got caught up in really loving their new young lovers and enjoying their time together. Yet they knew that they would never hurt their children, nor could they hurt their children's mother by leaving her. Ultimately, they ended their affairs, and in each case, both lovers ended up with hurt, anger, guilt, and loneliness.

The spouse almost always knows that there is something amiss in the relationship. When a lover pulls his or her emotions out of the marriage, the spouse can feel that. The spouse can't always verbalize it, but there is a lack of intimacy that goes with the lack of honesty. The same is true of children: they might not know about the affair, but they do know that their parent is not emotionally available to them.

One of the hardest concepts for spouses to understand is that there is not simply an offending partner and a victim of the affair. When an affair occurs, both spouses share responsibility for the loss of intimacy. Affairs do not happen when spouses are connected to each other with great emotional, mental, physical, and spiritual commitment.

Connected couples can withstand long distances, separation, temptation, trauma, and hardship without either person being drawn to a lover. The connection is such a powerful contributor to each spouse's joy, purpose, and happiness that having an affair just isn't in the picture. This is true intimacy, and it happens a great deal of the time.

Affairs happen when there is a crack in that intimacy. Affairs happen when at least one spouse does not feel noticed. He or she most often feels used, underappreciated, bored, lonely, angry, disconnected, and way too busy. When this situation is not remedied, there is a fertile ground for an affair. Affairs are a short-term answer to a long-term problem.

I do want to add that there are a few times that an affair is a prelude to a better way of life. When a relationship is truly broken and it cannot be fixed, sometimes an affair is the beginning of a bit of self-worth that allows a person to have the courage to work through a divorce and become free. This happens occasionally, but it is not the way it usually works. Everyone knows someone for whom this was the case, however, and it's this belief that leads people to an affair for relief from strife and a hope for intimacy. A great deal of introspection and honesty is necessary to see which is the true situation.

Another type of affair that takes place in today's culture uses the Internet to connect. Even if there is no actual sexual component, there can be a very intense and very serious relationship built through the computer. This is an emotional affair, and many hours are taken from the primary relationship and given to the computer lover. This kind of affair is also damaging, because it takes away intimacy from the primary relationship.

Over the past few years, the evidence of increasing infidelity has been mounting. There are many reasons, including the following:

- Affairs are glamorized on television.
- Both men and women have opportunities to share time together in the workplace.

• The availability of out-of-town travel for both sexes means that many partners are left at home while the other partner is on the road or in the air.

Most people begin a relationship filled with hope and commitment. They plan to be faithful. In my work with couples who have had affairs, I have observed that affairs tend to take place at maximal stress times: birth, death, illness, loss of job, geographical move, or retirement. For the couple who has trouble with intimacy, an affair will fill some needs and allow them to avoid intimacy with the partner.

To professionals who work with hurting couples, there is no such thing as a wronged spouse. There are only marriages in which there is conflict and pain. One person's unfaithfulness is often a manifestation of that conflict. Usually both partners play a role in the situation, so both must help to resolve it. Once the situation is fully understood, it is more likely that the couple will be able to work toward some reconciliation. Betrayal through an affair is a wound that sometimes can be healed and sometimes cannot.

Additional Reading

Black, Claudia. *Deceived: Facing Sexual Betrayal, Lies, and Secrets.* Center City, MN: Hazelden Publications, 2009.

Carnes, Patrick J. *The Betrayal Bond: Breaking Free of Exploitive Relationships.* Deerfield Beach, FL: HCI, 1997.

Carnes, Stefanie, ed. *Mending a Shattered Heart: A Guide for Partners of Sex Addicts.* Carefree, AZ: Gentle Path Press, 2008.

Jonson, Carol L. *Affairs: Emergency Tactics.* Syracuse, NY: Somerset Publishing Company, 2001.

Norwood, Robin. *Women Who Love Too Much: When You Keep Wishing and Hoping He'll Change.* New York: Pocket Books, 2008.

Schneider, Jennifer P. *Back from Betrayal: Recovering from His Affairs.* Tucson, AZ: Recovery Resources Press, 2005.

fourteen

Second Wife, Second Priority—Ouch!

Life isn't always that bowl full of cherries. It's sometimes very difficult and painful and we don't feel prepared for it.

—THELMA ELLIOTT

A SECOND WIFE IS any woman who marries a man who has had a previous wife. Being a second wife comes with many specific problems and possibilities. If the first wife was a difficult person and the marriage was broken and painful, the role of second wife suggests the possibility that a woman will be cherished and loved. Her husband has had a chance to compare, and he will do everything he can to appreciate his second wife.

If the first wife abandoned him or cheated on him, the husband will come to the marriage with lots of unfinished business with women, and this will affect the new marriage. With the addition of children, in-laws, and friends, this new relationship can be full of drama and trauma.

Second wives report that some first wives will not let go. When husbands pick up and deliver their children, they are invited in and offered a beer or a glass of wine. Sometimes the first wife uses the children's needs to manipulate the husband by inviting him to come to birthday parties and holiday get-togethers. The second wife often has a lower standard of living than the first wife; sometimes the children have huge financial needs, and the money is allocated for the first marriage while the second marriage gets what is left over.

Glynnis Walker, in her book *Second Wife, Second Best,* tells us that all wives are not created equal. She says that this inequality has nothing to do with economic status or even the relationship itself, and it transcends the boundaries of race and culture. It is merely a question of timing.

Being a second wife is not any easier even if the man is her second husband. Regardless of any other relationships the second wife has had, whether or not she has been married before, the reality is that she is going to be a second wife, with all the privileges and problems that come with that fact.

The dictionary defines *second* as that which comes after the first, the next below the first in rank and value, an article of merchandise not of first quality, and an aid or assistant. This is not a pretty picture. Is it any wonder that our society or culture, along with our

---

Seven Suggestions for a Successful Second Marriage

1. Seek support from a therapist, if necessary.
2. Keep all lines of communication open.
3. Minimize contact with painful situations.
4. Give a little more than you receive.
5. Set boundaries.
6. Attend marriage workshops.
7. Remember why you were attracted to each other in the first place.

---

family and friends, look at the first marriage or first wife as the original and the real thing? The second wife is just that: the second wife. This is a reason that a second divorce is frequent.

Janet was a second wife. Her husband, Dan, had already been emotionally bruised from a failed and frigid marriage. Janet spent a great deal of her time tiptoeing around the issues of the first marriage, trying to avoid getting caught up in Dan's fog of guilt and anger. She was the victim of a set of circumstances she did not create.

Janet is not included in the alimony conflicts, the children's anger and acting out, or the sale of the family home. It's not that she really wants to be included; it's that these issues demand great energy, emotion, and financial burdens that certainly affect her possible intimacy and closeness with her husband. Sometimes these events can be addressed, and sometimes they are too great. This is often when outside help and an objective third person is needed.

Money is a major issue for a second wife. Unless the man is very wealthy or had a good lawyer at the time of his divorce, the second wife will have a lower standard of living with her husband than the first wife did. Money will have to go two ways after the divorce, so there simply will be less of it. First wives most often keep the house. Most receive part of any savings plan and pension plan.

First wives also have access to the money that is part of the settlement for dependent children. For older children, there is insurance, college expenses, and weddings. There is much to consider. Second wives usually work to supplement the income, especially if there are children in both the marriages. Unfortunately, there are many recorded cases where the first wife goes after the earnings of the second wife, especially if she is successful in her work or the husband predeceases the second wife. It is a difficult and lonely situation for the second wife.

Money is one of the most important and effective methods of revenge if there is still anger in the relationship. By being an economic drain on her ex-husband and his new wife, the first wife is guaranteeing that through money, she is a constant presence in the marriage and is punishing him by receiving support without contributing.

The emotional strain is another big hurdle for the second wife. There is the internal feeling that because she is second, she needs to try harder. There is a drive to be included. This sets up a chain reaction of events and feelings. She goes from being a wonderful person to the man she married to being perceived as an outcast to his first family and his friends.

I remember one wife telling me about the devastation she felt at the wedding of her husband's daughter as the many photographs were being taken. She was the only female without a corsage and was waiting in the church pew alone while her husband joined the family for photographs. This kind of aloneness is very common in second marriages. A second wife loses some of her identity, evidenced in language that does not refer to her as Mom or even by name. She is often known as "the woman who married my dad."

If you are a second wife, it is important to realize that you are not alone. It is not just you personally who goes through the pain, confusion, hurt, and powerlessness of being the second wife. It's the position itself that causes much of the distress. Knowing that can be helpful and can give you hope that you will get through it. However, professional help might be the best investment you can make.

Being a second wife does have some positive aspects. A shift in attitude is important. The second wife has the opportunity to define what she wants her marriage to look like. She is able to be clear about what she wants and needs.

Very often the first wife fell into her marriage, following cultural and family norms. When it didn't work as expected, she was filled with anger, resentment, and fear. She demonstrated her pain by becoming controlling and trying to force her husband to fix the marriage. Nevertheless, it broke down, and the lifelong battle of how to end this broken relationship began.

A second wife has the chance to work out some of these problems before or at the time of the second marriage. She can articulate that what she wants is a union between two people who care enough about each other to make a life together. She is able to see some of the pitfalls yet is willing to work toward a physical, emotional, and financial commitment to each other. If she has good support, she can take the extra step and tell her future husband that she needs to be his first priority if they get married.

Very often, the situation is one in which the husband is prepared to make a better choice the second time around. He, too, may have fallen into the first marriage by meeting cultural expectations for men at that age and time, or perhaps he married because of an unplanned pregnancy or a desire for sex. In his second marriage, he is more mature and knows more about what he wants in his life. Even though it's his second marriage, it may be his first real choice.

Because the second wife may be a true choice in a way that the first wife was not, there are greater odds that she and her husband have mutual interests, mutual goals, and like spending time together. First wives often become parents sooner, and parent more intensely than, second wives. Second wives tend to put as much into being a couple as they do in becoming parents, and this is source of satisfaction for the second marriage.

People in a second marriage are often much more aware that the partnership is an economic one as well as a romantic one. They are able to plan better together for the present and the future. First wives often expect to be taken care of by their husbands. Second wives are prepared to contribute and also to be part of the financial planning and the execution of those plans. Because of a need for much discussion about finances, the future, goals, and interests, an intimacy is built in the second marriage that was never present in the first marriage. This is a bonus for both partners in the second marriage.

There is often a strong commitment to fidelity in a second marriage. Many remarried men and women have had affairs during their first marriages, or they were married to a spouse who had an affair. The pain and hurt of betrayal is a common occurrence in the first marriage. This lays fertile ground for discussion in the second marriage and puts fidelity on the table for serious discussion. Making a commitment to fidelity is also a benefit of the second marriage, because each partner does not want to revisit that pain.

All efforts are put to a severe test in a second marriage. Nevertheless, in the context of a loving, mutually supportive relationship, the complexities of a second marriage become opportunities to achieve great intimacy, maturity, and joy.

Additional Reading

Norwood, Robin. *Women Who Love Too Much: When You Keep Wishing and Hoping He'll Change.* New York: Pocket Books, 2008.

Paul, Jordan, and Margaret Paul. *Do I Have to Give Up Me to Be Loved by You?* Center City, MN: Hazelden, 2002.

Stuart, Richard B., and Barbara Jacobson. *Second Marriage: Make It Happy. Make It Last!* New York: W. W. Norton & Company, 1985.

Walker, Glynnis. *Second Wife, Second Best? Managing Your Marriage as a Second Wife.* Scarborough, Ontario: Doubleday Canada, 1984.

Workshops

Coupleship
Couples Intensive
Both programs available at:
Onsite Workshops
Cumberland Furnace, TN
www.onsiteworkshops.com
1-800-341-7432

fifteen

Girlfriends and Giraffes

Let us be grateful to the people who make us happy.
They are the gardeners who make our souls blossom.

—MARCEL PROUST

MOST OF US WHO have a computer have received many e-mails entitled "Girlfriends." These e-mails are all the same and they are all different. The message of them is that girlfriends are important and maybe one of the most important relationships as we journey through life. Giraffe love is part of that—we'll get to that shortly.

Little girls know all about bonding. They want sleepovers and slumber parties as soon as they are old enough to call their friends on the phone. Right from the beginning, they tell secrets, laugh at private jokes, and talk about what is important to them. The subjects change, the clothes change, and the age changes, but the ability to bond does not change.

Teen years are full of get-togethers, long nights of talking, secrets shared, phone calls, text messaging, and e-mails. We tell our girlfriends what we do not tell anyone else. There are times in our lives when we tell them what we do not tell our boyfriends, our siblings, or our parents.

Sometimes there is a time-out. Sometimes our girlfriends have to be put on the back burner. That tends to happen when someone falls in love and the new loved one shoots right up to "most important" on the list.

However, girlfriends give showers, help to plan weddings, and drink wine together long into the night as everyone is finishing college and getting jobs. Everyone becomes busy and then real busy. Enter in-laws, jobs, children, baseball practice, and dance lessons, and the vibrant life of the girlfriends gets less time on the calendar. Life changes.

Enter "giraffe love." Giraffes are wonderful animals. They are exotic and strong and delicate, just what it takes to be special. Somewhere in adult life, girlfriends surface again. There is something that clicks between women, and that old feeling of female bonding comes forth. It happened to me a few years ago when seven women decided to meet once a year for a "same time next year" gathering. The goal was to have fun, see a little of Las Vegas, and share a long weekend catching up on the year's activities. We had a few meetings. They were absolutely great.

Then for different reasons some of the women could not continue with the meetings. Others chose to keep meeting, and they picked the giraffe as their mascot because giraffes have the largest heart of all mammals, they take risks (stick their necks out), and have great vision (with their long necks they can see long distances).

The women in this group liked to think that they had large hearts, could take risks, and had great vision.

They committed to meeting at least once a year and spending four days sharing their deepest thoughts and feelings and giving feedback to each other. All the women are therapists, and getting the insight of three therapists every time you speak is a rich experience. To have someone know you over the years and watch your behavior and listen to your feelings in total honesty is a treasure, and very few people have it.

These women have gone through the suicide of a son, the illness and death of a daughter, estrangement from children, a divorce, heart disease, cancer, and a serious fall. Yet their souls have triumphed. They are fully engaged in life, making wonderful contributions, and giving and receiving love. They know how to laugh, to cry, and to cherish. When they meet and share their pains and their triumphs, they give energy and inspiration to one another.

It's a sisterhood to be treasured. These annual meetings nourish souls, slow down lives, and open up hearts. If you have friends who make this kind of commitment to you, you are blessed.

I also meet annually with a group that is committed to a time-out for their minds, bodies, and spirits. There are twenty-five of us, and we have been doing our annual "spa time" for several years. Marion Woodman—a Jungian analyst, lecturer, and author of seven books about human consciousness—would say yes to these experiences. She would call them "experiences of the feminine." Each woman who attends this time-out brings with her years of rich experiences and knowledge.

What happens is that each person slows down and lets individual wisdom permeate the time together. We swim, we dance, we hike, we share meals. While we are slowing down our bodies, we let our minds rest and allow deep thoughts and feelings to surface. We share with one another as little or as much as we choose at that moment. In the sharing, our souls meet and spiritual happenings occur. New insights and directions seem clear, there is great understanding, and we feel a sense of peace and serenity. It is a great healing time.

To be sure that I have plenty of fun in my life, I also belong to a tap dancing company. Twice a week I put on my tap dancing skirt, tights, and tap dancing shoes. For about ten years, tap dancing has been part of my life with its music, sisterhood, costumes, and exercise. Feeling like a little girl again is fun. In addition, there are all the lunches, parties, and outings that are byproducts of this fun-loving group. It's one more group that gives me support, a sense of belonging, and a great reality check when I tend to get too serious.

Yet another group that brings me joy is what I call my "kindness group." This is a small group of women that meet every month. During the month, each woman spends a set amount of money buying something for a stranger. It can be anything: picking up a tab for someone she sees in a restaurant, buying a toy for a child in the store (with the parents' approval, of course), paying for parking or a toll for the person behind her, or taking a cup of coffee to a postal employee.

When we meet, we bring stories about our activities to share. It's our own version of "paying it forward." My favorite was picking up the tab for two teens in a pizza place. They were shocked when they went up to the counter and were told that their bill had been paid. I stayed in my booth to watch the reaction. They never knew who paid the tab, but they had big smiles on their faces when they left the pizza restaurant.

What to Look For in a Friend

F	Fun, forgiving, faithful
R	Reliable, real, reassuring
I	Inseparable, interested, inspiring
E	Exciting, energetic, easy
N	Nurturing, necessary, noncompetitive
D	Dependable, daring, delightful
S	Smart, silly, soothing
H	Helpful, hallowed, handy
I	Independent, imaginative
P	Pampering, pragmatic, pleasing

All of these encounters with other women enrich my life. I give and I take. My heart expands, and my breathing is slower and easier after I have been with my girlfriends.

Some girlfriends live close and you can see them every day, whereas others you must connect with by telephone and e-mail. One dances with you and one just wants to go to lunch. Another listens to you talk about your children or your grandchildren. Another listens to you talk about your boyfriends or your partner. One friend will pray with you, another will share a glass of wine. One will go walking with you to stay in shape, and another will go with you on a cruise. You may have one dear friend who can do all these things, or you may have many girlfriends, each bringing something different to your life.

Treasure these friendships. They are true riches in life.

Additional Reading

Allenbaugh, Kay. *Chocolate for a Woman's Soul: 77 Stories to Feed Your Spirit and Warm Your Heart.* New York: Fireside, 1997.

Coates, Jennifer. *Women Talk: Conversations Between Women Friends.* Hoboken, NJ: Wiley-Blackwell, 1991.

Woodman, Marion, and Jill Mellick. *Coming Home to Myself: Reflections for Nurturing a Woman's Body and Soul.* Berkeley, CA: Conari Press, 2001.

Wyse, Lois. *Women Make the Best Friends: A Celebration.* New York: Simon & Schuster, 1995.

sixteen

Girlfriends Make My World Go Around

No matter how good a friend is, they [sic]
are going to hurt you every once in a while
and you must forgive them for that.

—MARY ANN PLATT

THE FIRST PEOPLE WE know are family. We grow up belonging to a blood family, an adoptive family, or other people who care for us. However, at a very young age, we start to choose the people we want to be around. Little children call these people playmates, teens call them buddies, and eventually we call these people friends. Life changes forever when we find friends.

Friendship is born at the moment one person says to another, "What?! You too? I thought I was the only one," says C. S. Lewis. The person who tries to live alone will not succeed as a human being. Friends are the people with whom you dare to be yourself. You can bare your soul. We all need male and female friends—not lovers, but friends.

Life is full of ups and downs, and we all have great joys and our share of problems. When things get tough, women tend to turn to

93

their friends to talk it over. Part of the reason for this is that men and women generally look at problems differently. Men tend to go it alone, and women tend to want to talk about things.

For example, women tend to have a more adaptive and creative way of looking at problems. Men want to get to the point and make a decision. Women want to look at all the angles and consequences and find an answer that works in a more all-encompassing way. Women like to play around with an idea—talking about it, having fun with it, and even expanding on it. Men want to analyze the facts and decide. Another way of saying this is that women respond intuitively, whereas men want to be more logical. Women like to work with a group and form a team, men like to go it alone. (All of these generalizations are about the tendencies of women as a group and men as a group; there are, of course, individual exceptions in both sexes.)

Neither way is right or wrong; it is simply different. That's why women need girlfriends. Women are the keepers of each other's secrets. They are the coconspirators in life's adventures. They laugh, cry, and talk. Through this, they keep each other well.

Men, on the other hand, also need this kind of connection, but it's often hard for them to get together and talk about things. I simply see it as different. They tend to connect while working out, watching a ball game, working on a computer project, or playing sports. This may sound like stereotyping. However, check it out. It's true. I think one of the greatest examples is that while men gather around to watch the Super Bowl, women get together for lunch and a visit.

Through the centuries and in many cultures, females have banded together for protection and support. Anthropologists have seen female bonding as a mystery. Friendship between and among women is protective and nourishing. It buffers hardship, lowers blood pressure, boosts immunity, and promotes healing. Perhaps this is why women have higher life expectancies.

"Loneliness is simply one of the principal causes of premature death in this country," says Dr. James J. Lynch, a Maryland-based author and psychologist who works with cardiac rehabilitation patients.

There are certain types of girlfriends that every female needs to have, just as males need other males in different ways. I've identified the following eight different kinds of girlfriend:

1. *The encouraging friend.* This is the friend who says, "Go for it." You could tell her you are leaving a great job to become a belly dancer, and she would encourage you all the way. She is always standing by to be your cheerleader and constantly reminds you that the world is a better place because you are in it.

2. *The truth teller.* You can count on this friend to tell you that the outfit you're wearing just doesn't look good or that you are acting strangely. The friendship is established, and there are no overtures of jealousy or malice. This kind of friend is a keeper because you know there is always someone who will help you to see the truth.

3. *The secret keeper.* You can tell this friend that you are thinking about a divorce, leaving your job, or having an affair, and you know that she will never say a word. She is there to listen and support. Your information is completely safe with her.

4. *The fun friend.* With this friend there are no agendas and no secrets, just lots of fun. Her enthusiasm is unconditional and ever present. She gives you permission to put all your responsibilities on hold and head out for a night with Tom Jones or Zac Efron. She encourages you to wear last year's too-tight jeans and more makeup than usual. It's all about the good time.

5. *The old friend.* There is a song that goes "Make new friends, but keep the old one, one is silver and one is gold." It's a treasure to

have a friend who knew you when, who knew your parents, and was there when you were growing up. My life feels grounded and stable when I talk with my old friends. It's like having a living memory book. It reminds us that who we are comes from who we were. An English proverb says, "The best mirror is an old friend."

6. *The travel buddy.* Everybody needs someone to travel with who can take the ups and downs of adventure. Anyone can be a tourist and see the sights. Being a traveler is very different. It means taking risks, having some things turn out well and other things be a bust. This is the person who can take the roller-coaster ride with you and be totally happy with the flexibility and excitement of a new adventure.

7. *The lunch friend.* Twice a month, my lunch friend and I settle in for a three-hour lunch and catching up on each other's lives. This sharing is the glue that holds us together for three hours. Trust, laughter, occasional tears, and learning take place. We save our stories, ideas, and questions for this special time. Our three hours together feels cathartic and renewing, and we each go on our way to begin to build our life stories until the next time.

8. *The confident friend.* This woman is very comfortable with herself, and she's a great reminder that we can all be a little more generous and thoughtful. She sends out Valentine's Day cards, birthday cards, and holiday greetings. She brings over a pot of chicken noodle soup if she hears you are sick. She is content with herself and doesn't feel as though she has to be a part of everything you do. If you have a party and don't invite her, she will call to see if you want to borrow her card table and chairs. She is an inspiration of simple goodness.

Each type of friend is special in her own way. You might have even more, or you may only have two or three, but they embody the above characteristics. It's often been said that life is partly what we make it and partly what is made by the friends we choose. Leadership coach Jane Nakken says, "Friends should be chosen carefully, because loving them will change our hearts and souls."

Changing friends and eliminating friendships is sometimes necessary and a difficult part of life. There is no way to keep all friends for all time.

Once, in a workshop on personal growth, the facilitator asked me to come up in front of the group. She said that she wanted to make a visual point about friendship. It was a cool day, and we were in a room with the windows open. Most of the people were wearing sweaters or jackets. She asked me to describe my closest friends by putting on a different sweater or jacket to demonstrate each friend. My list was long. As I mentioned each friend, I had to find a jacket or a sweater to put on. I was borrowing from everyone in the room. Soon I had on so many sweaters and coats that I could not move.

The point was well taken. There were so many people in my life that I was tired and unable to move. I felt stuck. There was no way for me to feel free or available to any of my friends because I was so overwhelmed and uncomfortable. The facilitator had made a very valuable point with me: there comes a time when one ends or limits some friendships in the interest of time and energy.

She pointed out that we should never just drop a friend and have the person wonder what happened. Rather, we should say good-bye after thanking the person for being in our lives, and then we move on. This felt coldhearted to me until I tried it; then it felt really good. The first time I told a friend that times had changed and my life was full of grandchildren, health care, and new activities, it was scary. We were at lunch, and my friend replied, "Thank you for being part of my life. I understand your changes. Let's try to have lunch once a year and catch up." We do, so we now have an annual friendship instead of a monthly one, and it is rich.

I then tried it out with more friends. Only one friend told me that she felt rejected and hurt. I acknowledged her hurt and told her that my time was so limited that this decision was necessary. I let her know that I cared about her and hoped we could keep in touch. She really couldn't understand, but that's just the way it is. I felt okay, since I was very honest with her. She e-mails me occasionally and I respond. It's comfortable for me.

My friends make my world go around, just as my family does. The friends who have become very important to me are the ones who give me plenty of breathing space and accept that my family is most important and requires lots of time and energy. My best friends are those who even help me to keep bonding with my family. My very best friend often gives me little gifts for my family. She knows that my time is limited, so she shows her love for me by honoring my family.

Here's a suggestion for an activity: make a list of your girlfriends and meditate on each one's gift to you.

Additional Reading

Girlfriend Getaways magazine, www.girlgetaways.com

Lynch, James J. *The Broken Heart: The Medical Consequences of Loneliness.* New York: Basic Books, 1978.

seventeen

Coupleship: I Need Closeness with My Partner

*A successful marriage requires falling in love
many times, always with the same person.*

—MIGNON MCLAUGHLIN

INTIMACY IN A RELATIONSHIP is one of the greatest joys of life. How can we make that come true for ourselves? The Danish philosopher Soren Kierkegaard tells us, "To cheat one's self out of love is the most terrible deception, it is an eternal loss for which there is no reparation, either in time or in eternity." Relationships are both "what makes the world go 'round" and infinitely challenging.

The hope of every relationship is to find a close partnership. The word that I have invented to talk about the optimal relationship between two people is *coupleship*, and I will use that word throughout this chapter.

Eight Ways to Build Closeness

1. Ask for and respect your partner's opinion.
2. When stress gets too high, take a break: go to dinner, see a movie.

3. Support each other's interests.
4. Keep your sense of humor; help each other when one loses perspective.
5. Make time and money decisions together.
6. Say "I love you" each day. If you can't, something is wrong.
7. Plan some "timeless time" each day. Try for thirty minutes a day and half a day each week, with no plans and no agenda. Just see what happens.
8. Do a ten-minute daily listening time. Each partner listens to the other and makes no response.

Coupleship is a passionate spiritual, emotional, and sexual commitment between two people that nurtures both people and maintains a high regard for the value of each person. *Passionate* simply means "full of feeling," being full of life. Each of us is responsible for bringing energy, excitement, plans, and joy to the partnership. It can be a challenge to keep doing this once both partners become busy with jobs, in-laws, children, friends, and the rest of life, but it is essential that both partners bring themselves fully to the partnership.

Fifteen Ways to Enhance Coupleship

1. Be honest when sharing feelings.
2. Learn how to fight fairly.
3. Tell your partner that he or she is number one.
4. Take some romance responsibility.
5. Honor the sensual and sexual aspects of the relationship.
6. Say "I love you" often.
7. Be financially responsible.

8. Pray together.
9. Remember special dates.
10. Plan time for the coupleship.
11. Learn the magic words: "I'm sorry, it was my fault, how can I make it better?"
12. Find humor in stressful times.
13. Care about your mate's interests.
14. Eat meals together when you can.
15. Except when one of you is traveling, try to go to bed together regularly.

The first responsibility of each partner is to clean up any excess baggage that he or she is bringing to the relationship. Baggage can be emotions and relationships that are connected to childhood, former marriages, adult children, financial difficulties, or friends. Each partner must come to the relationship honest, unfettered, and ready to make a commitment. An exception is if there are children who must be cared for from a previous relationship. All other emotional baggage is the responsibility of each person to deal with and not bring to the coupleship.

The next responsibility is to discuss and agree on the possible "invaders" that could harm this relationship. Invaders are people, substances, behaviors, or attitudes that work against the intimacy of a relationship.

People invaders might be friends, parents and siblings, adult children, support systems, ex-partners, and affairs. They can be recognized when they undermine and impair the partnership. They deplete energy and interfere with the partners' capacity for each other. Friends have the ability to become invaders when they come between the couple. As long as the partnership is seen as sacred, people invaders will not pose a threat. However, if others take first place with either partner, there is likely to be stress, and the coupleship will show damage.

Invaders can also be chemical: excess alcohol, abuse of drugs (both illegal and prescribed), nicotine, and even food. These affect health, judgment, and attention. If any of these substances has the power to take the person out of the coupleship, it must be seen as an invader and as something that has to be addressed and handled. There is an emotional barrier when a partner is anesthetizing his or her emotions with a chemical, and it just gets worse if both partners are doing so.

Behavioral invaders include compulsive gambling, sexual acting out, workaholism, excess television watching, or an overinvolvement with computer activity or sports. These are harmful habits that take time and energy away from the coupleship.

Finally, there are attitudinal invaders. These are thoughts, feelings, and perceptions that color our outlook on life. They include family myths, constant negativity, terminal seriousness, intolerant religiosity, rigid political beliefs, constant hypervigilance, and worry. These invaders put a gloomy pall over the relationship.

For a couple to develop intimacy and trust, they need to learn how to set boundaries. Boundaries teach those around us that we are important and that our needs as a couple are important. Emotional baggage and invaders of any kind must not deplete the energy and trust of the couple.

Ten Dangers to a Fulfilling Coupleship

1. Giving your mother, father, or a friend more importance than your partner
2. Scheduling your partner's time without asking first

3. Projecting your insecurities (from job, parent, finances) onto your mate and expecting them to be fixed
4. Putting your partner down in public or in private
5. Bringing up old data or anger in a current fight
6. Talking frequently about an ex-anything
7. Holding back honest feelings
8. Being indecisive about decisions that have to be made
9. Acting fragile, inept, or helpless
10. Telling partial truths

Psychiatrist Ralph Roughton tells us about the benefits of just listening:

> When I ask you to listen and you start giving advice, I feel unheard. When I ask you to listen and you tell me I shouldn't feel that way, I feel discounted. Please listen! Do not talk or do—just hear me. Please!

Learn how to fight fairly. There are going to be differences, anger, and disagreements, but it's how you express these that is the issue. Here are eight tips for finding your way through fighting:

1. *Give yourself permission to fight.* Accept that disagreements and fights are natural when two people are trying to merge into a coupleship.
2. *Know why you are fighting.* Be honest and know what is happening.
3. *Establish a goal when you fight.* It's not about winning, it's about clearing the air and finding a solution.
4. *Have fair rules for fighting.* Stay away from what is hurtful and from bringing up old issues. Never yell or get physical.

5. *Take responsibility for yourself.* Use sentences that start with I, not you.
6. *Be respectful.* It's not about being right or wrong. It's about hearing the other person and finding a solution.
7. *Look for the feelings behind the issue.* That will help you get to what is really happening.
8. *Find anything you can agree on.* It might start with little steps before a full agreement can be reached.

If the argument is lengthy or hurtful, remember the following three *A*s:

1. *Apologize.* Admit that you might have said some harsh things when trying to negotiate or seek understanding. Be sure that you apologize for what you said or did.
2. *Assure.* Let your partner know that even though you are disagreeing, you love and respect him or her. Differences do not mean a lack of love.
3. *Accept.* Recognize that you feel differently and that discussion and negotiation is going to be necessary. No one has to be a winner or a loser.

Randy Pausch, who died of terminal cancer after giving a wonderfully inspirational speech called "The Last Lecture," and a bestselling book of the same name, noted that there are three important statements that come easily to people who are in respectful and loving relationships:

• "I'm sorry!"
• "It was my fault."
• "How can I make it better?"

Try these three sentences. They can help any relationship become stronger and more mutually rewarding.

No one—and no relationship—is perfect. There is a guideline called "the 80 percent rule." Sometimes 80 percent is enough. Just because someone doesn't love you the way you want them to doesn't mean that they don't love you with all that they have. For long-term happiness in love, if you can look at your partner and say, "I have at least 80 percent of everything I want in a mate," consider yourself blessed. Turn to your friends, other family members, and coworkers to get that last 20 percent. No one can be expected to fill 100 percent of your wants and needs.

Additional Reading

Sherven, Judith, and James Sniechowski. *The New Intimacy: Discovering the Magic at the Heart of Your Differences.* Deerfield Beach, FL: HCI, 1997.

Wegscheider-Cruse, Sharon. *Coupleship: How to Build a Relationship.* Deerfield Beach, FL: HCI, 1988.

Workshops

Coupleship
Onsite Workshops
Cumberland Furnace, TN
www.onsiteworkshops.com
1-800-341-7432

Resource

Couples Therapy *(intensive programs)*
John and Linda Friel 1-866-561-4916

eighteen

Losing Myself When
I Am in Love

Remember to let the winds of heaven dance between you.

—RALPH BLUM

ONE OF THE MOST difficult balances to achieve in a marriage is "what is me" and "what becomes us." This is true with money, time, recreation, vacations, and many other things. It's an ongoing tightrope, and often there is tension around what is "me" and what is "us."

This is the birth of the coupleship; it comes with the decision to marry and form a new unit. In marriage, we give up a claim on a totally separate self to become part of a new relationship. We honor that new "us." It doesn't mean that we cannot have separate interests and separate time, but it does mean that we give up wanting to maintain a concealed or private life in the context of a marriage.

This is often very difficult if one of the partners is still hooked into the unit of a former family. It may be the family of origin, to which one remains overly connected, or it may be a former marriage to which one still feels connected because children are involved. It may mean having a strong connection with a friend or even with a group.

The Bible (Genesis 2:24) says that "a man shall leave his father and his mother and cling to his wife, and they shall be one flesh." The idea (applying it to both sexes) is that when you get married, you should make other relationships secondary to your partnership with your mate. It's not that you have to choose between someone else and your partner. Marriage was the choice, and now the partner is forever the priority. Great marriages work from this principle. They hold sacred the bond of marriage and the other spouse. All other decisions are made in support of that bond.

The partners may take turns being the focal point in a relationship. Sometimes one person's career might require both people to contribute to what it takes to make that career work. Sometimes both people have to take turns with the primary responsibility for child care. They know, however, that the bond of their coupleship always comes first.

The key to making coupleship work is honesty and ongoing communication. So often people say that they have trouble communicating. The truth is that most people know exactly how to communicate *if* they want to do so. The basis of poor communication is usually anger. We simply do not want to share ourselves with someone who has hurt us or disappointed us, so we withhold sharing as a way of communicating our resentment.

Once we have decided not to share something significant with our partner, we rearrange our priorities and let the partner know, through our resistance and silence, that he or she is not a priority to us anymore. If communication has broken down, it is just a sign that the coupleship has become less important to us and that our personal wants and needs have taken first place.

Excess emotional baggage is the responsibility of each partner. It is necessary to clear it up and not bring the feelings surrounding this baggage into the marriage. Each person needs to bring his or her whole self to the coupleship. Unresolved emotional baggage can create a separateness that damages the intimacy the partners have with each other.

Intimacy is also damaged when the partners allow invaders into the relationship; these were discussed in the previous chapter.

One does not fall "in" or "out" of love. One chooses to grow and deepen in love, or one chooses to ignore the needs of love, and love withers and dies.

On the wall of a public building, I found the following message. Although it is sometimes attributed to Ann Landers, I have found no credit for it; if credit is ever found, I want to know about it. It is so beautiful that it must be shared:

Love is friendship that has caught fire. It is also quiet understanding, mutual confidence, trust, sharing, and forgiving. Love is elemental. Its nature is unselfish, for it seeks only to nurture the life to which it is given. With patience and tenderness, it opens the way for that life to grow, to unfurl, and to dream.

Love is patient, love is kind. It does not envy, it does not boast, it is not proud. It is not rude, it is not self-seeking. It is not easily angered, it keeps no record of wrongs. It always protects, always trusts, always hopes, and always perseveres. Love can get through times of no sex better than sex can get you through times of no love. Love does not fail.

If you have love in your life, it can make up for a great deal of lack. If you don't have it, no matter what else there is, it is not enough.

Additional Reading

Paul, Jordan, and Margaret Paul. *Do I Have to Give Up Me to Be Loved by You?* Center City, MN: Hazelden, 2002.

Stone, Hal, and Sidra Stone. *Partnering: A New Kind of Relationship.* Novato, CA: New World Library, 2000.

Stuart, Richard B., and Barbara Jacobson. *Second Marriage: Make It Happy! Make It Last!* New York: W. W. Norton & Company, 1985.

Wegscheider-Cruse, Sharon. *Coupleship: How to Build a Relationship.* Deerfield Beach, FL: HCI, 1988.

Workshops

Coupleship
Couples Intensive
Both programs available at:
Onsite Workshops
Cumberland Furnace, TN
www.onsiteworkshops.com
1-800-341-7432

PART FOUR:

FAMILIES

To the world you might be one person,
but to me, you are the world.

—Anonymous

nineteen

Birth Order Traits: Does It Matter Who Is the Oldest or the Youngest?

Family faces are magic mirrors. Looking at people who belong to us, we see the past, present, and future.

—GAIL LUMET BUCKLEY

THERE IS NO GETTING around it: we are each born into our spot in the family. There are many traits that are predetermined simply by our birth order. Circumstances and unique situations are definitely part of the equation, yet some of the birth order givens apply to most people.

All of us were children at one time. Whether we like it or not, we were influenced by our childhoods, by our position in the family and how we related to our parents and our siblings.

The firstborn child enters a family of two adults, and those two adults are the role models for this child. Is it any wonder that this child matures quickly and models adult behavior, acting like a little adult?

The firstborn child is most likely to become responsible at an early age and to develop adult skills very early. I have referred to this child as an *alert* or a *family hero*. Firstborns tend to be very concerned about themselves and their parents and to live on alert. They become little family caretakers. They remember to lock the doors and turn out the lights. They see to it that food is prepared. Later in life, they plan family get-togethers, double-check the airline times, replace the paper in the printer, take great notes, and speak up to break the silence.

Their strengths include confidence, leadership, and caring. Firstborns are often quite successful. They may feel that they are not accomplishing enough, because they are programmed to compare themselves with older, more mature adults. On the outside, they appear confident, capable, talented, and strong. On the inside, they often feel scared, incapable, inferior, tired, and inadequate.

Research shows that firstborns, as well as only children, lead the pack in educational attainment, occupational prestige, income, and net worth. They tend to be more conscientious, ambitious, and aggressive than the younger siblings. They often move toward careers in medicine, engineering, or law.

Dalton Conley, in his book *The Pecking Order: Which Siblings Succeed and Why*, observes the following:

> Every astronaut to go into space has been either the oldest child in his or her family or the eldest boy. More than half of all Nobel Prize winners and U.S. Presidents have been firstborns. Famous eldest children include: Hillary Clinton, Bill Clinton, Richard Branson, J. K. Rowling, and Winston Churchill.

Middle children seem to have less of a need for approval. Some middle children rebel against the extremely responsible oldest child. They tend either to become an opposite—rebelling against what the parents and the oldest child value—or to simply pull away and not enter the family circle.

The angry rebels I refer to as *scapegoats*, and the ones that pull away I call *lost children*. Either way, they don't often find the validation in the family that they so sorely need. Both the scapegoat and the lost child are trying to find their place in the family and in the world.

One of the strengths of middle children is the ability to make and maintain good friendships outside the family and in the world. They are loyal and trustworthy friends. Middle children are very independent and look outside the family for their self-worth. Sometimes they act out to be noticed, and sometimes they find a special sense of belonging in clubs, in other groups, and in their hobbies. They tend to excel in technology, computers, and other independent pursuits. On the outside, they can appear either as aloof or as trying to attract attention; this can be good attention or bad attention. On the inside, they often feel angry, lonely, inferior, and defiant.

Middle children are more easygoing and peer-oriented than other children. They build bridges to outside sources of support and have excellent friendship and people skills. They make great mediators, peacemakers, and caretakers. Famous middle children include Bill Gates, John Kennedy, and Princess Diana.

Youngest children have learned that they need to find and then take a place in the family. Often the way they do it is with whatever makes people notice them. Sometimes that is humor and sometimes it is acting out. This child might become the family clown or the mascot, the one who demands attention with antics. Many youngest children become comedians later in life.

As young children, they often appear hyperactive. They may feel tension in the family and act out just to change the atmosphere. Youngest children have a tendency to be loners and like solitary activities. They enjoy television, computers, and technical games. They are often very bright and enjoy puzzles and challenges. They tend to feel a great deal of responsibility to the parents, and the parents, for their own reasons, often keep the youngest child immature and close to one of them.

Whereas oldest children tend to be old for their age, youngest children are often young for their age. Their strengths are compassion, loyalty to the parents, intelligence, and a high level of energy. Inside, they often feel scared, helpless, lonely, and incapable.

Youngest children tend to be both charming and creative. They may champion a cause, and once they choose a cause, they give it their all. They are successful in journalism, advertising, sales, and the arts. Famous youngest children are Jim Carrey, Eddie Murphy, and Billy Crystal.

Only children are very much like firstborns and are often burdened with high expectations from their parents. They are confident, articulate, and have great imaginations. They are known to be perfectionists. Famous only children include Tiger Woods, Leonardo da Vinci, and Alan Greenspan.

This is obviously just a thumbnail sketch of the roles in the family; there is much more to them. For instance, even though the only child in a family is very much like the firstborn, he or she often takes on the characteristics of middle and youngest children as well. It's a very hard role to play, and many only children feel very lonely. In healthy families, all these roles are changeable as the children mature and grow up. However, in high-stress families or addictive families, these roles become much more permanent, and it's more difficult for the children to change.

Most researchers stipulate that we are talking only about traits and trends. The whole birth order theory can be changed depending on a child's personality, the age gap between siblings, the parenting that takes place, and each family's circumstances.

Additional Reading

Conley, Dalton. *The Pecking Order: Which Siblings Succeed and Why.* New York: Pantheon Books, 2004.

Isaacson, Clifford, and Kris Radish. *The Birth Order Effect: How to Better Understand Yourself and Others.* Avon, MA: Adams Media, 2002.

Leman, Kevin. *The New Birth Order Book: Why You Are the Way You Are.* Grand Rapids, MI: Revell Books, 1998.

Sulloway, Frank J. *Born to Rebel: Birth Order, Family Dynamics, and Creative Lives.* New York: Vintage Books, 1997.

Wallace, Meri. *Birth Order Blues: How Parents Can Help Their Children Meet the Challenges of Their Birth Order.* New York: Holt, 1999.

twenty

Why Are Families So Different?

*Call it a clan, call it a network, call it a tribe,
call it a family. Whatever you call it,
whoever you are, you need one.*

—JANE HOWARD

IT SEEMS THAT SOME families just work out and everyone likes living in that family. Then there are families that seem to have one problem after another. Why does that happen?

Although it seems that some families have better luck in every way than other families, it is not really about luck. It's about the way the family members feel about themselves and one another that makes the difference. I remember when I first heard a wonderful family therapist, Virginia Satir, say, "In unhealthy families, children are there to meet the needs of the parents. In healthy families, parents are there to meet the needs of the children."

When the parents are whole and healthy people, they have all the tools that are necessary to raise children who will also be whole and healthy. When the parents are not whole and healthy, the children will feel stress and chaos, and problems will flourish.

To be whole and healthy means that each parent has a well-developed sense of self-worth and has developed and nourished his or her physical, emotional, relational, spiritual, mental, and financial self. In addition, whole and healthy people have the courage to make the choices in their lives that keep them whole and healthy. When both parents have developed themselves, they are ready to have children and pass on their tools.

In our society, many parents are lacking this kind of maturity and development and do not have these tools to pass on to their children. Those children thus grow up to be parents long before their personal needs have been met, and the dysfunction passes on from generation to generation.

Rules That Build Self-Worth

1. Communication is open and everything can be discussed.
2. Feelings are valued and people are encouraged to share those feelings.
3. The rules that have to be followed are spoken and clear.
4. There is a respect for each person and his or her beliefs and values.
5. Requests are spoken and clear. There is no need for manipulation.
6. Value systems are discussed.
7. People are open-minded and differences are respected.
8. New traditions and ways of doing things are created.
9. There is a sense of physical and emotional health in the family.
10. Trust and love prevail.

One of the ways to understand the ability of parents to provide a healthy home for their children is to assess the rules in the family. Some rules are spoken: "You have to be home by 11:00 PM and you have to call if you'll be later." Spoken rules allow for discussion, modification, and negotiation.

Rules That Undermine Self-Worth

1. A no-talk rule: certain things cannot be openly discussed.
2. Feelings are not shared; only facts and opinions are.
3. Entangled relationships: certain people connect only with certain other people.
4. There is manipulation and control of one another.
5. Belief systems are rigid; there is very little flexibility.
6. Only past traditions matter.
7. There are many stress-related illnesses.
8. There is a sense of grimness in the house.
9. Jealousy and suspicion are common.
10. Family members exhibit dependent behavior.

Other rules are unspoken: *Women are less important than men* or *Mom makes the rules.* These rules are understood rather than spoken. Unspoken rules are very dysfunctional because there is no room for discussion or disagreement. They contribute to dishonesty, anger, and deceit. Rules that undermine self-worth create home settings that are stressful and painful for the people who live there.

Changing the rules and expectations of the house can make a big difference in how it feels to live there.

Author Caroline Myers tells us, "We evolve at the rate of the tribe we are plugged into. We need to let the old way of being go, so the new way of being can emerge."

Additional Reading

Satir, Virginia. *Peoplemaking.* London: Souvenir Press, 1990.

Wegscheider-Cruse, Sharon. *Another Chance: Hope and Health for the Alcoholic Family.* Palo Alto, CA: Science and Behavior Books, 1989.

twenty-one

Someone I Love Is in Trouble— How Can I Intervene?

> *You gain strength, courage, and confidence by every experience in which you really stop to look fear in the face.*
>
> —ELEANOR ROOSEVELT

THERE IS LITTLE THAT is more painful than to watch people we care about hurt themselves. It happens in many different ways: someone may drink too much, eat too much, gamble too much, or use nicotine in any form; enter unhealthy love relationships, fall down on the job, drift in their career, or mismanage personal finances. This list is endless.

For the person who is watching the self-destructive behavior, it's a painful scenario. There are feelings of anger, helplessness, and frustration. One can just stay in those feelings, or one can make a decision to do an intervention. An intervention is a structured, formal process that changes the circumstances. One can intervene with any self-defeating, negative behavior. The goals of an intervention address the following:

- Confront the negative self-defeating behavior of the loved person
- Support the person in making changes
- Take a look at the dynamics of one's relationship to the loved person

When we care for or love someone who is involved in self-defeating behavior, it brings out feelings and behavior in ourselves as well. Sometimes we enable such people to be irresponsible. We fix their problems, we give them money, we ignore the pain they cause, we blame them, and so on. Their problem becomes our problem. In the effort to help them, we often hurt both them and ourselves. We need to take a good look at our own behavior.

Early interventions mean that we become very honest about how we feel and what we see. We may try to share our honest thoughts and feelings with the person with whom we are concerned, and sometimes that is enough: we are heard, the person responds, and change can begin to take place. This is a great relief after we have taken such a risk.

However, sometimes that kind of confrontational sharing doesn't work. We are too angry or hurt, or the other person is too defensive and denying. When that occurs, it becomes necessary to do a formal intervention. That means hiring a professional interventionist and planning a structured process.

Counselors, coaches, and interventionists conduct interventions. You can look them up in the yellow pages or you can call any mental health center, alcoholism treatment center, or therapist for a reference. Sometimes clergy and school counselors will also do interventions. The preparation for a typical intervention looks like this:

1. Someone decides that an intervention is necessary and finds a professional to lead the intervention.

2. Those who are interested in participating in the intervention meet with the interventionist and learn about the situation. Together they decide what course of action must be taken to stop the destructive behavior.
3. Each person who will be involved in the intervention writes down the behaviors that he or she sees as self-destructive. This information must be accurate, clear, and honest.
4. The interveners prepare to share their feelings of pain about the situation.
5. The interveners prepare messages of love and support for the subject of the intervention.
6. The interveners look at whatever behaviors they are exhibiting that add to the problem and make a commitment to change those behaviors.
7. Each intervener prepares to share a consequence if the person is not willing to seek help or change. Consequences are important in an intervention.

The process of preparation may require one to three sessions before the actual intervention can take place. The interventionist sets the stage. There is an agreed-upon time and place; the group will find the loved one by surprise, or the loved one may be invited to join a session. The person often resists setting up a meeting, however, so it becomes necessary for the group to take him or her by surprise. It may be a time when you are sure the loved one will be at home.

Then the process begins. Each intervener shares his or her information, feelings, and message of love and support. The interventionist asks if the person is willing to get help and describes treatment and counseling options. Only at this time does the subject of the intervention have a chance to respond. If the person says yes, the intervention is over and he or she proceeds to get help. If the person says no, then the interveners share their consequences. Some of the most powerful consequences I have heard are as follows:

1. "Mom, if you don't stop smoking, the grandchildren cannot stay in your home and be exposed to secondhand smoke."
2. "Dad, if you don't stop drinking, the grandchildren cannot ride in your car when you are driving."
3. To a wife: "If you do not get help for your compulsive shopping, I need to take my name off all our joint credit cards."
4. To a husband: "If you are not able to manage your work and have some time at home as a husband and father, I need to get a divorce and start my life over."

The consequences must be stated with love, firmness, and a full commitment to follow through on them. Threats and scare tactics do not help in an intervention.

About 80 percent of professional interventions work well the first time. In about another 10 percent of cases, there is also success. The other 10 percent of interventions do not work. The primary reason interventions do not work is that people have waited too long to do them and the loved one is in too great a state of denial and resistance. There really is no such thing as a failed intervention, however, because something changes with every intervention.

Additional Reading

Eliot, Eve. *Insatiable: The Compelling Story of Four Teens, Food, and Its Power.* Deerfield Beach, FL: HCI, 2001.

Johnson, Vernon E. *I'll Quit Tomorrow: A Practical Guide to Alcoholism Treatment.* New York: HarperOne, 1990.

Wegscheider-Cruse, Sharon. *Another Chance: Hope and Health for the Alcoholic Family.* Palo Alto, CA: Science and Behavior Books, 1989.

Wegscheider-Cruse, Sharon, and Joseph Cruse. *Understanding Co-Dependency.* Deerfield Beach, FL: HCI, 1990.

twenty-two

Caretaking: Who Takes Care of the Caregiver?

There are four kinds of people in the world: those who have been caregivers, those who are currently caregivers, those who will be caregivers, and those who will need caregivers.

—ROSALYNN CARTER

CAREGIVERS ARE OFTEN THE last to ask for help. They are the people who manage the care of family members and friends, yet they may deny that they themselves need care. Caregivers are at particular risk for a host of mental and physical illnesses, many of which have roots in stress, exhaustion, and self-neglect. They are often so engaged in their responsibilities that they forget about their own needs.

Cindy was caring for her mother, who was suffering from dementia; her son, who was unemployed; and her husband, who was ill. Her life was full of phone calls to make, phone calls to return, shopping to do, meals to prepare, clothes to buy, bills to pay, and a home to care for—in addition to teaching school part-time.

When Cindy became ill with back problems, her doctor referred her to a support group. She resisted going at first, because she felt overwhelmed by having to add one more thing to her already demanding schedule. Finally, she tried one meeting. She found that she was not alone, and she was amazed at how many people were in the same spot as she. The leader of the group gave her a book on caregiving that became her bible. She found resources that could help and she found support for herself. She felt as if the gift had saved her life. She had been so tired and felt so alone, and now she had found some hope.

Kathleen didn't see herself as a caregiver. She had been married to her husband for fifty years and was now retired. Her four children were scattered around the country, but she saw them often. One of her children had a child with several physical problems, and Kathleen helped as much as she could. She babysat for the family quite often and did her best to help deal with the child's illness.

Another one of Kathleen's children had been through a difficult divorce, and there were children in that family as well, so Kathleen spent time, energy, and money trying to smooth things over for these grandchildren. Contributing to the divorce was her son's progressive alcohol abuse. As she tried to hold all the pieces together for the grandchildren, her son died from his addiction, bringing increased physical and emotional distress to his family.

Kathleen's husband helped in every way he could, but he was beginning to show signs of dementia. His career had been a successful one, and she could tell that he knew he was slipping, so she did her best to cover for him and make him feel important and needed. Rarely did she stop and assess her schedule and the stress she was feeling herself. She just kept going.

When a third child began to show signs of addiction, Kathleen was overwhelmed and began to show physical symptoms herself. She developed back problems, broken bones from falls, and depression. Her caretaking had taken its toll, and she died quietly. The people she cared for are still living and require further care. Caretakers pay a big price for their caretaking.

The solution might seem obvious from the outside: Speak up and get help. Say no to demands. However, that seems to be the hardest thing to do. Reaching out for help seldom occurs to caregivers, and they resist suggestions of help. They believe that they should do everything they can to help their families and friends. They are used to adjusting their own lives to fit the needs of others. They often pull away from friends and stop doing the things they do for themselves. They become preoccupied with the people of whom they are taking care.

It's often very hard for those who know a caregiver to step in and confront the behavior. Sometimes people don't know what to do. Should they step in? Can they offer any help? Many caregivers experience profound and regular sadness. Although their caregiving may be driven by empathy and love, they are also dealing with guilt over the anger and frustration they feel. There is a desire to protect pride and deny how bad things are. Some families are not used to talking about their needs or their personal business.

Caretakers prefer to do everything themselves. They perceive asking for help to be a form of weakness.

If the caregiver does allow any help, go slowly and just pitch in a little. It doesn't matter what you do for a caregiver—just do something. They often no longer know what they need, so any help will make a difference. Care for the person and give her a break, take her to lunch, bring over a casserole, help with some of the paperwork, run errands, or take her to a movie. "Can I help with anything?" is usually not a helpful question. Knowing what to suggest becomes just one more task for the caregiver. It's best to offer something specific and let her just say yes or no.

Careful listening is also a gift. Sometimes the caregiver is lost in an emotionally draining situation. Listening carefully might give a clue of what the needs are and whether you can help fulfill any of them.

READER/CUSTOMER CARE SURVEY

We care about your opinions! Please take a moment to fill out our online Reader Survey at **http://survey.hcibooks.com**.
As a **"THANK YOU"** you will receive a **VALUABLE INSTANT COUPON** towards future book purchases
as well as a **SPECIAL GIFT** available only online! Or, you may mail this card back to us.

(PLEASE PRINT IN ALL CAPS)

First Name _____ MI. _____ Last Name _____

Address _____ City _____

State _____ Zip _____ Email _____

1. Gender
❑ Female ❑ Male

2. Age
❑ 8 or younger
❑ 9-12 ❑ 13-16
❑ 17-20 ❑ 21-30
❑ 31+

3. Did you receive this book as a gift?
❑ Yes ❑ No

4. Annual Household Income
❑ under $25,000
❑ $25,000 - $34,999
❑ $35,000 - $49,999
❑ $50,000 - $74,999
❑ over $75,000

5. What are the ages of the children living in your house?
❑ 0 - 14 ❑ 15+

6. Marital Status
❑ Single
❑ Married
❑ Divorced
❑ Widowed

7. How did you find out about the book?
(please choose one)
❑ Recommendation
❑ Store Display
❑ Online
❑ Catalog/Mailing
❑ Interview/Review

8. Where do you usually buy books?
(please choose one)
❑ Bookstore
❑ Online
❑ Book Club/Mail Order
❑ Price Club (Sam's Club, Costco's, etc.)
❑ Retail Store (Target, Wal-Mart, etc.)

9. What subject do you enjoy reading about the most?
(please choose one)
❑ Parenting/Family
❑ Relationships
❑ Recovery/Addictions
❑ Health/Nutrition
❑ Christianity
❑ Spirituality/Inspiration
❑ Business Self-help
❑ Women's Issues
❑ Sports

10. What attracts you most to a book?
(please choose one)
❑ Title
❑ Cover Design
❑ Author
❑ Content

HEFG

TAPE IN MIDDLE; DO NOT STAPLE

BUSINESS REPLY MAIL
FIRST-CLASS MAIL PERMIT NO 45 DEERFIELD BEACH, FL

POSTAGE WILL BE PAID BY ADDRESSEE

Health Communications, Inc.
3201 SW 15th Street
Deerfield Beach FL 33442-9875

FOLD HERE

Comments

When the caregiver is the spouse of someone suffering from Alzheimer's disease, it's especially difficult. The caregiver is in a grief process of losing the spouse emotionally and mentally but not physically. The sense of loss and powerlessness is tremendous.

However you choose to help a caregiver, just connect in whatever ways are meaningful to that person. Recognize that the caregiver's stress contributes to a denial of how bad things are. Caregivers are tired most of the time, whether or not they recognize their own fatigue or depression.

A frequent caregiving role occurs when you become the parent to your parent. It can start with phone calls that seem to be more medical reports than sharing news. There are also phone calls that seem strange: perhaps the parent is sounding afraid at home or is quitting clubs or activities that used to seem important. You begin to notice a forgetfulness, some fantasies, and some things that just do not connect. If there is Alzheimer's disease, the early signs can be hard to detect. Something just doesn't feel right. However, if this journey has begun, it's best to start learning about it before the situation becomes critical and crisis becomes part of everyday life.

Crisis becomes the story of millions of Americans who are caring for elderly parents and maneuvering the murky worlds of medicine, law, hospitals, nursing homes, guilt, fear, and family problems. A recent study estimates that 34 million Americans serve as unpaid caregivers for other adults and spend about twenty hours a week helping out.

It is clear that caring for elderly family members takes a physical toll (through high blood pressure, fatigue, and depression) and an emotional toll (through guilt, fear, and anger). It can also reawaken sibling rivalries and conflicts.

This is a situation in which information, support, and help are critical. The decisions that have to be made are difficult and painful, and sometimes the emotional hangovers last a lifetime. In today's society, the problem is complicated by complex family situations, such as divorce, stepparents, and geographic distances among family members.

Family members who live nearby tend to carry more of the burden. Family members who live farther away feel more guilt. Children with children of their own feel pulled in two directions, the family they came from and the family they created. Single children sometimes take on the bulk of the caregiving.

There is much to consider, and outside counseling can help to suggest ways to navigate these murky waters and hold the family together. Too often, with the death of elderly parents, a family splits up, and sometimes this is due to the conflicts that arose during the caregiving time. Any efforts made to prevent this kind of scenario are well worth the time and effort.

Additional Reading

Backus, Henny. *Care for the Caretaker: How Jim Backus' Wife Did It.* Calabasas, CA: Jasper Publications, 1999.

Casey, Nell. *An Uncertain Inheritance: Writers on Caring for Family.* New York: Harper Perennial, 2008.

July, William, and James Lacy July. *A Husband, a Wife, and an Illness: Living Life Beyond Chronic Illness.* Bloomington, IN: AuthorHouse, 2008.

Resources

Lotsa Helping Hands
www.lotsahelpinghands.com

National Family Caregivers Association
www.thefamilycaregiver.org
1-800-445-8016

Alzheimer's Association
www.alz.org
1-800-272-3900

twenty-three

I Would Like to Be
a Better Parent

*The heart of a mother is the child's
most influential classroom.*

—Janet Marey

DURING A MEETING OF a group of parents, one mother mentioned that
she wished she had been a better parent. Now that she is older and
wiser, she is aware of how she might have done things differently. She
feels guilt and sadness. In her sadness and regret, she forgets that she
did the best she could with the information, time, and ability that
she had at each stage of parenting. When asked if she would ever have
hurt or neglected her children on purpose, she, of course, replied that
she wouldn't have. Most parents do the best they can in the circumstances they are in. Sometimes it is enough and sometimes it isn't.

It is very wise and prudent, however, to keep learning, experimenting, and trying to improve one's skills. Here are a few exercises
to try:

- *Try to look at the world through your children's eyes.* Imagine being
  with their friends, what they have to cope with, how they relate

to their teachers, and what their concerns are. You will find that many things look different when seen through a child's eyes. "Children are anchors that hold a mother to life," said Sophocles.

• *Imagine what your children are thinking about when they look at and listen to you.* Are you acting, talking, and appearing as you want them to be? Parenting is 80 percent role modeling, 10 percent caretaking, and 10 percent teaching. What are you showing your children? "If you give your life as a wholehearted response to love, then love will wholeheartedly respond to you," says author, activist, and lecturer Marianne Williamson.

• *Pay attention to expectations.* Your children will understand your clear and spoken expectations, even if they don't always meet them. The unspoken or implied expectations, however, will devastate your children, for they have no way to know about them. Always remember that parents are there to care for the needs of the children. The children are not there to meet the needs of the parents.

• *Try to blend seeing the needs of your children with taking care of your own needs.* Sacrificing time and resources for only the children will lead to subtle resentments.

• *Learn about silence.* Poet David Wagoner tells us, "The forest breathes. . . . Listen to what it is saying; the forest knows." Sometimes when things are tense between you and your child, be silent, and wait. When a situation is not clear, when we do not know what to do, the best thing is not to do anything until the action we should take becomes clear. Sometimes it is good to be silent.

• *Learn to live without solutions and just let tension be.* In that tension, work to find your own balance. Eugen Herrigel, in the book *Zen in the Art of Archery*, describes how he was taught to stand effortlessly at the point of highest tension in archery without shooting the arrow. At the right moment, the arrow mysteriously shoots itself. Simply wait, then practice seeing that whatever comes up is workable. Forcing doesn't help. Pay attention to what is, and your patience will be rewarded in the end.

- *Every child is special in his or her own way, and every child has special needs.* Hold a picture of that child always and be wishing him or her well at all times. Figure out what each child needs and try to anticipate the expression of that need.

- *There are times we need to be firm and not waiver in our expectations.* Good parenting does not mean being overindulgent, neglectful, or weak, nor does it mean being rigid, domineering, or controlling.

- *Listen, listen, listen.* Listen with interest and compassion. This will end the one-word answers that young people like to give.

- *Above all, keep learning.* Invest time and effort in knowing more about your child and what your child's needs are.

- *Try not to be indulgent.* Indulgent parents are often permissive because they want good things for their children. The tendency is to give too much freedom and too many things. If they don't provide structure and consequences, however, indulgent parents hurt their children rather than helping them. Structure helps to make the world predictable and enables children to feel safe. Children actually want structure; it teaches them to control their behavior and manage their emotions. When parents do not set limits, children often have more power than they know how to use appropriately.

- *Enforce consequences.* Children who do not experience consequences, or who get away with things that are wrong, grow up to feel as if they are above the law. This creates countless problems that will be present all their lives.

Parenting is a 24/7 job, and it lasts forever. It's the greatest challenge and by far the greatest reward in life. Children own a piece of your heart that no one else can ever reach or touch. Should you ever lose a child, it will leave a hole in your soul that never heals.

Parenting includes the obvious tasks, such as providing shelter, food, medical care, touch, comfort, and safety. These are basic needs that every child deserves to have fulfilled. Once these needs are met, the next level of parenting enters: providing learning opportunities, such as education, museums, travel, and fun.

Then there are the more subtle jobs of a parent. Parents must provide support when things aren't going well for a child, at any age. They need to be there when children hurt. Parents have to know when to take care of themselves so that they have something to give to their children. Later on, as the children grow up, the parents' role shifts to listening, offering support, and providing information and suggestions that meet the children's needs.

My personal experience is that children really need their parents in their thirties and forties, as they go through life's changes at these times. They need a good friend who knows them well. I believe we need to tell our adult children: "Don't ever give up your dreams, and never leave them behind. Find them, make them yours, and never let them go."

Someone once said that a mother can stop worrying after her child gets married. In reality, the marriage merely adds a new member to the mother's heart. A mother's job is not done when her last child leaves home; distance only adds more concerns. People have often said that a mother can love no one as much as she loves her children, but in reality, grandchildren steal grandmother's hearts just as much.

There are many tasks and events that bond mothers and children. There are the important years of learning to walk, talk, and recite the alphabet. Then come all the school events, everything from Girl Scout cookies to band practice. The most important job I felt as a mother was to make memories. Memories are the glue that hold all the other experiences together. "Do not follow where the path may lead," said Ralph Waldo Emerson. "Go instead where there is no path and leave a trail."

In our family, there were countless trips to Disney World. It wasn't just the excitement of driving in the entrance. The memory had to do with the expectation that we would be all together and the anticipation of what was going to happen. It was about the rain gear, the walk down Main Street after dark, the sights, the smells, and the music. At every level, we shared laughter, fatigue, and closeness. We would double up in rooms, tell stories, and make memories.

Family Christmases, summer vacations, and reunions have been full of card games, board games, and good food. We gather around the stove or the kitchen counter, tell stories, give hugs, laugh, and feel the warmth of belonging. "Give to the world the best you have and the best will come back to you," said the nineteenth-century poet Madeline Bridges.

For part of my life, I lived in South Dakota, the home of the Lakota Sioux Indians. They taught me an important word: *tribe*. A tribe is a group of people or clans who are descended from a common ancestor. My family's tribe includes aunts, uncles, and cousins. We add to our tribe when a good friend becomes like a family member. Our basic tribe is fifteen people, but sometimes it swells to twenty or more. There is great comfort in belonging to a tribe that makes memories.

Senator Elizabeth Dole tells us, "When you're in your nineties and looking back, it's not going to be how much money you made or how many awards you've won. It's really about what did you stand for? Did you make a positive difference for people?" Each of us is planted in a family, and that's where we can make the most important difference.

Parenting is love—challenging, hard, easy, 24/7 for a lifetime, exhilarating, heart wrenching, magical, frightening, and probably the most important thing a person can ever do.

Additional Reading

Bluestein, Jane. *Parents, Teens, and Boundaries: How to Draw the Line.* Deerfield Beach, FL: HCI, 1993.

Friel, John C., and Linda D. Friel. *The 7 Best Things Smart Teens Do.* Deerfield Beach, FL: HCI, 2000.

————. *The 7 Worst Things Good Parents Do.* Deerfield Beach, FL: HCI, 1999.

Herrigel, Eugen. *Zen in the Art of Archery.* New York: Vintage Books, 1999.

Kalas, Steven. *Human Matters: Wise and Witty Counsel on Relationships, Parenting, Grief, and Doing the Right Thing.* Las Vegas, NV: Stephens Press, 2008.

Satir, Virginia. *The New Peoplemaking.* Palo Alto, CA: Science and Behavior Books, 1988.

Williamson, Marianne. *The Gift of Change: Spiritual Guidance for Living Your Best Life.* New York: HarperOne, 2006.

twenty-four

Family Stress

*Not all fights are bad. In fact, they are preferable
to phony serenity. Letting go of old hurts
makes room for new possibilities.*

—MADELINE CAREY

FAMILIES FIGHT; THEY JUST DO. If they learn how to do it well, it
makes them closer and more honest with each other. Whether the
issue is holidays, how to care for parents, how to spend money, or
whom to vote for, it seems that we are always at one another's
throats. Experts have said that the family that fights fair is more
likely to stay together and more likely to be happy together. Such
families are more likely to continue a lifetime relationship and much
less likely to drift apart.

It is the families that avoid stress and disagreement that drift apart
and lose their closeness. What fighting does is clear the air, much
like a strong wind on a smoggy day. Fighting in a healthy way is an
art that has to be learned. The time to set the ground rules is when
there are no issues on the table and the people involved are feeling
cooperative, fair, and of good will.

It stands to reason that there is much to be preserved in the family system. After all, these people have shared parents, time, and growing up together. There have been vacations, holidays, graduations, weddings, and countless other bonding experiences. At the same time, there have been different family situations, different positions in the family, and individual family memories. As my mentor Virginia Satir has said, "In every family system, there are opportunities and handicaps."

New people often enter a family system, and each new person impacts the family in ways that are not always clear. They bring their history, opinions, and strengths, and the system changes. For those who choose to preserve family closeness, it's important to find ways to navigate differences and feelings to best honor the people involved. There will inevitably be disagreements and different points of view.

The rules of respectful disagreements include honesty, patience, the ability to listen, and the desire for resolution and understanding. When the outcome is needing to be right, hurting someone else, or having your own way, disagreements do not seem productive.

There are naturally going to be differences, divergent opinions, and tensions when people live together. From time to time, those situations can lead to frustration and irritation. When a person knows that he or she can share these frustrations and irritations safely with another person, there is less buildup of feelings that lead to hostility, judgment, and explosive anger.

I remember, years ago, when I learned that it was good to argue in front of other family members, especially children. That was a rather shocking idea. As I learned more, it became clear that if we fight by the rules of cooperation, not only do we get better results, we are also role-modeling for others that fighting can be fair and productive. As a debater in both high school and college, I learned the value of a difference of opinion.

Virginia Woolf had a great ability to hit below the belt and esca-late a fight into a battle. Some use the expression "throwing in the kitchen sink," because in this kind of fighting, the issue that starts the fight is soon lost in the fray because someone keeps bringing up subjects connected to feelings about totally different issues. One sub-ject adds to another, and the quarrel becomes so big that there is no way to resolve any of the issues. Hurtful things are said, and there is pain for everyone involved.

There are two other forms of sabotage that poison healthy fight-ing. One is called "bagging it." This happens when someone holds in little irritations and lets them fester instead of confronting and discussing. It then takes only a trivial incident to stimulate all the festering anger, hurt, and blame to erupt. It's a form of blindsiding and serves no purpose other than trying to hurt the other person.

Ten Tools for Fair Fighting

1. Honesty
2. Commitment
3. Emotional sharing
4. Willingness to be responsible
5. Clear and specific needs
6. Trust
7. Forgiveness
8. Affection
9. Plans for resolution
10. Negotiation

There is no reason to fear the expression of feelings if the parties have determined that the goal of fighting is to express each person's truth, listen to each other, and reach a solution. Anger is a healthy feeling. When anger is expressed in a healthy way, people usually feel much closer because they have spoken their truth to each other.

Some people believe that fighting can lead to separation and estrangement, but it is really just the opposite. Intimacy cannot happen without complete sharing. When we avoid that kind of sharing, intimacy is weakened and sometimes dies. Families will feel such a breakdown in communication. When sharing and communication break down, everyone has less satisfaction and closeness with everyone else. This leaves family members looking outside the system for someone else with whom to share. It pushes family members away from the family to find the closeness they crave.

Some families love to do a great deal together. Family members who enjoy being with one another tend to have a more open attitude about fighting. They want to keep the closeness alive, and they do not want the tensions to build. They want to protect their connection, they want to enjoy one another's company, and they treasure their togetherness.

Other family members might want more time alone but not know how to negotiate for that time. They tend to play "uproar." This means that they pick fights to achieve distance and silence. As a result they have more time to themselves. They tend to play cards, join clubs, play sports, and become involved in activities that take them away from home. They are more likely not to fight fairly. They often use the silent treatment or play the victim to get their point across.

Then there are family members who try to exist alone, psychologically. They are loosely connected, but they don't become emotionally involved. They coexist in relationships rather than jumping in with all their feelings. They usually stay busy with jobs, children, clubs, or hobbies.

Connected family members are engaged with one another emotionally, mentally, physically, and spiritually. They make one another's world go around. They enjoy some individual interests or hobbies, but a portion of their time is spent in family pursuits. When they spend time together, they share their thoughts, ideas, and feelings on a regular basis. They might live thousands of miles apart, but they share by phone, through e-mail, and on periodic visits. This intimacy is so valuable to all of them that they would rather fight to protect it than settle into a distant connection.

Here are a few tips for productive fighting:

1. *Fight by appointment.* Gather your information and make plans. View disagreements like settling a labor dispute rather than waiting until there is a strike.
2. *Decide if the fight is public or private.* Is it a fight that would best be done in front of others, or is the subject matter private?
3. *Decide where to fight.* Restaurants and public places are not good fighting places. Save your bedroom for closeness; avoid fighting there as well. A closed office or den might be the best place.
4. *Do not drink and fight.* Alcohol simply causes a whole series of problems that keep the fight from being productive.
5. *Plan to give something of yourself.* Commit to working toward a mutual understanding and resolution.

Most fights can be resolved by using the above steps. Some quarrels have such depth and emotion tied to them that it is best to seek outside therapy to work on them. If the same issue keeps recurring, it's a sign that resolving it will require some outside counseling. A significant aspect of any relationship is whether everyone is willing to seek outside help when it is called for.

One of the most frequent situations is a person who shows up for counseling and says that the other family members refuse to come to counseling. The question then is "What can I do if my family will not seek help?" As a counselor, I ask, "What do you want to do about it?" No one can get well or make changes for other people.

A true relationship shares the high times as well as the low times of daily life. It means being included and brought into each other's private world of feelings, wants, and fears. A true relationship is like the safety of a private harbor in a sea of troubles. People crave this type of intimacy, and clearing the air of frustrations, anger, and differences is part of the price one pays to have it. It is worth every fair fight.

Additional Reading

Faber, Adele, and Elaine Mazlish. *Siblings Without Rivalry: How to Help Your Children Live Together So You Can Live Too.* New York: HarperCollins, 2004.

Parker, Jan, and Jan Stimpson. *Raising Happy Brothers and Sisters: Helping Our Children Enjoy Life Together from Birth Onwards.* London: Hodder Mobius, 2004.

Satir, Virginia. *Peoplemaking.* London: Souvenir Press, 1990.

twenty-five

How Can I Be a Special Grandparent?

Grandmothers aren't hot from cooking and baking these days. Grandmothers are hot because they're swimming in the mainstream of life.

—Lois Wyse

The entry of a child to any situation changes the whole situation.

—Iris Murdoch

GRANDPARENTING IS A wonderful opportunity. The little innocent people who come into our lives have the potential of changing many things. They deserve our love and protection; they deserve role modeling and hugs. Yet with all that they deserve, they give so much more. They give joy, laughter, and a chance to try again in helping to shape a youngster's life. As a family therapist with decades of experience, I have seen time and again that the shared love of parents and grandparents for a child can promote the healing of past wounds. That love is a true inspiration.

Being a grandparent holds great joy, but it also comes with responsibilities and challenges. In good times and hard times, all these elements are present. Always remember that a grandparent has a unique position in the family. The grandparents know at least one of the parents better than anyone else does. They are invested in that parent. As a grandparent, you can bring to the relationship something that no one else can. You can bring the history of that parent and a feeling of the connectedness of generations. No one else can do that.

A grandparent can play many roles. When the parents are meeting all the basic needs of the child, the grandparent can simply add the frosting to the cake and be the extra everything to that child. In today's culture, sometimes it is difficult for parents to provide all the basic needs of their children. In that case, the grandparents can provide some of the cake, too, and not just the frosting. Grandparents can provide resources for vacations, extra special clothes, help with purchasing lessons, or help with learning experiences. Each family can determine the best way for the grandparents to help their grandchildren.

Parent educator Marcia Jacober says, "To be told we are loved is not enough. We must feel loved."

Giving and receiving unconditional love is a great gift between a grandparent and a grandchild. The parents can take the role of teaching discipline to the child, and the grandparent can simply provide love and acceptance.

This chapter is mostly about grandmothers. I am one, and I also had a wonderful experience with my own grandmother. I did not know my grandfather as well, because he died early in my life. What I have learned about grandfathers I have learned from my partner, who is a wonderful grandfather. My life has been blessed by watching him grandparent. All that I say here applies to grandfathers as well. The singer Helen Reddy tells us, "Gentleness is not a quality exclusive to women."

One of my grandmothers loved me without condition and very openly. She was always asking how I felt and what I was thinking. She laughed with me, we had secrets, and she was generously affectionate. I know that much of the security I have felt as an adult came from the security I felt being the grandchild of someone who gave me so much love and acceptance. For many people, the seeds of self-worth were planted by a grandparent, long before word or even thought. They were planted at the level of feeling and touch.

Vitality and fun are other gifts that grandparents can give to their grandchildren. Parents are often extremely busy with responsibilities during their children's growing up years. Right from the start, grandparents can step in with extra hands, extra time, and extra resources. There are countless ways the grandparents can help: babysitting, working around the house, planning vacations, and giving the parents breaks.

We are so lucky today to have cell phones and e-mail. It is possible to stay very connected to our grandchildren. Even with the great geographic distances that separate my family members, we are able to stay connected and involved in one another's lives. It's a form of social security for children to know that their grandparents are available to them.

Another role that a grandparent can take is being the historian. Grandparents can take time to organize photos, make scrapbooks, and let their grandchildren know about their history. I love to take my grandchildren around my house and show them my father's (their great-grandfather's) German beer mugs, the many pillows that my mother (their great-grandmother) cross-stitched, and the dishes that I had as a child. It's important for them to know that they came from somewhere and that there is love that has come through the generations just for them.

Some items I have marked so that my grandchildren know that

these things will be theirs someday. This is another form of social security, which brings a sense of belonging and self-importance. If enough is shared, the children will come to know their history even though their ancestors are gone and they can never meet them. Self-improvement guru Dale Carnegie (best known for *How to Win Friends and Influence People*) tells us, "Remember that happiness doesn't depend upon who you are or what you have, it depends solely on what you think."

Being a mentor and teacher is a very important role for a grandparent. Mentors support us and teachers challenge us. Both help grandchildren to thrive and learn. Grandparenthood is the perfect opportunity to share whatever special skills one has. My grandmother taught me the ability to accept all people and look for the good in them. She also taught me to love to cook. Making homemade soup, special cookies, or a wonderful roast beef are skills I learned from her. She also taught me about having fun. When we were together, we would always buy an ice cream cone before dinner in case we would be too full after dinner.

My grandmother also provided me with the ability to become a leader, because she would take on the role of student. She was always interested in what I did, so I would share my learning and ideas with her. I taught her how to dance, and I shared recipes with her so she could learn some new ways of cooking things. She loved to be my audience when I was learning how to speak in public. She taught me that it is never too late to learn.

Another role a grandparent can take is travel guide. My love of travel was stimulated by the many trips I took with my grandmother. She worked for a railroad, so there were many opportunities for train rides. We would pack a picnic basket and go on trips, sometimes for the day and sometimes for much longer. Some of my greatest bonding activities with my own grandchildren have been to take them on trips. A wise grandma once said, "Presence is more important than presents."

Meeting Special Challenges

There are special challenges in some families that parents, children, and grandparents have to face. Sometimes children have to grow up too fast and assume extra responsibility. At times the grandparents can provide extra love and help.

A grandparent might be ill or disabled in some way. It is important that the grandparent acknowledge that this is happening. Perhaps it is impossible to drive a car, go the beach, or keep up during some family activity. It is best to be honest with the grandchildren and tell them what is happening. Grandparents have the opportunity to reassure the children that they are loved and then do however much is possible.

A grandparent's death is often painful for children, and it can be the children's first major experience with loss. Whatever the circumstances, it is important for the remaining grandparent to be there for the grandchildren. It is important to comfort, to be honest, and to reassure them that they are going to be okay. They will have to navigate this important loss and will need all the support they can get. Encourage them to ask questions and learn to talk about their feelings. Tears should be welcomed rather than discouraged. The grandchild should be made to feel comfortable expressing fear, sadness, hurt, grief, and anger.

Children need to learn to understand that death is a natural part of life and not to be feared. Each family's way of explaining death will come from its own belief system and tradition. Include the children in conversations and planning. Leaving them out will promote isolation and loneliness.

Divorce is another common and painful time for families. When parents get divorced, the foremost task of the grandparents is to preserve their relationships with their grandchildren. Divorce doesn't happen just between two adults, it happens to whole families. Usually, all family behaviors—constructive and destructive—are exaggerated at times of high stress. Families with good coping skills will get through this time with as little hurt and scarring as possible. Families with poor coping skills (such as alcohol abuse, smoking, or quick anger) will exaggerate these behaviors. Tension can be high, and stress can be very high. This might be a good time to seek outside therapy.

Children of divorce often feel pulled between each hurting parent, and that dynamic can extend to the grandparents. Grandparents can offer a safe place and a relationship that refuses to take sides; they can simply offer comfort to the children for all they are going through. The grandparents might be the safest and most comfortable relationship the children have at this time. It is important for the grandparent not to get embroiled in the competition, jealousy, hurt, and anger between the parents.

If one of the parents decides that you cannot see your grandchildren, you are going to have a tough time and will need a great deal of support. You might even want to seek legal counsel to ensure that you know your rights in this regard. Begin by seeking help from a competent family therapist and/or legal aid.

In the context of a divorce, or at any other time, if you ever believe that something is happening that is harmful to your grandchildren—such as parental drug abuse, abandonment, neglect, or physical or sexual abuse—you will need both therapeutic help and legal counseling. For the sake of your grandchildren, do not hold back. This is an appropriate time to intervene.

Additional Reading

Elgin, Suzette Haden. *The Grandmother Principles*. New York: Abbeville Press, 2000.

Freeman, Criswell. *Grandmothers Are Forever*. New York: Simon & Schuster, 2006.

McBride, Mary. *Grandma Knows Best, but No One Ever Listens*. Minnetonka, MN: Meadowbrook Press, 1987.

Wegscheider-Cruse, Sharon. *Grandparenting: A Guide for Anyone Who Plays a Grand Role in a Child's Life*. Palo Alto, CA: Science and Behavior Books, 1997.

Wyse, Lois. *Grandchildren Are So Much Fun, I Should Have Had Them First*. New York: Random House, 1995.

Part Five:

HEALTH CONCERNS (GETTING WELL)

Only I can change my life.
No one can do it for me.

—*Carol Burnett*

twenty-six

Breast Cancer:
The Words Strike Fear

I entrust myself to God with a sure knowledge
that my healing is now taking place.

—ROKELLE LERNER

THE SENTENCE "You have breast cancer" changes the life of the woman who hears it. Her feelings of safety, beauty, normality, confidence, and manageability are challenged to their core. She is immediately thrown into a world that is foreign to her. It's a time of great upheaval. It is as though the world had been in color and has suddenly gone black-and-white. She continues to function and do what must be done, but it all feels different.

When I heard that sentence, I felt denial and panic at the same time. At first, I thought there was a mistake: it couldn't be me. Someplace deep inside me, I started to panic when the doctor called me back for more x-rays. That had never happened before; why was it happening now? Part of me said that the doctor was just doing a good job and wanted to make sure everything was okay. Another part of me knew that something was different.

It is that feeling of things being different that is often the most confusing and painful. Not only are there important steps to be taken, such as identifying treatment options and visiting oncologists and surgeons, there is the surreal feeling of it all. As the oncologist spelled out the choices and options for me, I thought that maybe she was talking about someone else. Yet she was talking to me, and there were decisions to make.

I couldn't run away from this information. I needed to share this new journey with my closest family members and friends. Perhaps the most difficult sharing was with my partner, since this was my most intimate relationship. If someone is single and still has dating years ahead of her, that, too, is a major concern. How will she share not only her cancer journey but also the effects of that journey on her body?

Another level of sharing is necessary if the woman has daughters. I had two daughters.

Given the statistics that are available about family involvement in breast cancer, I had much to share with my daughters and a desire to give them courage, hope, and comfort in case they ever had to take the same journey I was being forced to take.

Is it any wonder that a woman faces a daunting and difficult time as the words *breast cancer* become part of her daily life? It is imperative that the following three events take place to return some safety, beauty, normality, confidence, and manageability to every woman who is diagnosed with breast cancer:

1. *She must do all she can do to get the best medical care for her particular situation.* She will undoubtedly see more than one physician to achieve this goal. She will need to choose among the options for treatment. The treatment often involves a major change in her body image regardless of the option she chooses. This is all an emotional roller-coaster journey with questions and concerns.

2. *She must do all she can to return to beauty, function, and normality.* During this difficult time in her life, every effort must be made to help her return to feeling that life and her situation are manageable. Fortunately, there are ways in which this can be accomplished. There are many treatment options, including implant surgery and nipple restoration. She can find the best possible way to achieve an acceptable outcome for her body.

3. *During the time of surgery, treatment, and, for some, reconstruction, it's important that she find her own belief in her safety and beauty.* Sometimes it requires new clothes. There might be body changes that have to be addressed. If there is extra time spent in bed, new sheets and pillows are sometimes a nice treat. Fresh flowers and soothing music are important daily treats. It helps if family and friends understand these special needs.

A return to normality is imperative for the patient. She needs to rebuild her self-image in regard to her body. This will ultimately have a profound effect on the rest of her family. With the return of a positive body image and a new self-worth, she will be able to continue or rediscover her sexuality. This in turn affects how she enters a sexual relationship with her partner. It allows her to feel as though she is bringing her whole self to the relationship.

Husbands respond to the cancer diagnosis in a variety of ways. Some respond with total support, some are frightened by the illness, and some are even more frightened by the surgery results. Some do not know how to deal with the differences and so they pull away. This causes stress for both people. When a full reconstruction has taken place and the nipple looks real, it is often easier for a husband or partner to think that everything is going to be all right.

If the woman feels good about her recovery and about her body, it affects the whole family. She will be much more confident and feel like her prediagnosis self. Her emotional life will even out, and she will be able to be available to her partner and/or family. If her relationship to her partner returns to the way it was before the illness, their relationship will affect the family as well.

This is extremely important if there are daughters in the family. If they can watch their mother recover from this illness, regain her sense of manageability in her life, and learn to love her body again, it goes a long way toward reducing their fear of someday having to face breast cancer.

It is important right from the beginning that children know about the breast cancer and are given age-appropriate information. There will be many changes in the family when there is a diagnosis of breast cancer, and when the children do not know why the changes are taking place, they often wonder if it's because of them.

Early information for very young children can simply be something like "Mommy has a problem that is health related, and she is going to take care of it with her doctor." They can be told that she will need more time at the doctor's, may even have to go to a hospital, and may need more rest. Children can handle any truth that is given to them if it is done in a way that assures them that while change is taking place, they will be cared for and secure.

Older children can handle more information. If the girls are teens or older, they can go through the experience with their mother. This starts with the doctor's visits right up through the surgery. The final step of surgery is often the nipple restoration. This is the best way to alleviate the fears of daughters. They need a role model, and the mother can offer that.

It's important for older daughters to know that there is a risk; this will encourage them to be diligent about their own breast exams and mammograms. It can be explained to the older daughters that the risk is similar to diabetes or heart disease. It is not a certainty, only a risk. It is important not to frighten older girls, but it is important that they know their risk factor.

Breast cancer is always a frightening diagnosis, but today, fortunately, it is for many women only a crisis that has to be managed. With proper diagnosis, competent medical help, and now nipple restoration, it does not have to be a disfiguring event. It is important that every woman learn her rights about each step of recovery and that physicians and insurance companies fulfill their obligations and responsibilities to every woman who is diagnosed with breast cancer.

Additional Reading

Gawler, Grace. *Women of Silence: The Emotional Healing of Breast Cancer.* South Yarra, Australia: Hill of Content Publishing, 1994.

Harpham, Wendy Schlessel. *Happiness in a Storm: Facing Illness and Embracing Life as a Healthy Survivor.* New York: W. W. Norton & Company, 2006.

Love, Susan M. *Dr. Susan Love's Breast Book,* 4th ed. Cambridge, MA: Da Capo Press, 2005.

Lucas, Geralyn. *Why I Wore Lipstick to My Mastectomy.* New York: St. Martin's Griffin, 2005.

twenty-seven

Technology Overload

Learn to get in touch with the silence within yourself
and know that everything in this life has a purpose.

—ELIZABETH KUBLER-ROSS, AUTHOR AND HEALER

IT IS CLEAR TO ME that we are drowning in knowledge and information and still starved for healing and direction. Information and connection overload is a problem for many people. The very time-saving tools that excited us when they first became available are now taking their toll on our health as they cause stress. If you add up the ringing of the cell phone and the landline phone, the text messaging, the BlackBerry, and the e-mail alert dings, you will find that there is frequently continuous interruption. This techno-stress increases the output of fight or flight chemicals such as adrenaline. The result is an ongoing stage of overload that can trigger anxiety, a racing heart, sleeplessness, tension, and a feeling of being overwhelmed.

Years ago, before all the technology that is available today was invented, I was receiving many calls after the workday ended. It seems that when people couldn't reach me during the day because I was busy, they figured they could find me at home after work. Some people were direct and told me they wanted counseling. Other people disguised their request for help by sounding as though they were checking in with me, and I would find myself listening to their problems and then advising, providing informal counseling.

I finally reached a point at which I had the number removed from my landline phone. That is, I could call out, but I could not receive calls on it. We kept one phone line in our home just for intimate family, and everyone protected that line.

Even with an unlisted number I had received more calls than I could comfortably handle. My role as president of a company, international speaker, and marriage and family therapist brought with it countless calls a day. Hiring someone at my office to take and return my phone calls gave me almost two extra hours a day, which I put to good use. Most people, but not all, accepted that this is the way I handled phone calls. I remained calm, focused, and productive.

There are many things you can do today to relieve some of the stress of constant connection and interruption. Here are some suggestions:

1. Disable the alerts on your e-mail and choose specific times to read and answer incoming mail. This can be done as little as once a day or, if you are at work, once every hour.
2. When you want to be away from your e-mail for longer periods, create an auto-reply message to notify senders that you are currently not available and will get back to them as soon as you can.
3. Inform family and friends of a window of time in which you will take phone calls, and simply let all other calls be picked up by an answering machine or voice mail, then respond to them at a specific time. This will help you to maintain a feeling of manageability over your time.
4. Web surfing raises the adrenaline level, and this increase makes it difficult to sleep. Several studies have shown that if you turn

off your computer an hour before you go to bed, your sleep will be deeper and more sound. Sound sleep is critical to memory and mood.

5. Inform family and friends that you cannot handle all the e-mail forwards you receive. During the last political season, my friends understood that I did not want to receive political e-mails. That one gesture saved me almost an hour a day.

6. Work at becoming focused on website searches and eliminate wasted minutes and hours with general surfing. The time and energy you save can be put toward more important things that you would like to be doing.

John Naisbett points out in his book *Megatrends* that as our world becomes more high-tech, we need for it to be balanced with equal amounts of high touch. With more communication tools than ever before, people are having much less real-time interaction. It has been aptly stated, "People who live in virtual communities have virtual lives."

When I purchased my digital camera and printer to make my own photos at home, I realized that I would no longer be having my short chat with the photo developer I have used over the years. He knows me and has watched as my photos changed from gatherings with my grandchildren when they were little to when two of them had become almost six feet tall. He has watched my hair go from being very black to gray and blond. I will miss our interactions.

It led me to start thinking about all the people with whom I used to interact on a regular basis. One of them was my butcher; now it's hard to beat Costco meats for variety and value. I also miss the young man who used to fill my car with gas; now I pump the gas, wherever I am. An important person in my life as a writer used to be my printer; now I can do much of what the print shop once did. For years, I played the piano for relaxation and enjoyment; now I am more apt to listen to a CD or my iPOD.

I have fond memories of going shopping, driving the car, taking a walk, and reading a book at the airport without the phone ringing. I have a cell phone now, and I know that all I have to do is turn it off and that quiet time will still be mine. Nevertheless, there is a little nagging feeling that I now should be available in a way that I never had to be before.

Don't get me wrong. I feel no shortage of gratitude and support for all the technical advances that make my life easier, safer, and more productive. It's just that it's important for me to know how to learn to use technology instead of being used by it. With conscious thought and choice, I know when and where I want my phone turned on. My mood tells me when it's important to turn off the TV for a few days and read and relax. I can slow down my world by returning phone calls in a few days and not feeling compelled to answer the phone every time it rings.

Some have talked about the harm that speeding up the world is doing to individuals and families. We live in a culture of more, and more powerful technology and gadgets. When people have a hole in their soul, they sometimes believe that what they can acquire will fill up that hole.

What people need more often is human touch and contact. It becomes very important to be sure that touch, contact, and communication is part of our lives. When that is a priority, we have a better chance of using technology to add to our happiness and connection rather than allowing it to pull us further apart.

One of the ways to check out your relationship with technology versus human contact is to go on a technology "fast" and see how comfortable or uncomfortable you are. Years ago, I was speaking on a panel with Dr. Andrew Weil. At that time I was juggling many commitments in my schedule. There were many stressful things going on in my daily life. Andrew mentioned to me that it is a very healthy thing to take a thirty-day news fast every once in awhile and simply let yourself settle down and balance a bit. I couldn't imagine doing that. However, I was feeling stressed out and decided to give it a try.

I picked February of that year and turned off my TV and canceled my newspaper. Just in case the world came to an end or there was a worldwide earthquake, I did not give up my radio. It was a surprising and healing month. At first it was really hard. I missed the noise of the TV, the early morning ritual with the morning paper and coffee, and the Sunday paper. I felt tense, disconnected, and a little empty. However, I made it through the thirty days. My blood pressure was better, my appreciation of music was heightened, my spirits were lifted, and nothing bad happened.

Through doing that, I changed some of my daily habits. Now in the morning I meditate and take an early morning walk. The only time I read a newspaper in the morning is when I travel and pick up *USA Today*. By choice, there are times when I want a *USA Today*, a local paper, or the *Wall Street Journal*. When I want them, I buy them. The Sunday morning paper is part of a ritual, so I do subscribe to it. As for TV, a show has to be good, and it has to be recorded and watched at a good time, or it just doesn't fit into my schedule. Once a year, I still do the thirty-day news fast, and I learn something every time.

Technology and instant information are available to us for use and abuse. Have the fun and choice of deciding what you want in your life, one choice at a time, one change at a time. The choice is ours.

Additional Reading

There seems to be very little literature on this subject. It might be a subject to discuss with a therapist or coach. If you should decide to make choices and changes in your relationship to your cell phone, Blackberry, or computer, I recommend these books.

Dispenza, Joe. *Evolve Your Brain: The Science of Changing Your Mind.* Deerfield Beach, FL: HCI, 2008.

Fishel, Ruth. *Change Almost Anything in 21 Days: Recharge Your Life with the Power of Over 500 Affirmations.* Deerfield Beach, FL: HCI, 2003.

Fishel, Ruth. *Take Time for Yourself: Meditative Moments for Healthy Living.* Deerfield Beach, FL: HCI, 1995.

Naisbett, John. *Megatrends: Ten New Directions Transforming Our Lives.* New York: Grand Central Publishing, 1988.

twenty-eight

The Emotional Consequences of Smoking Cigarettes

Remember, we all stumble, every one of us.
That's why it's a comfort to go hand in hand.

—EMILY KIMBROUGH

Okay, I have heard it all:

Smoking is not good for me.
Smoking is an addiction.
Smoking is a social stigma.
Smoking will shorten my life.
Smoking is not allowed here.
Smoking is not allowed there.

The messages are everywhere. I know what it's like to do the following:

- Have to leave an event and go outside to smoke
- Fork over plenty of money to feed my habit
- Smell smoke on everything I own
- Notice the disgusting stares I get from strangers

- Feel the craving coming more often than I would like
- Sneak in a cigarette here or there
- Wish I could quit, but I can't

Then again, maybe I don't want to quit. Smoking is one of the few pleasures I enjoy. Maybe I wish everyone would just back off and leave me alone about smoking.

I know what it is like to feel the following:

- Shame if someone I love asks me to quit and I don't want to quit
- Guilt when I sneak a cigarette
- Inadequate when I try to quit and fail
- Angry when I get pressed about quitting
- Sad when I realize what I am doing to my body
- Afraid when I hear the long-term results of smoking on my body
- Self-loathing when I realize how much money I spend on cigarettes

So I keep smoking.

How Smoking Affects Emotions and Sexual Intimacy

Smoking cigarettes dulls our emotions by covering them up and sedating them. When we light up and let the nicotine do its job, it can quiet anxiety, fear, hurt, anger, and other emotions for a short time. However, this early relief is intense and short. We have to keep lighting up to keep our emotions sedated. Thus, we develop an emotional craving for relief. Our emotions are our beacon of understanding and the guide to our behavior. When we are fearful, we protect ourselves. When we are guilty, we say we're sorry. When we are hurt, we talk about it. When we feel happy, we express it. When we feel creative, we create. When we feel close to someone, we share that feeling. The dictionary says that our feelings are our passion.

I know that someone who smokes is going to say, "How can that be? I get angry and afraid. I still feel guilty, and I also feel sad." I am not saying that smokers have no feelings. I am saying that their feelings are fuzzy and unclear. Someone might say that she is angry, when underneath she is really fearful or lonely. Someone might say that he is sad, when underneath he is really angry. Feelings are distorted and confusing when someone is under the influence of nicotine.

We all have heard people say, "I'm missing out on intimacy with my partner." The partner looks befuddled and says, "I don't understand. I feel close to you. What are you talking about? This intimacy—what does it mean?"

Intimacy is simply the sharing of intense emotion with each other. Cigarette smokers and drug users cannot do that. They have sedated their true and most honest feelings and are disconnected from even knowing what they feel. Because they cannot feel their feelings, they cannot share those feelings. There is a sense of disconnection or space in their relationships.

We have the capability to feel passion about many situations, and one of those situations is sexual. Not only can we feel passionate about music, nature, travel, and learning, we can also feel passionate about another person. We are actually able to feel safety, trust, and commitment with another person.

When we sedate our emotions, it is very hard to feel passion. We can think about passion and get away with it, but we cannot fake emotional passion when we try to be a sexual person. We become less able to perform sensually and sexually. Therefore, we find that smokers and drug users have very complicated sexual lives.

In the absence of emotional passion, it becomes necessary to find sexual arousal and satisfaction in other ways. Common substitutes are pornography, violence, excessive masturbation, affairs, and danger. When we are not capable of an *emotional* physical response, we have to find a mechanical way to artificially stimulate a physical response. We then become dependent on mechanical sex. Seduction and affairs help us to become aroused sexually because they wake up our feelings and thus our emotional life. It's exciting, it's new, and there is the stimulation of secrecy.

Sexual intimacy and intercourse are much less satisfying with artificial stimulation. There are at least a couple of reasons for this.

For one thing, it's natural that men are able to be stimulated faster than women most (but not all) of the time. In a mechanical rather than an emotional encounter, it is therefore common for the man to reach orgasm before the woman does. If the woman feels angry or hurt or left out, there is no way for the sexual partners to be really fulfilled—certainly not emotionally. This frequently leads to a fight and a cigarette, and comfortable distance is then established.

Even if both people are artificially orgasmic at a similar rate, there is very little intimacy that follows orgasm. Emotions are uncomfortable, and a smoker will then have a cigarette rather than feel the pain of the lack of intimacy. There is a need to set up emotional distance. The cycle continues to repeat itself.

How Smoking Affects Daily Behavior

Our emotions are the clues to how we want to behave. When our feelings are distorted, it leads to distorted behavior. Protecting the smoking habit leads to all kinds of new and often uncomfortable behaviors. For instance, there is the need to find and keep a supply, and it's very stressful if a supply is not at hand. The need to go buy cigarettes can supersede any other activity, no matter how important that activity is.

Then there is the need to find places where it's permitted to smoke. Many workplaces do not allow smoking during work time or meetings anymore, so it has to be squeezed in on breaks. Certain buildings do not allow indoor smoking, so the employees have to go outside. Many restaurants no longer allow smoking; if they do, it's usually in a separate room from nonsmokers. Nonsmokers don't want the smell or the secondhand smoke, so smokers who go out to dinner with nonsmokers must be prepared to compromise and sit in the nonsmoking section.

There is often emotional stress between smokers and nonsmokers. Smokers group together around ashtrays, and nonsmokers withdraw from them. Each group has less interest in the other. This is hard on relationships. Emotional pain is part of every smoker's life.

There is a great deal of literature available about the physical consequences of smoking cigarettes. Smoking is deadly. There are Smokers Anonymous or Nicotine Anonymous groups in many cities, and there are structured intensive treatment programs. If you want to quit, make the decision and choose the way you want to find support in quitting.

Additional Reading

Cruse, Joseph R. *"I Don't Smoke!": A Guidebook to Break Your Addiction to Nicotine.* Deerfield Beach, FL: HCI, 2009.

Resources

Yahoo! Health
http://health.yahoo.com/smoking-overview/

The Quit Smoking Company
http://www.quitsmoking.com

Your Total Health
http://yourtotalhealth.ivillage.com/quit-smoking-what-works

twenty-nine

Cancer: The Dreaded Diagnosis (My Story)

> *When we move out of the familiar here and now,*
> *we set in motion a series of events that, taken together,*
> *bring about changes at the very root of our being.*
>
> —JOSEPH DISPENZA

THERE ARE MORE THAN 10 million cancer survivors in the United States. I am one of them. It's been more than fifteen years since I have heard that frightening word in reference to myself. My memories of the journey are still very clear. It started when I went in for my annual mammogram, and my life was turned upside down.

First, there is the uncomfortable feeling that starts your heart pounding when you hear the sentence "We need a few more pictures." The next phase of fear comes with the suggestion that you bring someone with you to the meeting with your doctor. When you hear, "We have some bad news," your heart begins to flutter even more, and you feel as if someone has punched you in the stomach. You listen as if your life depends on it. The biopsy is scheduled, and you lie on a polished steel table, naked except for a thin cotton gown.

Then there is the magic time. This includes anesthesia, the biopsy, the trip back to the recovery room, and a few hours of deep sleep. My next memory is the trip from the recovery room back to the hospital room and, through the fuzzy images, seeing my partner walking beside me. In a thick voice, I hear myself say, "What did they find?" He replies, "It is cancer."

I have taken the journey from wife, mother, grandmother, and friend to becoming a statistic: one more breast cancer patient with big decisions to make. I feel my former life fading. My home, my interests and hobbies, and my work seem to belong to another life. My life now is full of phone calls to family, x-rays, options, fears, lots of tears, and questions and more questions.

My story is one of the lucky ones. My partner was at my side through it all. My family—including my grandchildren, all from out of town—gathered at the hospital. My prognosis was good, and my care was the very best. The Mayo Clinic in Rochester, Minnesota, managed my medical care. I received many phone calls, including one from Former First Lady Betty Ford to offer her support. There are others in this situation without spouses, with dependent children, with a poor prognosis, and with limited care. Yet we are all bonded by shock, fear, pain, and sadness. Our lives are changing in ways we do not even understand at this point.

Today's medical approach to breast cancer is to involve the patient in the decision making. There are many decisions to make. My partner and my son took the information we could gather from the Internet and added to it what we were learning at the clinic. In one day, we opted for a mastectomy and a reconstruction, all to take place within the same surgery. In two days, I was back on that polished steel table waiting for the next phase.

When I awoke, it was over. My partner never left my side. He, my children, my grandchildren, and my sister were there for me. My room was filled with flowers from all over the United States. There was a wonderful woman from the organization Reach to Recovery sitting in my room, ready to tell me her story. Phase one was now over. I had gone from shocked patient to a recovering survivor.

Phase two begins. There is the recovery time. In about three weeks, the reality and enormity of this experience became clearer to me. There was less information available about how to enter this new world than there was about the diagnosis and treatment. My emotions were raw, my body had changed, and there were questions but no one to ask for answers. A new frontier was emerging; it's called *survivorship*, the rigorous task of finding out how to be a living, recovering cancer patient.

There are many unknowns, such as which further treatments to choose. There are decisions about chemotherapy. Then there is the question of how someone with a changing body handles her body image, her sexual life, and her relationships in a world obsessed with beauty and physical perfection. There are ongoing physical challenges. There is still fatigue and some pain, possible arm swelling, insurance and employer problems, and chronic depression, for some.

In a poll taken by Lance Armstrong's foundation, 57 percent said that although cancer leaves their bodies, it is always part of their lives. Many said that the practical and emotional consequences of the disease were more painful than the medical issues. Just adjusting to the concept of the loss of health when one receives the cancer diagnosis is a major grief. Then there is the never-ending recurrence of fear with every doctor's visit during the first five years. After being shocked once, there is the fear that we will be shocked again. We all know that five years isn't a magic number, but it is one that we all wait for with hope.

My oncologist told me that people who reach out for support show a better recovery rate. I listened and responded to everything she told me. I started a cancer support group in my area and attended another in a local hospital. The incredible book *Getting Well Again* by O. Carl Simonton, Stephanie Matthews-Simonton, and James L. Creighton became my bible. I set out to remove toxic people and toxic situations from my life. This in itself was a really big task, because I had to leave certain people and certain circumstances behind.

One thing was clear to me, however: my recovery was up to me, and I was going to do what had to be done, no matter what happened and no matter who had to leave my life. I had switched from the world of the well to the world of the sick, and I was determined to switch back to the world of the well. Today, fourteen years later, I live in the world of the well, and I am grateful. Along the way, I learned—and challenged—some myths about cancer.

Your doctor knows best. It is true that Susan Love is a doctor, but her message is that you yourself know your body best and must enter into the treatment process with all your thoughts and feelings. She feels that the support of other women is also a healing factor. She also believes the patient needs to be an active part of her recovery. Perhaps the myth to be broken should read, "Medicine, Surgery, and Medication are the only healing factors." My doctors at the Mayo Clinic were terrific, and they were there for me in all the ways I needed. Yet the most helpful information I received came from a book that was written by another doctor, Susan Love. Her writings answered every question, fear, and challenge that I faced. I have since had the opportunity to listen to her speak in person, and she is the best resource and solid caring person on this subject. Her writings are invaluable.

There is nothing funny about cancer. Cancer is too serious not to take lightly. The best thing I did for myself when I got out of the hospital was to go to a four-day workshop led by Dr. Bernie Siegel.

He and his wife talked about all the aspects of disease and created an atmosphere of laughter, seriousness, humor, and wit. It was as important to me as any of the medications were at that point. I laughed again, hope settled in, I had a sense of being understood, and my feeling of control over my life seeped back in, gradually. Participating in that workshop was healing.

Treatment will be terrible. Actually, I had minimum pain with the cancer itself. Discomfort with the new and unusual was more like it. Lying on a steel table was uncomfortable, yes, but not painful. There was a little pain after the operation, but it was manageable. Learning to live with a reconstruction and a changed body brought me discomfort, but the pain was again manageable. I didn't need chemotherapy, but my friends tell me that it creates an unpleasant taste in the mouth, a little nausea, and some fatigue—but not pain, really.

Life will never be the same. Life isn't the same, but is life ever really the same, day after day? Life has its ups and downs, its constant changes, so it is indeed true that life will never be the same. However, for the same reason, life is the same. The situations are different and the challenges are different, but life does settle into normality again. The sun comes up, we go about our daily lives, we connect with the people in our lives, and we face the same challenges we always have (money, taxes, vacations, jobs, cars, and so on). In that sense, life remains the same.

You will be strong and never be afraid again. This is not true. Sometimes you wake up in the middle of the night and are scared to death. Having a partner is a great comfort. Think about getting a pet. When your mind plays tricks on you, it's wonderful to have something alive and warm that you can hold.

You will be damaged goods. This is not true. Cancer survivors work hard to be great and look great. When you work hard, you are bound to get results. Survivors report that their hair has grown in more beautiful than ever, their skin is smooth and clear, and they feel better than ever. I don't know when it happened, I don't even know exactly how it happened, but one day I woke up, saw the sun, and realized that life was ready to go on.

At that point I decided to write my own ABCs of coping, and I want to share them with you:

A: **Always** keep going. Life will change, but you can handle it, and someday it will feel normal again.

B: **Build** a bridge between being a healthy person and now a sick person. Know that you can cross that bridge back to being healthy again.

C: **Cancel** anything that is not essential.

D: **Do** not let anyone tell you how to feel or diminish your truth about those feelings.

E: **Emotions** are your friends. Feel them and express them.

F: **Find** a good support group and use it.

G: **Go** to your treatments with the feeling of a warrior out to do battle.

H: **Have** some fun, whether it's a movie, a play, a workshop, or a special dinner. Carve out some time for pleasure.

I: **Ice** cream; it's soothing and comforting. Find your favorite and enjoy that pleasure.

J: **Journey** to see someone you care about. It could be a friend, a coworker, or a family member. Reconnect a friendship.

K: **Keep** a journal of your experience. Someone in your world would like to know about it someday.

L: **Learn**, learn, and learn some more. Look for ways to spruce up your recovery and dare to try new experiences.

M: **Moment** by moment, live and savor. Do not postpone anything you can do today to bring more happiness into your life.

N: **No.** Say no to whatever you don't want in your life. Give up obligations and expectations that have been placed on you. Grab freedom.

O: **Own** your values and your integrity. Let people know who you are and what you need for your own health.

P: **Pray.** Find whatever prayer means to you and pray. It's a link to a Higher Power and the power within you.

Q: **Quiet** yourself a bit each day. Develop some quiet time when you can meditate and relax.

R: **Reexamine** your priorities. Your quality of life will improve as you keep and eliminate people and situations based on your priorities.

S: **Share** what you have learned with family and friends. This is a journey they are taking with you, and your intimacy will grow through sharing.

T: **Timing** is important in recovery. Give yourself whatever time you need to heal, to find your energy, and to feel hope once again.

U: **Utilize** all the resources that are available to you: the Internet, books, workshops, support groups, and talks with family and friends.

V: **Volunteer** and become involved. Being with others and helping them is one of the best ways to help yourself.

W: **Walk,** walk, walk. The exercise is good and healthy, and the medical benefits of walking are huge. Regardless of the weather, walk, and if weather is impossible, play a tape and walk inside.

X: **X-rays** and continued medical care will always be part of your life. Learn to appreciate the great help that medical care has been to preserving your life.

Y: **Yes.** Say yes to the people and things that make you feel alive, loved, and engaged. Say yes to experiences that bring joy and that let you share your gratitude at being healthy and alive.

Z: **Zap** any negative thinking or preoccupation. Know that negativity will limit healing and slow down your progress. Get rid of any thoughts that even suggest the possibility of negativity.

Additional Reading

Coping with Cancer magazine, www.copingmag.com

Love, Susan M. *Dr. Susan Love's Breast Book,* 4th ed. Cambridge, MA: Da Capo Press, 2005.

Potts, Eve, and Marion Morra. *Understanding Your Immune System.* New York: Avon Books, 1996.

Siegel, Bernie. *Love, Medicine, and Miracles: Lessons Learned About Self-Healing from a Surgeon's Experience with Exceptional Patients.* New York: Harper, 1990.

Simonton, O. Carl, Stephanie Matthews-Simonton, and James L. Creighton. *Getting Well Again: The Bestselling Classic About the Simontons' Revolutionary Lifesaving Self-Awareness Techniques.* New York: Bantam Books, 1992.

Workshop

Any workshop with Bernie Siegel
http://www.berniesiegelmd.com/

thirty

Alcohol: Am I Drinking Too Much?

> *Do not look back in anger, or forward in fear, but around in awareness.*
>
> —James Thurber

> *The booze that leaves you breathless also can leave you careless, homeless, family-less and jobless.*
>
> —Lee Silverstein

JANE WOKE UP WITH a headache and thought, *I wonder if I am drinking too much. I certainly wouldn't ask anyone to tell me what they think. And why wouldn't I? Am I afraid of what they would say? Lately it seems that I have been drinking more than my friends. They have a glass of wine, and I have two, sometimes three. Sometimes they have a cola or an iced tea. I always have wine. Dinner is not dinner without a drink of some kind. Then I noticed that the five o'clock cocktail signaled the end of my productive day. More concern.* But, she rationalizes, *I never get drunk, never drive a car after drinking, and no one has mentioned my drinking to me.*

Jane is beginning to recognize that drinking has become a good friend. She can't imagine not having a regular alcoholic drink. This would be a good time to stop drinking for awhile—just to see if she can do so comfortably. She might not be headed down the road to addiction, but she is clearly becoming dependent on alcohol.

Alcohol is sneaky. At first, it's a fun, tasty social experience. It lubricates the feelings and makes it easier to socialize. It's relaxing and a ritual. This can go on for some time. However, for people in certain circumstances, it can turn into a problem. These circumstances are the following:

1. The genes that make one vulnerable to alcohol addiction
2. The availability of alcohol
3. A permissive environment

One might ask, isn't that just about everyone? Nevertheless, if you do not have certain genes, you simply will not become addicted. You may abuse alcohol, get drunk, and cause problems for yourself and others, but you will not become addicted. If you have any concerns, talking this over with an addictionologist, or someone trained to recognize addiction, is a way to assess the situation.

Alcohol is readily available in our culture, and our culture is mostly a permissive environment. One could argue that our culture almost promotes the use of alcohol.

There is plenty of literature available to self-assess one's use of alcohol. One of the more personal ways to do so is to ask the following questions:

1. Am I aware that I drink more than the people around me?
2. Do I drink to excess once I start drinking?
3. Am I uneasy when I know that there will not be alcohol available?

4. Do I ever behave differently in social situations once I start drinking?
5. Have I ever embarrassed myself when drinking?
6. Do I hide or keep secret the amount that I drink?
7. Am I aware of how much money I spend on alcohol?
8. Do I ever socialize without alcohol?
9. Am I comfortable with friends who do not drink?
10. Have I ever done anything dangerous to myself after drinking? Have I driven a car, gone home with a stranger, had sex when not planning to, or missed work?

All the above are serious clues to alcohol dependency and maybe addiction.

Social drinking tends to shift into abuse of alcohol when, instead of recognizing that alcohol eases pain and stress, we *seek* that mood change when we are stressed or in pain. It's a subtle shift. Some drinkers will notice that over time, they seem to be drinking more to feel that mood change. One drink used to do it, then two became necessary, and now three drinks are needed to feel the mood change.

What is happening for those who will become dependent and addicted is that tolerance is developing. That is, it takes more alcohol more often to achieve a positive mood change. The problem is that while the mind and emotions are feeling better, the body is slowly adapting its chemistry and requiring more alcohol.

Exactly how and why the body develops this increased tolerance for alcohol is still a subject of pharmacological research. Yet we know it happens. Years ago surgeons noticed that patients who drank heavily required larger amounts of anesthesia to become anesthetized. Whatever the explanation, one thing is certain: acquired increased tolerance is an important warning to the heavy social drinker that serous trouble lies ahead.

A second major symptom of addiction is that a person will develop blackouts. By this I do not mean passing out. Blackouts are temporary times of amnesia while remaining conscious. When they begin, they may be for a very short period, just a minute or two. You will think that you forgot something, or you will deny that you or someone else has said something. For that minute or two, nothing records on the brain.

As dependency develops, blackouts can last for minutes, hours, and sometimes an entire day or evening. It is a very frightening situation and contributes to the self-denial of drinkers. They truly believe their own reality; it's just that they are missing big pieces of their reality. When big pieces of reality are not available to the drinker, it's easy to see why personal and job problems become very serious. When does that person pass from social drinker to dependence to addiction? What is the magic line? No one knows the answer to this for sure, but we do know that blackouts happen only to someone who is in serious trouble with alcohol.

The last major symptom of addiction is a loss of control. This happens when people who are drinking are not able to control how much they are going to drink at any given time. They still have the option of not taking the first drink, but after that drink, they lose control of how many more drinks they will have.

This means that any use of alcohol starts a chain reaction in which the drinker feels a physical demand for alcohol. Usually, by this stage, others have noticed the drinking and there have been instances of hurt, anger, broken promises, and what appears to be dishonesty. The drinker promises not to drink and breaks the promise. More personal and professional problems occur.

By now, Jane has a lot to think about. Denial of her increasing tolerance, blackouts (seemingly forgetfulness), and loss of control are starting to cause personal and relationship problems.

The best way to determine the seriousness of her drinking would be to seek an assessment from a professional. Most alcoholics resist this option. It would make the problem too real, and it is more comfortable to deny what is happening.

Another good way to learn more about addiction is to attend an Alcoholics Anonymous (AA) meeting and just listen. You can go as often as you choose to just listen. As members share their histories, strength, wisdom, and hope, one can sometimes make a self-assessment.

There are also many books to read that will help you to make a self-assessment. The chances are that once a person begins to wonder if there is a problem, there most likely is a problem.

Additional Reading

Johnson, Vernon E. *I'll Quit Tomorrow: A Practical Guide to Alcoholism Treatment.* New York: HarperOne, 1990.

Wegscheider-Cruse, Sharon. *Another Chance: Hope and Health for the Alcoholic Family.* Palo Alto, CA: Science and Behavior Books, 1989.

thirty-one

Please Help Me with My Grief

All of us grieve differently.

—JOAN GILBERTSON

EVERY HELLO BEGINS WITH a good-bye, and every good-bye makes possible a new hello. Life is about saying good-bye and hello—and so it goes until the day we say good-bye to this life and hello to the mystery over yonder.

Life is more than just a relentless presence of random tragedies, accidents, disease, and death. Relationships die, possibilities die, and dreams die. To welcome anything means to let go of something else. There are many kinds of loss, but all of them involve grief.

Grief has many forms. Nostalgia is grief over lost innocence. Despair is grief that we feel when we have lost hope. Longing is grieving for a future yet to arrive. Cynicism is grieving that we no longer believe in what is good. Guilt is the grief we feel when we abandon our own values.

Some cultures teach and value dramatic and emotional expression. Other cultures teach and value the restraint of emotion. Unfortunately, some cultures actually intellectualize and deny grief.

To grieve honestly and well, we need to give up control. We have to sit quietly with our sadness and breathe it in and out. There is often a lump in the throat, weeping, crying, wailing, shoulders shaking, and breath coming in gulps. Sometimes we go a bit crazy. Our legs fail, we make noises and moan. We hold our guts.

It's a kind of dying, but it is holy and necessary. Unacknowledged grief turns to poison and malice. Couples who can't grieve sometimes divorce and sometimes settle into polite distance. Depressed people are often angry people, and angry people are often sad people.

To stay healthy, we must learn to say good-bye often and well. We must give thanks for what was good, forgive what we can, and let the rest go. We have to surrender to grief. Broken hearts don't kill us. In fact, it's just the opposite: the denial of a broken heart can become destructive and lethal.

We do not heal by gritting our teeth and distracting ourselves. We mustn't let time merely pass, because it's not true that time heals all wounds. The only way to heal is to grieve.

One day we wake up in the morning and realize that life has changed permanently in ways that will touch us forever. We realize that someone or something that we love has died. Our pain may happen at the time of the loss or come sometime after the loss, but on a given day, the realization will hit hard that this is a permanent change in our lives.

At the time of the loss, there is shock if the event was not expected; if it was expected, there is often a weary feeling of surrender. There is almost a feeling of walking through mist or fog, as if nothing is really clear. We wonder why other people are grocery shopping, going to work, and going to movies. How can they do that when I am in such pain? No matter how badly your heart is broken, the world doesn't stop for your grief. It's a brutal time of agony, breathlessness, sleeplessness, and no appetite. There is much to do in this chaotic time of loss. There are decisions to make, papers to sign, and days to get through. One day, you simply know that your heart has been broken.

Each person grieves in his or her own way, and we need to be respectful of what gives comfort. I know a mother who kept one of her daughter's sweaters without washing it for several months just to smell her daughter's perfume, which was left on her sweater. A widow slept with her husband's wedding ring under her pillow for years as she went to sleep thinking about him. Some cry very easily, and some can't cry at all. Some become chaotically busy, and others tend to isolate. Some reach out to friends, and others want to be alone.

Joan Didion tells us in her book *The Year of Magical Thinking* that she went crazy with grief for a while. She takes us on her journey. She had lost her husband to a sudden death and her daughter to an illness, both in a very short period.

Frequently, in the course of my counseling with someone on some other subject, the conversation will turn to an area of hurt and sorrow over the death of someone close. As we talk more, tears often begin to flow and pain is relieved. Then there is an apology, with the following words: "I'm sorry, I should be over this by now." There is no need for an apology, nor should the person feel "over" it by now. We never get over death and loss, we only get through it. It's an unhealthy expectation that one should get over the grief process. Why should we even want to get to the point where the loss of someone dear and loved is a matter of emotionless intellectual reflection?

The person you lost was part of you, and you cared and loved deeply. You will go on without him or her, but there may never be a point in your life when the memory of him or her will not evoke feelings.

The tears, emptiness, loneliness, and guilt that are part of the consequences of the death of a loved one will diminish with time, but only diminish. It's unfair and unreal to expect them to totally disappear. They will be there forever. Life will go on, and that is important. New friends, new dear ones, new loved ones, new activities, and new joys will enter your life, but they can coexist with precious memories.

The first level of healing is in the first year after the loss. There will be all the first reminders. In the case of death, there will be the first birthday, the first anniversary, the first holiday season, the first vacation, the first tax season, and so on. Each first will have a set of memories attached to it, and these feelings must be experienced. These experiences will get easier with time, but they will always evoke feelings.

Another difficulty comes when just for an instant you forget that you are grieving and find yourself laughing. It might be because of an incident that happens. You laugh and feel like your old self. It feels good to laugh, and then it hits you: you are grieving, and laughter isn't part of grieving.

Then the guilt starts. How can you be happy when your loved one is gone? There are mixed feelings. Grief keeps us connected to the one we have lost, and at some level, we believe that we should stay sad.

There is, however, another way to stay connected. I borrow from Steven Kalas, a talented Las Vegas journalist. He says, "Thriving is another way of honoring the life of your loved one." When you affirm your life, you affirm your lost person. "Did your loved one begrudge you happiness when she/he was alive?" Kalas asks. "Would she/he be happy or sad that you are reluctant to enjoy your life?"

Perhaps the best way to stay connected to your loved one is to remember a time you were happy together and know that your loved one would really enjoy seeing you happy. Grieve whenever you have to, but allow yourself to stay connected to your loved one by showing your happiness as well.

For several years, I have been meeting with some very wonderful women. They are all women who have lost an adult child to an early death. Their courage, their rawness, their honesty, and their willingness to grieve is a testament to the life force.

Those who have experienced the loss of a child have learned that there is a particular emptiness in their hearts that can never be filled. Nor would they want it to be filled. The poet Alfred Tennyson expressed it beautifully: "Oh for the touch of a lost hand / And the sound of the familiar voice that is still."

Although the loss is crushing, those who are blessed with a faith in and an understanding of God will know that the loved one is safe and peaceful far beyond our understanding. We can take solace in the safety of the souls of our loved ones.

Life goes on—never quite the same, never as complete as before, but we have our memories, which nothing can destroy. They are our treasure, and those memories will become gold to us as we continue our journey.

Instead of hurting over the fact that nothing lasts forever, accept it as one of the truths of life and learn to find meaning and purpose in the changes and the joys that fade. Learn to savor the moment, even if it doesn't last forever.

Moments of our lives can be eternal without being everlasting. Close your eyes and see if you can remember a special person or a special moment: a loved one, an event, a city, a sunset, or a beach. In one way, it didn't last long at all, but in another way it has lasted for-ever because we still remember it. That is the only kind of eternity that we know about for sure.

We can have these memories whenever we choose, and they will do more for our souls than any one major religious experience. It is our spiritual right to have these precious memories. The good life is not about big or spectacular experiences. It's about knowing how to have those precious moments and letting them add up to something.

There are two important lessons in life: Belong to the people who love you, and accept pain as part of life.

Healing isn't easy. Frustration tends to set in quickly. We hurt and we feel defeated. Sometimes we want to give up. We want to walk away and pretend nothing matters. We won't, however, because we are people of faith and people who care.

We all have to feel down sometimes before we can feel up. We have to cry sometimes before we can smile. We have to hurt before we can feel strong. Nevertheless, if we keep on working, sharing with others and believing, we *will* heal in the end.

Somewhere I read the following piece about Earthbound angels, and I cannot find a reference for it. Should anyone know where it comes from, please let me know, and I will be happy to credit it. It is so good that I want to include it, and so I pray that the author will understand.

> Occasionally, we are graced with the presence
> of Earthbound angels. They are unable to
> stay with us for long, but while they do,
> they bring unprecedented joy and happiness
> to all they touch.
> While they are here, we bask in their
> goodness and marvel at their contribution to the world.

When they leave, we are left with the devastation that comes with
losing such a wonderful being.
But we must remember: the Earthbound angels
are not ours to keep. They are ours to
enjoy, learn from, and behold until they
return home.

It's important to remember the following:

1. Your grief will take longer than most people think.
2. Your grief will take more energy than you thought possible.
3. You may grieve for lost opportunities as well as the person who
   was lost.
4. You will have many emotions and they are all okay to have.
5. You may feel lost and unimportant for some time.

The fact must be faced that grief is never fully resolved, that the
hole in the soul is never filled up for us again. There is a permanent
pain of loneliness, which is a valuable witness to our ability to love.

Additional Reading

Dayton, Tian. *Heartwounds: The Impact of Unresolved Trauma and Grief on Relationships*. Deerfield Beach, FL: HCI, 1997.

Didion, Joan. *The Year of Magical Thinking*. New York: Knopf, 2005.

James, John W., and Russell Friedman. *The Grief Recovery Handbook: The Action Program for Moving Beyond Death, Divorce and Other Losses*. New York: HarperCollins, 1998.

———. *When Children Grieve: For Adults to Help Children Deal with Death, Divorce, Pet Loss, Moving, and Other Losses*. New York: HarperCollins, 2002.

Kalas, Steven. *Human Matters: Wise and Witty Counsel on Relationships, Parenting, Grief, and Doing the Right Thing*. Las Vegas, NV: Stephens Press, 2008.

Kübler-Ross, Elisabeth. *Questions and Answers on Death and Dying*. New York: Scribner, 1997.

Kushner, Harold S. *When Bad Things Happen to Good People*. New York: Anchor Books, 2004.

Manning, Doug. *Don't Take My Grief Away from Me*. Oklahoma City, OK: In-Sight Books, 2005.

thirty-two

Suicide: A Pain with No Second Chance

*All human wisdom is summed up
in two words: wait and hope.*

—ALEXANDRE DUMAS

*I believe in the sun when it is not shining.
I believe in love when I do not feel it.
I believe in my God even when there is silence.*

—KARL LOES

IT WAS CHRISTMAS EVE, and I was a young woman with a toddler and a baby, waiting for my parents to come to my house to celebrate. They lived 100 miles away. My concern grew as they were late. When I called them on the phone, I got a steady busy signal. That was strange, because they should have been on the road by then.

Finally, the phone rang, and the voice on the other end simply stated, "Come home, your dad is dead." It was surreal. How could my dad be dead? He was forty-six years old, I had talked to him earlier that morning, and he had said that he would see me later. Because no explanation was given, I thought there must have been some kind of accident. Leaving my little ones with other family members, I started the 100-mile ride home. As I arrived at the home in which I had grown up, I saw the Christmas tree lying in the front yard in the snow—strange.

Walking in, I saw my mom sitting in a chair with people all around her. She was crying. My much younger sister was nowhere in sight, and my brother was upstairs. Even though it was Christmas Eve, there were family and friends everywhere.

My uncle took me aside and said, "Sharon, your dad killed himself this afternoon."

Oh! I thought. *There must be lots of things to do.* I went to the phone and started calling people. Then I talked to my brother and checked on my sister. I asked my mom what I could do for her. It went on like this for several days, until a funeral was planned. People arrived and were cared for, my dad was buried 100 miles away, my mom was connected to her family members, and the initial trauma was over. I remember leaving my mom and my brother with relatives. My sister went home with friends on a dark and cold night—it was twenty-six degrees below zero. I went home one last time to empty the ashtrays, pick up dirty dishes, and walk through the empty house. Then I drove the long 100 miles back home, wondering if it is safe to drive while crying.

I told my friends that my dad had had a serious bronchitis attack and died. Disconnection from the truth became my motto. I had broken from the reality of what was happening and was using my extreme sense of responsibility to keep from feeling pain. My feelings of loss, hurt, anger, and shame were numb. This numbness and denial stayed with me for a long time. I functioned, but I did not feel. It was too scary to go into my feelings. This was where I needed to stay to feel safe. The only feelings that I was aware of were the following:

- Love for my children, which resulted in my overprotecting them
- Sadness for my mother, which resulted in fear for her
- Fear for my brother and sister, which resulted in my feeling responsible for them.
- Abandonment, which resulted in my isolation

There just wasn't a right time or place for me to feel safe enough to feel my own feelings of loss. Ultimately, my stuffed-down feelings turned to depression. My depression also lasted a long time, until I reached out and sought help. Ultimately, I realized that I wasn't being a good mother. Concern for my children propelled me into getting help for myself.

Help came in the form of finding a safe place in which I could revisit that painful time of my father's suicide and have a chance to express my grief and my anger. This was therapy. Finally, when I said good-bye to him many years later, I was able to let him know how much I loved and missed him. In therapy, I was also able to let him know for all time that I love the parts of me that are like him. As the fear and ice that were in my heart began to melt and my emotional life began to warm up, the healing started. Today, in a spiritual way, I feel very connected to my dad and blessed to have been his daughter.

Survivors of suicide have difficult and painful journeys. Some say that losing a parent is the most difficult suicide, because a parent is supposed to be your safe place, the person you can count on forever. Others say that losing a spouse is most difficult, because it usually seems like a permanent abandonment by someone old enough to make adult decisions. Still others say that losing a child is the worst of all, because a parent is supposed to give children a reason to live and make them feel safe. To me, all suicides are painful in a way that is not easily understood or able to be discussed. The anguish is simply too overwhelming.

Later in life, as I worked with families in which a suicide had taken place, there were some harsh concepts to confront. Some researchers say that suicide is an expression of anger. When people cannot turn anger onto the object of their anger, they turn it on themselves. The researchers say that it is a choice between being angry enough to commit murder or to commit suicide. Those who choose suicide over murder have chosen the lesser violent path.

Other researchers say that guilt is a major factor. When guilt is so great that it feels impossible to make amends and get some relief, suicide seems as if it will bring relief.

Still others say that hopelessness is a major factor. When people believe that they have tried and tried to do something important to themselves and they have failed repeatedly, suicide stops the cycle. It is just a way out.

When working with a sixteen-year-old girl who had failed in an attempt to take her life, I said to her, "Mary, why would someone so young, with so much to live for, try to kill herself?" She was in a hospital, recovering from cutting her wrists.

She answered, "Sharon, I didn't mean to really die and have it be forever, I just wanted to die awhile." She explained that she was in conflict with her dad, had broken up with her boyfriend, and was failing a class in school. She didn't know how to rest, and she thought that maybe suicide would feel like a rest. She had not thought through the permanent consequences of dying.

My partner, Joseph Cruse, a long-term suicide survivor, told me that he felt a book about suicide could be written in just three chapters:

Chapter 1: Whew! (Relief)
Chapter 2: So there! (Anger)
Chapter 3: Oops! (I didn't really mean to die.)

There are some steps that loved ones can take after someone they loved commits suicide. These are as follows:

1. *Let all the feelings come forth.* Recognize that it may take some time. The freezing of emotion that comes with a major shock might allow only a few feelings at a time. As feelings surface, talk about them with someone who will simply listen. A loving and active listener is the most important person for the family to find. It might be a friend, a rabbi, a pastor, another family member, or a coworker. What is important is that the person will listen. This is not a time for advice or pity. It's a time to be heard. This is not something you will get over; it is something you will get through.

2. *Make a conscious decision to accept the fact that you will never have many of your questions answered.* The person who could answer those questions is dead, and those answers went with him or her. This is very hard, and sometimes the decision to let those questions go has to be made several times a day. The Serenity Prayer can help at this time: "God, grant me the serenity to accept the things I cannot change, the courage to change the things I can, and the wisdom to know the difference."

3. *Give the person the right to have made his or her own decision.* Somewhere in your process and in your own time, let this happen. My feelings were that I should have helped my dad with his depression, I should have seen the signs, I should have made him feel better about himself, and on and on. At some point, I had to realize that people who are capable of taking their own lives have the right to make their own decisions. For me, it was another step in the healing process to realize that although I did not like or approve of the decision my dad made, it was his decision to make.

Additional Reading

Dayton, Tian. *Heartwounds: The Impact of Unresolved Trauma and Grief on Relationships.* Deerfield Beach, FL: HCI, 1997.

Goodman, Sandy. *Love Never Dies: A Mother's Journey from Loss to Love.* San Diego: Jodere Group, 2001.

James, John W., and Russell Friedman. *The Grief Recovery Handbook: The Action Program for Moving Beyond Death, Divorce and Other Losses.* New York: HarperCollins, 1998.

_____. *When Children Grieve: For Adults to Help Children Deal with Death, Divorce, Pet Loss, Moving, and Other Losses.* New York: HarperCollins, 2002.

Kübler-Ross, Elisabeth. *Questions and Answers on Death and Dying.* New York: Scribner, 1997.

Kushner, Harold S. *When Bad Things Happen to Good People.* New York: Anchor Books, 2004.

Manning, Doug. *Don't Take My Grief Away from Me.* Oklahoma City, OK: In-Sight Books, 2005.

Resources

Suicide Hotlines
www.suicidehotlines.com

Crisis Link
www.crisislink.org

The National Suicide Prevention Lifeline
1-800-273-8255

Part six:

CREATIVITY

Take a risk a day—one small or bold
stroke that will make you feel
great once you have done it.

—*Susan Jeffers*

thirty-three

My Home Is My Nest:
How Can I Improve It?

A house is who you are, not what you ought to be.

—JILL ROBINSON

LIVING SPACE IS ONE of the most important subjects we can discuss. We divide our time among work space, living space, and option space. Work space is where we do our job. It may be one place or it may be several spaces, but it is where we spend regular time working. Option space might be a gym, a spa, a sports facility, a friend's home, or a club. Most important, we live somewhere. The space we develop for our living is the most essential space of all because it feeds us, it defines us, and it is our nest.

In the animal world, the nest is where a newborn animal is safe, where it learns its independence, and where it develops into an adult animal. In the human world, our nest is where we get support and nourishment, where we relax and rejuvenate, and where we know we belong.

Nests that feed us with energy and good feeling are usually filled with music, color, comfort, art, learning, connection, friends, food, and safety. We love being there. It's where we connect with ourselves and others, with computers, phones, and technology; where we share food and have parties with family and friends; where we learn by reading books and magazines and listening to recordings; and where we feel comfortable in soft warm beds and relaxing baths. Happy and satisfying homes have friends who come to visit and an ease of hospitality.

In my home, there are a few special places. A big comfortable bed is very important. Down pillows and comforters welcome us at the end of a full day. A television in the bathroom is a great way to start and end each day, catching up on the news. A bathtub with candles and bubble bath guarantees a special place to relax at the end of a busy day. The TV swings around so one can have a bubbly soak while catching a special TV show. It's a great place to relax—and to use when we need a treat.

One of the most important places in every home I have had is a meditation corner. We have two rocking chairs facing each other with a table between them. On the table is a candle, a miniature fountain, a fresh flower, healing stones, and several papers holding the names of the people we pray for daily. The table sits in front of corner windows covered with beautiful stained glass hangings and special artifacts that we have collected: rose quartz, the stone of healing; sand from Hawaii; and an acorn, to remind us that acorns grow to become mighty oaks.

Next to one of the rocking chairs is a basket full of meditation books. Each morning my partner and I spend half an hour reading meditations and sharing some of our spiritual thoughts. One has to get up early and plan for this time, or it can't happen. There is never enough time. We have to choose this time and protect it.

Next to the other chair is a CD player and a collection of meditation music. Spending this time with music, meditations, and each other is our guarantee that this day will not unravel. It's a high point of the day, and it's only 7:00 AM.

Another important part of our home is our work and project area. This includes our computers, our books, a television, and a large table. Each of us has many special projects, and to have a space where we can work, explore, and create is very important to us.

We have a special area where we can share time with family and friends. We love to entertain, and we keep this spot ready for company. It has pillows, books, comfortable furniture, and candles. We love to add fresh flowers to the mix. There is also some wine chilling and some snacks in the cupboards and freezers, so we are always ready for someone to stop in for a visit.

We have three fountains, two indoors and one outside. Seeing and hearing water is a great mood soother. We have three salt lamps, in three different rooms. The golden glow of a salt lamp brings a soft feel to a room, and we leave the lamps burning 24/7.

In a guest room, I keep exercise tapes. That way, if the weather is such that I can't walk comfortably, I can still walk two to three miles to the exercise tapes.

Finally, bringing the outdoors into our indoor life is important for us. We choose flowers, mostly roses, to welcome people to our home. We live in the desert, so we use rocks and flowers to make our home feel beautiful and alive. The beauty of nature is important even though our access to outside space is limited.

It doesn't take a mansion to feel like a king or a queen in one's home. What is important is to know what makes you feel special, safe, and beautiful in your surroundings. Choose what is of value to you and then develop your nest. Your nest will no doubt be different from my nest. We are all different. All that matters is knowing that each of us needs a nest that fits our values, our comfort, and our pleasure. Go for it, and develop your own nest.

The size of your living space doesn't matter. It may be a house, a condo, or an apartment. Susan Susanka, author of *The Not So Big House,* says the following:

> A house should encourage connectedness. People lose touch with one another when every function is done in a different room. . . . Big living spaces tend to fuel big lives. They promote a cycle of desiring more stuff, time spent working to pay for the acquired stuff, and lots of rushing to fit in everything else—followed by going shopping as a stress release, resulting in more stuff.

This is not exactly good role modeling.

Ultimately, a loving family home is determined by the size of your heart, not your hearth. Your children's values, self-worth, and closeness are what they take from that home, whether you live in a tiny apartment or a big house in the suburbs.

Additional Reading

Breathnach, Sara Ban. *Simple Abundance: A Daybook of Comfort and Joy.* New York: Grand Central Publishing, 1995.

Stoddard, Alexandra. *Creating a Beautiful Home.* New York: HarperCollins, 1993.

———. *Living a Beautiful Life: 500 Ways to Add Elegance, Order, Beauty, and Joy to Every Day of Your Life.* New York: Avon Books, 1988.

Susanka, Susan. *The Not So Big House: A Blueprint for the Way We Really Live.* Newtown, CT: Taunton Press, 2008.

Wong, Angi Ma. *Feng Shui: Do's and Taboos.* North Adams, MA: Storey Publishing, 2000.

Resources

For a feeling of peace and calm, use salt crystal lamps in several of your rooms. Salt lamps are crafted from crystalline rock salt that is mined from an ancient seabed, millions of years old, in the foothills of the Himalayan Mountains. The primary purpose of salt lamps is to purify the air in your home, but the secondary

198 Part Six: Creativity

purpose—a warm exotic elegance—will enhance the beauty of your surroundings. Salt lamps are available from the places listed below.

SpiritualQuest
www.spiritualquest.com

Solay Wellness
www.natural-salt-lamps.com

thirty-four

Playtime: I Need More Fun in My Life

Life is what we make it, always has been, always will be.

—GRANDMA MOSES

REGULAR BREAKS IN YOUR routine will boost your overall sense of well-being. Dr. Mel Borins, author of *Go Away Just for the Health of It*, says, "I've seen patients with chronic headaches and mood disorders return from a vacation feeling better about their work and the things going on at home." Time off, whether an extended vacation to the Pacific Islands or merely a ten-minute break, can make a big difference in a person's life.

People who take regular vacations have a lower rate of death by heart attack than people who do not take time off, according to many studies. Whether the vacation involves a swanky spa, a historical tour by bus, or a campout, what is important is the break in routine. Dr. Borins says that "even planning a trip boosts your positive thoughts." Collect brochures, read magazines, and start that dream trip. It puts you in a different frame of mind.

Stepping out of one's routine clears the head and starts different "juices" working. Some people say that planning a trip and traveling is just too hard and confusing. There are transportation problems, it's expensive, and it takes too much effort. It's easier to just stay home.

The journalist Sydney J. Harris said, "A winner takes a big problem and separates it into smaller parts so that it can be more easily manipulated. A loser takes a lot of little problems and rolls them together until they are unsolvable."

Try something new and different. It might be planning one night a week to try new eating places. It could be monthly or on a weekend, trying a new hobby or sport. It might be a class in something fun to do, or it could be vacationing in a dream spot or taking a trip around the world.

If a small effort works, and you begin to notice the benefits, that is just great. If you are disappointed, try something else. Sydney Harris also said, "A winner learns from his mistakes. A loser learns only not to make mistakes by not trying anything different."

Next to my most comfortable chair is a table where my monthly magazines are kept. When I need a quick fifteen-minute break, one of my favorite magazines and a cup of tea are within my reach. My iPod is on a shelf near the back door, so if there is time for a half-hour walk, my favorite music is handy. Just breathing in the outside air and noticing the neighborhood flowers is a mood elevator for me.

On the days when the house has to be spruced up, my Jerry Lee Lewis or Elvis music is there to help me dance through the tasks. I challenge anyone to be depressed or lethargic when listening to Jerry Lee Lewis make that piano come alive.

A favorite activity that is good for me personally and also gives my relationship a boost is to simply stop what I am doing, leave everything as is, and run out to a daytime movie. If that's impossible, a nighttime movie will work. Days, however, are especially fun. Grab a sandwich, sneak it into the theater, and have a picnic with a friend. There are times we pay extra and do a double matinee. It feels like a vacation.

Explore your own town. Rent a room and buy a bouquet of flowers. Eat in a special restaurant and explore shops, stores, and areas of your own town that you haven't seen for a while. Buy something by which to remember this special time. A mini-vacation in just twenty-four hours. If you can stretch the time, make it a weekend and go somewhere within a 100-mile radius.

Another way to have fun is to spend it with a child or a teen. When I was young and single, I joined Big Sisters and spent time with a twelve-year-old girl. Caring for foster children and foreign exchange students added more adventures.

Most of my fun-filled and fondest memories are times spent with my children and grandchildren. My children have made me go on carnival rides and have inspired me to make many trips to Disneyland and Disney World. They have taken me to the state fair, made chocolate chip cookies at midnight, dragged me camping, and taught me many card games.

My grandchildren have brought baseball, ballet, more card games, board games, backyard swimming parties, football games, movies, laser tag, bowling, and more into my life. It's really hard to grow old with children and grandchildren in your life.

One thing I have learned from children and teens is to plan play. Their play is fun and intentional, and it has a specific agenda. They ask, do you want to go play? Then they begin to plan what, when, and how they want to play. Adults are not as direct or clear about simply wanting to play. They will ask, do you want to go to lunch or dinner? Do you want to do a round of golf or go bowling? They hide their idea of play in some plan for eating, drinking, or a sensible activity. Young people will just hang out together.

Fun is even an integral part of work for many successful people. A *60 Minutes* episode, "Get Me the Geeks," featured Robert Stephens, founder of the Geek Squad, which helps people at home with their technology problems. He started the business at his kitchen table and became very successful. Robert Stephens has made the point that work doesn't always have to be about the task. It can be about having fun and pleasure in doing the task. He has added a sense of whimsy and color to his surroundings, his home visits, and even the cars the Geek Squad drives. He has had fun doing it. His business plan was "Be nice and fix it."

Richard Branson, the founder of Virgin airlines, has had fun creating his style of airplane comfort. His airline features special music, dim lighting, and pilots in black shirts and pants instead of uniforms. His box lunches are gourmet, not humdrum turkey sandwiches.

When Ben Cohen and Jerry Greenfield started their ice cream business, they decided to have a little fun with it. Long before they were making any money, they decided to play with their customers. They started by having a sale in which you could buy one scoop and get one free. Thus you could experiment with a new flavor. On Mother's Day, they would give all mothers a free ice cream cone. If a woman was visibly expecting, she would get a double dip. They also gave baby cones to people waiting in line. Is it any wonder that their business grew by leaps and bounds?

How about all the successful computer start-up companies where people wear jeans, eat pizza, and listen to rock music while working? They have fun and end up making millions doing so. Who says we have to wear stiff clothes and have structured jobs? Adding a little fun to the work can foster creativity and success. Many companies have found that when fun is part of the business, they end up spreading joy to their customers and employees alike.

Here are some fun ideas to try by yourself:

1. *Chose your wildest fun music and do laundry and straighten the house while listening to it.* It has to be loud if it is going to work.

2. *Place a small television on the counter near your bathtub.* Fill the tub with lots of warm water and bubble bath, light three candles, pour a plastic glass of a good chilled wine, and turn on your favorite TV show. Add hot water as you need it.

3. *Explore your neighborhood.* Put on your most comfortable walking shoes. Grab your MP3 player or iPod, a bottle of cold water, and your sunglasses and head out for at least a half hour—an hour, if you can find the time. If your neighborhood is not good for walking, find one that is.

4. *Pick a night and have a date with yourself at home.* Inform family and friends that you are busy that night. You don't have to explain. Your time and your life is your own, unless you are in the habit of always letting people know what you do. (If you are in that habit, you might take a look at it and see if that's really good for you.) Be sure to turn off all phones and your computer. Prepare some favorite comfort food; we all have dishes we just love. Take a bath using the ideas above, put on your most comfortable pajamas, grab a good book, put your food on a tray, and settle onto your sofa or into your bed (whichever is more comfortable). Read, eat, relax, doze, and start all over again. Your whole body will reach a state of deep relaxation, and your cares will diminish. You may be amazed at how rested you feel and how many cobwebs leave your thoughts. Repeat as often as you need it.

5. *Go out for an evening or an afternoon by yourself.* Plan to spend about fifty dollars. Go to a great bookstore, buy a special cup of coffee, and experiment with authors. After an hour, choose one book to bring home. Then drive to a theater, choose a movie, and settle in with hot popcorn. This will be about a three-hour date with yourself that will provide fun and relaxation that will last for several days. Next month come up with another idea for a three-hour date, and enjoy yourself.

Be sure to keep all these special times to yourself. You owe it to yourself to have some special plans and memories. You do not need anyone to make comments about your choices, you do not need to share all of your life's activities with another, and you certainly do not need anyone to plan to spend these special renewing times with you. This is a gift you give yourself.

Additional Reading

Carter-Scott, Cherie. *If Life Is a Game, These Are the Rules*. New York: Broadway Books, 1998.

Davis, Martha, Elizabeth Robbins Eshelman, and Matthew McKay. *The Relaxation and Stress Reduction Workbook*. Oakland, CA: New Harbinger Publications, 2008.

Boxed Cards

Self Care Cards, Cheryl Richardson

Heart and Soul, Sylvia Browne

Goddess Guidance, Doreen Virtue

52 Ways to Energize, Lynn Gordon

Calling All Women Meditation Cards, Sharon Wegscheider-Cruse *thirty-five*

Storytelling

We are each the hero of our own story.

—Mary McCarthy

The reason we survived, when so many other bands from the eighties didn't, is that we made a decision to become great storytellers.

—Jon Bon Jovi

STORYTELLING IS A GREAT SKILL. It can put you at ease in social situations, make your business memorable, and keep your curiosity on high alert. People connect through stories, and we all have them. At different times in our lives, stories can heal, offer hope, and build faith. Here are a few of my own.

The Red Rose

There was a time in my life that I felt scared and alone. I had just accepted a job in Austin, Texas. After years of personal and professional life in Minnesota, I felt the need for a change. Several

circumstances in the winter of 1982 indicated to me that it was time
to leave. With the offer of a meaningful job in Texas, I sold my home
and left my family, friends, and career.

I headed for Texas on a cold December day. I was driving a small
gray Honda and was dressed in a gray snowsuit with a red knit hat
and red down-lined cowboy boots. A few hours into the three-day
drive, I was battling a snowstorm. By the time I neared the Texas
border, after two days of driving on treacherous ice, my emotions
were tense and vulnerable. I was feeling personally alone and totally
uncared for. I also felt professionally isolated from friends and peers.
The tears began to flow. After about two hours of crying and driving, I prayed.

*Dear God, I feel so alone and so unsure. If You have anyone who cares
about me, please give me a sign.* I continued to drive. Shortly thereafter,
I saw a roadside diner and decided to stop and take a break.

As I entered the restaurant, I picked up a magazine. I sat down in
a booth, and the waitress came over to take my order. The first thing
she said was, "You must be the Red Rose." Puzzled, I asked her to
explain. She said, "The truck drivers are all talking about the Red
Rose. Some lady left Minnesota in a small gray Honda in the middle
of a snowstorm, and they've been concerned and watching out for
her from Minnesota to the Texas border. They have followed her on
their radios to make sure she was okay. I see you have made it, and
I'll let them know."

My tears began to flow again, this time from relief and gratitude.
I felt watched over and protected. The sign had been given to me. I
was personally being cared for.

As I began to eat my sandwich and sip a cup of coffee, I opened
the magazine. The article I was drawn to was entitled "Families of
Alcoholics Recover." The article began, "Sharon Wegscheider, in her
work, reports. . . . " I could not remember giving an interview to this

particular magazine, yet here was an article about my work. Even professionally, I felt protected—divinely protected. The tears were replaced by a smile.

My lesson learned: We can be cared for even in the risks we take. Sometimes we need to take a leap of faith and change our lives. It may be scary, but if we have the courage and strength to make changes, some wonderful surprises might be waiting for us.

Amazing Grace

Speaking at a conference in Seattle, Washington, I had planned to end my presentation with the song "Amazing Grace." Picture one thousand people in the audience at the finale of my presentation. I had arranged for the crewmen to lower the lights, and I was to press a button that would start the song. The presentation had gone very well, and there was a mood in the room. The lights dimmed, and I announced the song.

Then every speaker's nightmare happened: something didn't work. I pressed the button—nothing. I pressed again—still nothing. I tried one more time and was just about ready to have the lights brought on when I heard a rustling in the dark on the stage. There was a keyboard behind me on the stage, and I could hear someone approach. All of a sudden, a beautiful voice started to sing "Amazing Grace," and the singer accompanied himself on the keyboard. It was beautiful and it was perfect.

He was a professional musician who just happened to be in the audience for my presentation. His name was Jerry Florence. We became great friends, and he traveled with me for four years, doing music for my presentations.

My lesson learned: there are angels who walk on this earth, and every once in a while we get to meet one.

The Law of Attraction

I had attended a workshop about hopes and dreams. Each participant was asked to make a collage with pictures torn out from magazines to represent some of his or her hopes and dreams. As the workshop leader was walking around, she glanced down at my collage and said that it was way too bland and didn't have big enough ideals.

Trying to do better, I started over and added several far-reaching photos. The workshop leader told me I needed bigger dreams and bigger plans. I needed to choose photos that had scenes less likely to be mine. So I went back to the magazines and found photos that seemed to me very big ideas indeed. I had a beautiful fur coat, a luxury hotel in a big city, a big-screen TV, a limousine, a driver, some beautiful flower arrangements, and soft falling snow. She said to me, "Much better." After the workshop, I took the collage home and put it away in my office.

About two years later, I was working in my office one day, when I received a phone call. Could I come to New York and be on *The Phil Donahue Show*? Phil Donahue was the Oprah Winfrey of those years—the preeminent late-afternoon talk-show host. He wanted to interview me about my book, *Another Chance*, which had just been published.

I ordered my plane ticket and checked the weather in New York. The television station sent a limousine for me and delivered me to the Plaza Hotel in New York. As I stepped out of the limousine (complete with driver) in my fur coat, it was snowing.

The scene felt very familiar. Then I remembered my collage. As soon as I arrived home, I found the collage, and sure enough, the hotel in it was the Plaza. I had fulfilled the dream pictures in my collage.

My lesson learned: Dream big, fantasize, and attract into your life whatever it is that you would like to have.

Grand Ole Opry

When my daughters were teenagers, I was working and traveling a great deal, and we didn't get to spend as much time together as I would have liked. I was scheduled to lead a five-day workshop, but it was canceled and I found myself with five free days. We were living in Minnesota, and I decided to take my daughters to Tennessee to visit the Grand Ole Opry. We jumped in the car and left immediately. I assumed that we could get tickets when we got there.

A few days later, we arrived in Nashville, and I called the Opry to order tickets. I was told that the Opry was completely sold out for several days due to the Country Music Awards program that was being held there. I was heartsick and pleaded my case, but to no avail.

Working in the field of addiction, I knew that people in that field try to help each other out. I didn't know anyone in town, but I thought that maybe I could meet someone who could help. I called the Alano Club, the local club for support for families. I asked if there was anyone who could help me to buy tickets.

About an hour later, the hotel clerk at the front desk called and said that an envelope had been delivered for me. I went down to the desk, and to my amazement, there were tickets for the entire Country Music Awards presentations, front row center. There was a note saying, "For all that you have done for the field of addiction—please enjoy." It was signed "An anonymous friend." We had a wonderful and exciting time in Nashville.

My lesson learned: What goes around comes around. We reap what we sow.

The Flat Tire

One night, as I was driving home from teaching a class at our local university, I could feel my front tire going flat. Soon I was driving on the rim. It was about 11:00 PM, pitch black outside, with only a sliver of a moon. I had taken a shortcut and was in a pretty bad part of town. This was in the days before cell phones. I sat awhile and finally decided that I needed to do something, so I got out of the car and began to walk.

In the distance, I could see a dim yellow light, so I walked toward it. As I got closer, I could see that it was a porch light and that the front door was a screen door. I could just barely see inside the house. As I got closer, I could see that there were about ten rather scruffy-looking men sitting in a circle. My mind raced with imagining the scenario of what was going on in that house. I was frightened.

Nevertheless, I had to do something. The neighborhood was rough, and I had no car and no phone. I walked up to the house and knocked. One of the men came to the door and asked what I wanted. I told my tale and he listened. Then a second man came out and took a long look at me. He then said, "Are you that lady who has her picture on the back of a book about alcoholics?"

I had just published a book with quite a large picture of me on the back jacket. When I said yes, he said, "I read that book. It helped me a lot." I had interrupted an AA meeting that was just ending.

He went to get his buddies, and all ten men walked back with me to my car, changed the tire, and sent me on my way.

My lesson learned: Never be too quick to judge. You might miss a great adventure.

I love telling stories and I love listening to stories. Stories can heal, make us laugh, and give us thoughts to ponder. We all have a need to be heard and to connect with others. Stories can provide the wonderful attraction that brings us to each other.

Additional Reading

Allenbaugh, Kay. *Chocolate for a Woman's Soul: 77 Stories to Feed Your Spirit and Warm Your Heart.* New York: Fireside, 1997.

Bolsta, Phil. *Sixty Seconds: One Moment Changes Everything.* New York: Atria Books, 2008.

Gilbert, Elizabeth. *Eat, Pray, Love: One Woman's Search for Everything Across Italy, India, and Indonesia.* New York: Penguin, 2007.

Kidd, Sue Monk. *The Secret Life of Bees.* New York: Penguin, 2008.

Martin, Katherine. *Women of Courage: Inspiring Stories from the Women Who Lived Them.* Novato, CA: New World Library, 1999.

Martin, Katherine. *Women of Spirit: Stories of Courage from the Women Who Lived Them.* Novato, CA: New World Library, 2001.

Wegscheider-Cruse, Sharon. *Dancing with Destiny: Turning Points on the Journey of Life.* Deerfield Beach, FL: HCI, 1997.

Wyse, Lois. *Women Make the Best Friends: A Celebration.* New York: Simon & Schuster, 1995.

thirty-six

Holidays Are Hard
for Many People

> *Giving presents is a talent, to know what*
> *a person wants, to know when and how*
> *to get it, to give it lovingly and well.*
>
> —PAMELA GLENCONNER

ONE OF THE DEFINITIONS of the word *holiday* in Webster's dictionary is "a day of freedom from work." Somehow that doesn't really ring true for many people. *Holiday* also means a day of celebrating something. It doesn't really matter what the holiday is, too few people manage to have a restful day of celebration. There is too much to do and too many people to visit—all when we are eating and drinking too much and not taking time to exercise.

There are people who do have great holidays. They are the ones who truly take a break for themselves and find a way to relax and refresh themselves. They listen to music and read, sleep in, take a hike through a park, and share time with the people in their lives. For the most part, however, our culture struggles with downtime. People often want more and more, and in the process of getting it, they create their own stress.

It seems that with food, gifts, travel, and the disruption of schedules, there is tremendous stress and strain during holiday times. The bigger the holiday, the more stress there is. In addition to doing all that has to be done to prepare for the day, there is the pressure of the expectation of joy. Combine this with the forced togetherness of family and friends, and the stresses and strains only multiply.

I remember when my children all had partners who were added to our family system, one by one, and this added more expectations to the celebration of Christmas. To minimize the stress, my partner and I chose the second weekend of December to be our Christmas holiday. That freed the children to spend December 25 with their new families. My partner and I then went on a vacation over the actual holiday.

Now that there are grandchildren, we sometimes choose another time of year to celebrate as an extended family and let each individual family celebrate its own way on Christmas Eve and Christmas. Occasionally, we all get together, all fifteen of us, but it isn't an annual expectation anymore. It's very special whenever we can get together. Understanding, listening, flexibility, and love are the ingredients that make for family closeness and feelings of belonging.

Hope springs eternal in families, however, and too often people will try to find the same holiday feeling that is depicted in books, in stories, and on television. When this feeling is hard to attain, then sadness, depression, and feelings of failure flourish. Each year, people try over and over, thinking that this time things will be different.

If only for a little while, people often deny what the truth really is. They can be dealing with the loss of a family member or a friend, the loss of a job, broken relationships, divorce, financial problems, health problems, alcoholism, or pill dependence—the list goes on. Holidays also tend to be a time when people drink more, smoke more, eat more junk food, exercise less, and pick fights with loved ones.

So what are we to do during holiday times? Here are some suggestions:

1. *Stay aware of what you feel and share those feelings with at least one other person.* My father died, by committing suicide, on Christmas Eve. Each year I need to share my feelings about it and remember my utter sense of loss and abandonment. Then I can let it go and remember him with love and tenderness.

2. *Set boundaries with people who want to get together.* There are usually more gatherings and company than is good for us. Choose people you enjoy being with and turn down other offers. You do not have to accept every invitation. For me, it works well to do some entertaining around Thanksgiving and in early December and again in late January and on Valentine's Day, then save lots of time for myself and my partner during the actual Christmas and New Year's weeks. If you visit relatives, stay at a hotel and limit the time you spend together. When we have plenty of space and time to ourselves, the together time is much easier and much richer. Visit for hours, not days. If you have invited company to your home, carve out some alone time for yourself. This may be a good time to get a massage, do some shopping alone, or meet friends for coffee. Constant togetherness is a setup for stress.

3. *If you have a large family gathering, add a little structure.* When we all get together in my family, because we are of different ages, we have different interests and levels of energy. It helps a great deal to plan to have a meal all together and then divide into smaller groups for the rest of the day. Some play cards, some play golf, some take a walk or a hike, some just sit and visit. Late in the day, before breaking up, we might have a storytelling session or a card game with everyone together again.

4. *Attend a support group meeting.* Holidays are times of the year when belonging to a support group is especially valuable. Get out and go to meetings. Share your thoughts and feelings with others who understand and support you. There is always acceptance and love to be found in these meetings.

5. *Plan ahead as much as possible.* My family lovingly laughs at my little charts and maps that I put together before each family gathering. Yet when the visit is over, everyone can see that these things have invariably helped. Well before we get together, I send out an e-mail to find out what each person would like to do and what his or her expectations are. Sometimes we can meet them and sometimes we can't, but everyone feels heard. I have some teenage grandsons who really want to play golf. My granddaughters want to shop, and my son loves a good restaurant. My husband wants to sing with one of the granddaughters. These are like pieces of a puzzle. We take the time we have and divide it into different segments and try to do as much as we can for as many as we can.

6. *Keep mealtimes simple.* Food is always an important part of every get-together. I have learned to keep it simple, make it good, and do takeout and order pizza as much as possible. Every visit and trip includes one meal from In-N-Out Burger. When you're cooking, invite people into the kitchen and let them make their own favorite dishes. It's like a potluck, only you provide all the food. To me, fancy dinners and table settings are for small groups and extra time. Holidays are for festivity and fun.

7. *Remember why the holiday is there.* If it's a religious holiday, allow time for each person to celebrate in his or her own way. If it's a spiritual gathering, you can plan some readings, music, and sharing that is appropriate. If it's the Fourth of July, Thanksgiving, Valentine's Day, or Super Bowl Sunday, there are many

fun games and activities that will make it special.

8. *Go light on gift giving.* I keep a big box in one of my closets for storing gifts, and then I shop a little all year. I am always seeing things that remind me of someone to whom I would like to give a gift. I also take advantage of sales throughout the year. On the Saturday after Thanksgiving, I pull out all my treasures and decide who would like what gift. I spend that day bringing out my Christmas music and wrapping gifts. If there are some gifts I still need to get, I spend Sunday at my favorite bookstores and coffee shops and either purchase items or buy gift cards. By December 1, my Christmas shopping is done, and there is lots of time for seasonal enjoyment.

9. *Learn from the experience, and each year will get better and better.* Have fun with holidays. They are the times that we can give to ourselves to connect with those we love. My grandmother was very wise when she told me, "Follow some traditions, but start plenty of your own."

Additional Reading

Black, Jan, and Greg Enns. *Better Boundaries: Owning and Treasuring Your Life.* Oakland, CA: New Harbinger Publications, 1998.

Breitman, Patti, and Connie Hatch. *How to Say No Without Feeling Guilty: And Say Yes to More Time, More Joy, and What Matters Most to You.* New York: Broadway Books, 2001.

thirty-seven

Hopes and Dreams

Inside you there's an artist you don't know about. . . .
Say yes quickly, if you know, if you've known it
from before the beginning of the universe.

—JALAI AL-DIN RUMI

WHY DOES IT SEEM as though other people have all the creativity? They cook like Rachael Ray, decorate like Martha Stewart, dress like Cindy Crawford, think like Barbara Walters, and date someone who looks like George Clooney. It is easy to feel frumpy and a bit behind the times.

Great accomplishments seem that way only to the person who is observing. To the artist or to the master, it seems easy. It feels easy to them because they are simply doing something they love. Great works are labors of love.

Art is like a relationship. It is a uniquely personal expression of oneself, opening a bigger window through which others can see something, such as hope, beauty, or understanding. Great art, whether in cooking, dance, painting, or speaking, is simply one person sharing all that is important to him or her. The artist's love for this medium is so great that it brings energy to the viewer.

If you want to become more artistic, make a commitment to something or someone. All art is really a living echo and message of human relationship. People create and re-create themselves with one another.

In her book *Write It Down, Make It Happen,* Henriette Anne Klauser urges us to have artistic goals. You must have long-range goals to keep you from being frustrated by short-range failures. Keep trying—try new things, try new mediums. Keep experimenting until you find your passion. When you do find your passion, have fun with it, play with it, follow it wherever it takes you. Motivational speaker Jim Rohn says, "A fuzzy future has little pulling power. To really have your future pull you forward, your dreams must be bold and vivid."

Billionaire Warren Buffet was working at what he loved long before he became wealthy. He says the following:

> You know, they say that success is getting what you want and happiness is wanting what you have. I don't know which one applies in this case, but I do know that I wouldn't be doing anything else. I always worry about people who say, "I'm going to do this for ten years. I really don't like it very well, but I'll do ten more years of this and . . . " I mean, that's a little like saving up sex for your old age. Not a very good idea.

Someone once said that creativity is God's gift to us, and using that creativity is our gift back to God. Julia Cameron, in her book *The Artist's Way,* warns that we can squander our own creative energies by investing disproportionately in the lives, hopes, dreams, and plans of others. She urges us each to find our core and begin to follow our own dreams and goals. This is a tricky process.

As we search for our own authentic dreams and hopes, we may find regret. We may realize that we have wasted a great deal of time and have let many ideas and hopes wither away and lose energy. We may see that others have gone before us. As we focus on lost times or lost dreams, there may be some regret and grief that has to be faced. If we choose resiliency, however, we can walk through the grief and find ourselves beginning to feel excited about where to go from here.

When tennis champion Billie Jean King said, "I think self-awareness is probably the most important thing toward being called a champion," she was telling us to go inside and find what we value and what we want to create. It's impossible to do it wrong when it comes from within, for there is no judge of our creation.

Once you decide what it is that you want to create and share, it becomes easy. We become dogged and persistent in breathing life into our creation. Estee Lauder, the creator of a dynasty of cosmetics, tells us, "Toughness . . . is not dependent on being crude or cruel. You can be feminine and tough. I love my femininity as much as I rely on my toughness. What others call tough, I call persistent."

It's a spiritual journey to be creative, and we all have to do it while we live in the world. My late mentor Virginia Satir used to tell me to keep one foot on the ground, to stay grounded in reality. Pay the bills, do the grocery shopping, make dinner, pay taxes, take a bath, and put on your lipstick. With your other foot, you can step as high as a visionary. Reach for the stars, do something different, imagine, and create. Walt Disney said, "If you can dream it, you can do it." Muriel Siebert, the first woman to own a seat on the New York Stock Exchange, tells us, "You don't have guarantees in this world. You've got to take chances."

Years ago, I had the opportunity to meet the wise man Baba Ram Dass. We were in a workshop together. He shared with me that "the next message you need on your creative journey is always right where you are." This message has had a great impact on me. It keeps me listening, paying attention, and waiting for and recognizing teachers in my life. The universe gives us what we need. If we are too busy looking for what we need, we might miss the gift. In other words: "Bloom where you are planted." Leo Tolstoy reminded us, "True life is lived when tiny changes occur."

While creating, keep your dreams to yourself or tell them only to people who share your dream. Take to heart the words of Bette Midler: "The worst part of success is trying to find someone who is happy for you." When outer critics question your work, it's too easy to lose creativity.

Sometimes family members want more time from you, sometimes a job demands your close attention, sometimes friends are threatened, and sometimes people are jealous. Treat your creative ideas like a small child who is counting on you to take care and provide nourishment. As the ideas grow and mature—like a child—you will be able to bring more people into your space. Treat your ideas with love and safety. They are not there for the opinions and curiosity of the people around you. My good friend Claudia Black says, "Surround yourself with people who respect and treat you well."

In her book *The Aquarian Conspiracy*, Marilyn Ferguson wrote that each of us is born a visionary. She said that our life task is to learn to access our inherent powers, unique strengths, and creativity. She noted that the great visionaries of history saw something that needed to be done, and their purpose became doing their part to get it done. That fits with one of my beliefs, I believe that the "communion of saints" referred to in certain prayers is simply all those who are visionaries and workers, doing their job of unifying and supporting one another's vision and wisdom.

Today much of our world is broken and needs healing and beauty. Each of us has the ability to listen to his or her inner voice and find a way to create something that will soothe, fix, enlighten, touch, or comfort. We have hunches or intuitions that nudge us to do our part. We experience joy and fulfillment when we find our purpose and our contribution. When we live a creative and visionary life, we come to know inner peace.

Additional Reading

Breathnach, Sarah Ban. *Simple Abundance: A Daybook of Comfort and Joy.* New York: Grand Central Publishing, 1995.

Cameron, Julia. *The Artist's Way.* New York: J. P. Tarcher, 2002.

Ferguson, Marilyn. *The Aquarian Conspiracy: Personal and Social Transformation in Our Time.* New York: J. P. Tarcher, 1987.

Klauser, Henriette Ann. *Write It Down, Make It Happen: Knowing What You Want—and Getting It.* New York: Touchstone, 2001.

McMeekin, Gail. *The 12 Secrets of Highly Creative Women: A Portable Mentor.* San Francisco: Red Wheel/Weiser, 2000.

thirty-eight

The Writer and the Artist

> *You can have anything you want if you want it*
> *desperately enough. You must want it with*
> *an exuberance that erupts through the skin and*
> *joins the energy that created the world.*
>
> —Sheila Graham

SOME WOULD SAY THAT creativity and art are important aspects of our lives. Many of us know that art and creativity are much more important than that; they are part of our soul. Creativity is about vision; it is sacred and defines how we live. Artists have vision, take risks, and change environments.

My own story of creativity is a miracle. In the 1970s, there was little awareness of the needs of and challenges for the children of alcoholics. There was also very little interest from the professional community in this population. My personal interest pressed me to develop programs that could intervene and offer help to this population. There was no path to follow and no support for programming. It has been said that in the absence of financial support, creativity has to flourish. That was very true for me. I found a house, called it "The House," and started programs of support and healing.

Because I had no money to hire staff, I went to many organizations and asked if their interns could help me. This brought me nurses, pastors, teachers, and community organizers. We trained together and executed our programs. Children responded, and the research was done that led to developing a model of treatment for families of alcoholics. It might not have happened if I had had the financial resources to do it all on my own.

Creativity is actually a leap of faith, believing in something that can be rather than something that already is. I remember hearing that when we are looking at a block of marble, we have the chance to imagine all the different items and people who are already in that marble, and it's our creativity that will bring them out through carving. That's the time to trust our process, releasing what is already there.

Creative expression is one of the satisfactions and joys of my life. It includes living in a creative space, meeting with creative people, and trying new actions in my life. Instead of watering down our creativity by trying to meet the needs of others, we find our satisfaction by investing in ourselves and making our own creative life.

As we search for our creative selves, it is good to avoid the gloom-mongers. These are the people who discourage us. They tell us all the problems that could occur with the wonderful and exciting creations we might produce. They're long on problems and short on answers and support. We need to limit their contact in our lives. They feed off problems and put up roadblocks and brick walls.

Each of us is endowed with special gifts. We have the chance to expand on those gifts and find a way to bring our specialness to the world. One of the lessons we learn with creativity is that the universe supports it. If something is not meant to be and is not in harmony with universal energy, it will be hard to make it work. There will be stuck times and more stuck times. However, if something is part of the universal energy, it will flow, and we have only to respond.

At times the whole process of the universe comes together to support a person's efforts. Mythologist Joseph Campbell calls this connection "a thousand unseen helping hands." My own life has been touched in this way. When I look back over my journey, I see that there is a connection among my parents' addictions, seeking help for myself, facing my own depression and pain, wanting help for all children of alcoholics, going down a path that had not been paved, believing in myself, mentors coming into my life, meeting my soul mate, having the support of my children, and meeting and connecting with influential people. There is a synchronicity of events that I could not make happen. I believe that there is a God, a Higher Power, a Universal Energy, and that I am a link in a chain.

As our creativity is bursting forth, it is important to know when to discard the old and when to embrace the new. It's an energy that starts deep inside. We feel ready to discard old dishes, old ideas, old clothes, old papers, and old belief systems. We are willing to face the vulnerability and the loss involved in letting go. The old and familiar has to go so that we can make room for new ideas, new thoughts, new plans, and new belief systems. We feel both fear and excitement.

However, we must take action and follow our intuition. Julia Cameron speaks eloquently about "reading deprivation." She reminds us, in her book *The Artist's Way*, that many people are blocked in their own creativity by having a reading addiction. She says that "we gobble the words of others rather than digest our own thoughts and feelings, rather than cook up something of our own." What creativity demands from us is a strong, steady, slow pace. The dancer Agnes De Mille once said, "No trumpets sound when the important decisions of our life are made. Destiny is made known silently."

Many people are held back from expressing their creativity because they demand too much from themselves. They see the big picture, but not the steps that it takes to get to the big picture. Artists and writers tend to think of big books, publicity tours, and the feedback from critics before they complete three really good chapters and an outline.

At the basis of this leaping ahead is the feeling of fear, especially long-term fears. There is the fear of not doing it right, the fear of not doing it in a timely way, and the fear of producing less than a great work. This keeps many people stuck in always getting ready to get ready. Some call this *procrastination*. I call it *fear*.

Seek your bliss and follow it. When the idea for this book began to germinate in me, I felt a great sense of enthusiasm. It was important for me to exercise each day and get the sleep I needed. There were jobs to do, roses to prune, and meals to prepare. Yet I just wanted to get to the book. It was fun doing research, even more fun putting it on paper. I reminded my friends and family that writing a book was bringing me great clarity, satisfaction, and joy. That has been my bliss. To do what we think we need to do, write, or create because we have a good idea that "should" be out there-that is, to do work with drudgery—is not the same as working with one's bliss.

We need to feel excited upon waking each day that we have a chance to create. There will be days that are slow or feel like a failure, but most creativity and success is built on learning from those failures. Creativity is also a leap of faith, the space between the trapezes. When we let go of a fixed direction, then our faith, God, the universe, or a Higher Power steps in and helps us to grab the trapeze that is coming to us.

We need to develop trust, intuition, and skill and let the direction of our creative endeavor happen. When I began this book, I was headed in another direction, but as I was taking the path I had planned, I let go of one trapeze and grabbed onto the other trapeze I was offered, and a new direction was given to me. My bliss increased and my creativity flourished. Author Adrienne Rich tells us, "The unconscious wants truth. It ceases to speak to those who want something else more than truth."

As we unleash our creativity, there is an interplay of autonomy and input. Some people want input from many people before they start writing or doing their project. Others treat their ideas and project with great autonomy. There is not a right or a wrong way to do it. There will sometimes be a perfect product, and there will sometimes be many false starts. Each artist must find his or her own balance or style. As the Renaissance philosopher Francis Bacon once said, "The job of the artist is to always deepen the mystery."

I have found that my style requires autonomy. When a project is looming inside me, I find that I want to walk more, meditate more, pull away from social events, and live quietly in my nest. There is something stirring inside me that is demanding my attention. I simply start to write. It is very difficult to dismiss this feeling of wanting to create. If I try to ignore it, I become irritated and sometimes even depressed. My writing demands expression.

In many ways, being a writer and an artist defines part of who I am. It demands that I pay attention to my feelings, surround myself with nurturing people, keep my home and nest comfortable, and listen carefully to whoever turns out to be a teacher. It keeps me vigilant about the world around me in a caring and interested way. When I am writing I find that I take good care of myself. Buddha said, "To keep the body in good health is a duty, otherwise we shall not be able to keep our mind strong and clear."

My dear friend and mentor Virginia Satir inspired in me the love of "process." As much as I enjoy the product, the process itself is a rich time. It is a time of letting go of control, or rather the illusion of control, and waiting for the inspiration to present itself. It is a time of dreaming and experimenting and making something from only your inner self. As a small girl—and a poor little girl, at that— I enjoyed the pastime of making mud pies. I could go outside with the dirt, water, leaves, stones, seeds, and beans and make the prettiest and most beautiful pies and cookies I could dream up. I would put them in the sun to bake. I loved the process and the creation. My memories of creating this beauty still make me smile.

Joseph Campbell wrote, "Follow your bliss, and doors will open where there were no doors before." Accept that there will be dry times; they are necessary while the creativity in us is germinating. These are the dark times.

Theologian Anthony Padavano believes that much is happening when we are in the dark and creativity is not available to us. However, when we let our natural energy flow and pay attention to how we feel and what is happening in our lives, the sun will come out, and with it will come clarity, direction, and the fire in our souls.

Additional Reading

Bryan, Mark, with Julia Cameron and Catherine Allen. *The Artist's Way at Work: Riding the Dragon.* New York: Harper, 1999.

Cameron, Julia. *The Artist's Way.* New York: J. P. Tarcher, 2002.

_____. *The Right to Write: An Invitation and Initiation into the Writing Life.* New York: J. P. Tarcher, 1999.

Lindskoog, Kathryn. *Creative Writing for People Who Can't Not Write.* Grand Rapids, MI: Zondervan, 1989.

Rich, Adrienne. *On Lies, Secrets, and Silence.* New York: W. W. Norton & Company, 1995.

part seven:

PERSONAL GROWTH

Change happens when the discomfort
of the familiar outweighs the
fear of the unknown.

—*Anne Parker*

thirty-nine

Guilt Has Its Purpose

*The willingness to accept responsibility for one's own
life is the source from which self-respect springs.*

—Joan Didion

FEELING GUILTY IS SO uncomfortable that we want to avoid it at all
cost. Yet who can avoid feeling guilty about something or other? The
"coulda, woulda, shouldas" creep into our lives so easily: I could have
been a better mother, I should have been a more fun partner, I wish
I had been a kinder daughter or a more thoughtful friend. It is so
easy to feel guilty about our behavior.

Guilt has often received a bad rap. It is often associated with feeling really bad about ourselves and wishing we had been different. It
is usually connected to something we wished we had done or something we did do and wished we had not done. Another way to look
at guilt, however, is to see it as a message, not a place in which we
live. When we feel guilty, we have a heavy feeling. It's clear and it's
noticed. We feel bad. The chances are that there is something we
need to do.

If we can learn to recognize this heavy feeling, we can use it as a clue to see what is going on, and why we feel this way, and if there is some action we should take. Once we understand the situation, we can take whatever action is necessary to change the situation.

There are many possibilities. Maybe we need to say, "I'm sorry" to someone, or maybe we need to make a phone call or send an e-mail. Maybe there are bigger actions to take. Staying in the feeling of guilt without making amends or finding a resolution is self-defeating and produces more guilt.

No one can make us feel guilty. They may try, by telling us things about ourselves that they think are wrong, mean, or unacceptable. They may try to guilt-trip us, but we cannot be *made to feel* guilty. Guilt is a feeling that comes from deep inside ourselves when we act in a way that does not fit our values. It's our own internal feeling. When someone tries to guilt-trip us, the healthy response is to feel anger at being manipulated. When people try to guilt-trip us, we have to let them know that it doesn't work with us. Guilt comes only from within.

Guilt is actually good for us. Studies show that guilty feelings are associated with healthy emotional functioning and satisfying relationships. If we didn't have guilty feelings, we would live in a world full of chaos where we would all hurt one another and behave in terrible ways without any order or structure. Guilt is a motivator to take corrective action. We try to repair situations and relationships, and we also change our behavior to avoid feeling further guilt.

Jan is married and the mother of three small children. Her life is full of school events, meetings, a part-time job, and social responsibilities with her husband. She has very little time to herself. To give herself a break, she signs on for a year at a fitness center. She works out twice a week. She has a few misgivings about the money she is spending and the time she is taking away from her family.

Yet her value system tells her that she needs exercise, that she needs some time away from the family responsibilities to reduce stress, and that she is a better mother and wife when she has her exercise. Even though she has some misgivings and sometimes a questioning feeling, she does not feel guilty, because she is acting within her value system. She has shared these feelings with her best friend, who has encouraged her to continue her self-care.

About six months into the fitness center routine, Jan becomes aware that she has developed affectionate feelings for Ken, a man who is there at the same time she is there. At first, it is only a smile and a hello. Later, on a break, they talk with each other. They both have very full family lives. Jan looks forward to the fitness center more than usual and has even found herself taking special care with her clothes and hair. One day Ken asks her to join him for lunch, and she does. Now she is feeling very uncomfortable, and the feelings are heavy. She keeps the lunch a secret.

Jan starts to feel guilty. The first time Ken makes an attempt to kiss her, she knows she is in trouble—mostly because she knows she *wants* him to kiss her. She starts feeling very guilty. She doesn't sleep as well, but she continues to go to the center even though she knows she is doing something outside her value system. As time goes on, she starts to compulsively eat, a bad habit she hasn't indulged for years. She becomes irritable with her family, and she doesn't like herself at all. She feels depressed.

Jan eventually goes to a therapist to discuss this situation. She learns that she needs the break that the fitness center gives her, but she has allowed herself to be drawn into a relationship that she really doesn't want. What she wants is more time with her husband. She wants to feel attractive again. She enjoys the relaxation of exercise. With the help of her therapist, she takes action.

She thanks Ken for his friendship and says that she needs to pull away from what is a risky relationship. She then chooses to go to a different fitness center. She asks her husband for more time, and he gives it to her. She also asks her husband if he will take a walk with her two or three nights a week for exercise, relaxation, sharing, and time together. These walks become very important to both of them.

Once Jan takes action, her guilt lifts and she begins to feel like her old self. She starts to lose the weight she has put on during the time of compulsive eating. She sleeps better, and her attractive personality returns. Guilt has helped her to make changes that she treasures.

Guilt is only as good as the motivation to act that it creates. There is nothing to be gained by the paralysis of guilt. Taking action includes the following steps:

1. *Take responsibility for yourself.* Know that guilt means that some part of your behavior is out of step with your values. There is a reason for guilt.
2. *Try to understand what is going on.* See yourself as a good person who has made a mistake or has some behavior that is not good for you. Try to understand why you made this mistake, and it will be easier to make changes. Jan realized that she was lonely and in need of stress relief. She knew she had made a mistake, but she was not a bad person.
3. *Make amends, if appropriate.* Sometimes making amends would further hurt someone. In those cases, change your behavior, but it is not necessary to inflict more hurt.
4. *Be kind to yourself.* We all make mistakes. Learning from and fixing the mistake is what is important.
5. *Plan the repair.* It will be easier to make behavior changes if you have a plan. Jan decided to leave her fitness center and find a new one, said good-bye to Ken, and asked her husband for more time. These are all concrete, clear steps. If you need to talk to a trusted friend or a counselor, do so.
6. *Take the necessary action.* Do not repeat the behavior. If you find that you do and can't seem to stop, then see a therapist and figure out why this is happening.

When you feel guilty, remember that it's like having a flickering light on your car that signals something is wrong. Do not stay in the guilty feelings. Use the six steps above to get out of that heavy place. Guilt can be an opportunity.

Additional Reading

Borysenko, Joan. *Guilt Is the Teacher, Love Is the Lesson.* New York: Grand Central Publishing, 1991.

Dryden, Windy. *Overcoming Guilt.* London: Sheldon Press, 1994.

Middleton-Moz, Jane. *Shame and Guilt: Masters of Disguise.* Deerfield Beach, FL: HCI, 1990.

Tangney, June Price, and Ronda L. Dearing. *Shame and Guilt.* New York: Guilford Press, 2003.

forty

Forgiveness: Does That Mean I Have to Forget?

There is no healing without forgiveness.
I love the peace I feel with forgiveness.

—HELEN CASEY

WHEN I WORKED FOR a national agency years ago, I was held back in my job because my employer was very sexist: he did not believe that women should have positions of recognition or power. It was in my early years as a professional, and I did not have what it took to stand up for myself and call him on his behavior. For a while I was very angry with him, and even the sight or sound of his name could bring up emotional pain for me.

As time went by, my feelings softened. For one thing, I realized that I had learned a powerful lesson: I would never again let myself be the subject of sexism. I would speak up. Also, as I heard more and more stories about this man, I came to realize that I was not the only person he had hurt. He had hurt several other people, so I didn't feel singled out.

As I thought about this situation, it became clear to me that I needed to forgive him—for my sake, not his. It wasn't good for me to carry around this amount of hurt and resentment. I sat down one evening and wrote a long letter telling him how I felt when he hurt me. My letter was full of concrete examples and stories.

When the letter was finished, I read it over a couple of times. It was cathartic; I felt angry, relieved, and finished. This man had died a few years earlier, and there was nothing to be gained by mailing the letter to anyone else. However, it was very important for me to put my feelings of pain into words. I forgave him for his behavior and then I burned the letters. Since that time, the situation, the feelings, and the memories have been healed. His name no longer holds any emotional punch for me.

Another example of forgiveness that is very real for me is when I forgave my parents for what I experienced as neglect and danger while I was growing up in a home with alcoholic parents. There was much that was hurtful for me. The feelings were real, and they were painful.

Yet in my grown-up years, I have learned a great deal about the homes in which both my father and my mother grew up. My parents were not given the tools and the examples that would have helped them to know how to care for me. As I learned about their circumstances, it became clear to me that they gave me all that they had, and then some. They gave me more than what they had been given. With that knowledge, it became very easy for me to forgive them for what I had not been given. They did their best, and seeing them through my grown-up eyes, I now feel only gratitude and love for them.

Just what do we mean by forgiveness? Does it mean that we have to let go of our anger and our pain? That is a big part of it, because it's unhealthy to hang on to resentment and bitterness. These feelings make us irritable and on edge. They can also bring about blame and a sense of righteousness. When we decide to forgive someone, we are doing it basically to help ourselves.

We live in a society with many broken elements; our culture brings us pain on a fairly regular basis. If we harbor irritation at every little transgression, it becomes a hard way to live. The scales of justice will never be in perfect balance. Revenge is a waste of time. Do we really want to contribute more to the broken world in which we live?

The best thing about forgiveness is that we do not have to involve anyone else in the act of forgiving. We do not even have to notify the person we are forgiving. It's a personal exercise.

Nevertheless, the fact that I've forgiven doesn't mean that I have to forget what happened. If I have been treated badly, it would be folly for me to forgive and forget. That would be a way of setting myself up to be hurt again. That's not part of forgiving.

In forgiving, I set the other person free and I set myself free. I let the feelings heal and encourage myself to be vulnerable and available again to others with all my feelings and emotions. However, with the person I am forgiving, I protect myself. I do not have to be vulnerable and available to that person.

If something meaningful ever happens with the person who has hurt me, if he or she expresses accountability and sorrow for the hurt, I can make new decisions about my connection to that person. However, if that never happens, by forgiving I can go on in life and set the relationship aside without malice or resentment.

Forgiveness becomes the gift we give ourselves. It implies that we admit that we do not know the complete circumstances of the people who have had an impact on our lives. It acknowledges that we do not have the wisdom to play judge, jury, and executioner over people who have hurt us. Forgiveness is a choice.

We choose life for ourselves and for others when we forgive. We relieve ourselves of the burden of carrying around hurt, anger, pain, and loneliness. Healing happens for us. We give others the freedom to live their lives, rest in peace, or work out their own behaviors, feelings, and consequences.

As an exercise in forgiveness, try the following:

1. Make a list of people who have hurt you.
2. Make a list of people you have hurt.
3. Examine how you feel when someone has hurt you.
4. Examine how you feel when you know you have hurt someone.
5. Ask yourself honestly, "What is the payoff for my not forgiving someone?"
6. Ask yourself honestly, "What could be the payoff if I do forgive someone?"
7. Choose to forgive—or not.
8. If you choose forgiveness, write forgiveness letters and make a decision whether to send them. The criterion for sending them would be whether the letters would release both of you and not open the wounds again.
9. Take the healing that comes from writing the letters.
10. Let all feelings heal over time.

In forgiving, give up the fantasies. There are no perfect families or relationships. Most of us are simultaneously talented and flawed, doing the best we can in walking through life's gifts and challenges.

Former UN Secretary-General Dag Hammarskjöld said, "Forgiveness is the answer to the child's dream of a miracle by which what is broken is made whole again, what is soiled is again made clean." Feeling all our feelings and forgiving someone else is a gift we can give ourselves. This gift is called *serenity*. When we let go of the energy it takes to hold on to blame and resentment, we have the energy we need to get our own needs met. If there is no way to be able to forgive, you might want to seek the help of a professional counselor.

Instead of waiting for someone to send you flowers, plant a garden.

Additional Reading

Casarjian, Robin. *Forgiveness: A Bold Choice for a Peaceful Heart.* New York: Bantam Books, 1992.

Dayton, Tian. *The Magic of Forgiveness: Emotional Freedom and Transformation at Midlife.* Deerfield Beach, FL: HCI, 2003.

Dowrick, Stephanie. *Forgiveness and Other Acts of Love.* New York: W.W. Norton and Company, 1998.

Enright, Robert D. *Forgiveness Is a Choice: A Step-by-Step Process for Resolving Anger and Restoring Hope.* Washington, DC: American Psychological Association, 2001.

Nelson, Mariah Burton. *The Unburdened Heart: 5 Keys to Forgiveness and Freedom.* San Francisco: HarperSanFrancisco, 2000.

forty-one

The Courage to Change

Our aspirations are our possibilities.

—SAMUEL JACKSON

THE FIRST TIME THAT you think you would like to do or have something very different from what you already do or have, you have made a major commitment. Maybe you want to change the color of your hair, take a different kind of vacation, have a different career, move to a new city, or change your lifestyle. That kind of thinking can take your breath away. It's at once frightening and exciting.

When we feel confused, stuck, and helpless, we often do not know where to begin. The most important thing we can do is to look outside ourselves for more information and possibility. If we could have already gotten out of the stuck spot we find ourselves in, we would have done so. There are very few problems in life that have not been experienced by someone before us. If we look around, we will see that others have been in our situation; they have struggled, some have suffered, and many have healed.

The thoughts come first, then the small steps start in the direction of what you want to have for yourself. At first, no one will even notice the small steps you are taking. However, you will notice, and these small steps give you a bit of confidence and hope. It's called *private courage*. Each step becomes a defining moment, making your goal seem real to you even if no one else knows about it.

My first big change was when I knew I needed to go through a divorce. I had made every single effort I could to save my marriage. One day, I knew that I could no longer keep trying to make things better by myself. I needed to divorce. The idea of divorce was so foreign to my own way of thinking that I needed to take several smaller steps to prepare myself. It took many weeks of making small changes.

First I went back to school and focused on getting a degree that would help me when I became single. Then I began to develop a support system of friends who I knew would be there for me. I opened a private bank account and started to save money. Finally, the day came when I filed for divorce. It may have looked impulsive, but in my heart of hearts, I had been making plans for some time.

The same was true when I changed my career. Raising three children on my own had been a financial challenge, but my job was a dream job, in many ways. It included creativity, travel, and a great deal of contact with the public. It was in the field of family therapy and addictions, which was my passion at the time. The downside of the job was that my very sexist and passive-aggressive boss was holding me back, both professionally and financially. The idea of giving up that job was simply too much. Where would I work, and how would I support my family?

I began taking little steps. I started writing and designing some training programs. I did some volunteering and built up a professional support system. Then the day came when taking the risk was less frightening than staying in a stuck place. I quit my job and went to work for myself. That work turned into the development of a successful business and the publication of several successful books.

The first task we have in making a successful change is to become clear about what we want. We can't go on the journey of change without having an idea of where we want to go. Once we have a direction, it becomes easier to figure out how to get there. There may be many conflicting aspects of the change. What is good for one person might cause pain for someone else.

All aspects have to be explored, and decisions must be made. Decisions for an adult must always include the well-being of any dependent children who are involved. Sometimes, as an adult goes forward, there are many negotiations and compromises to be considered. Sometimes there is short-term hardship to protect long-term possibilities. Some of the pain is necessary, and this can be a good time to get professional help.

We have all known people who, in a big act of courage, look as though they have done something great and claimed something they truly wanted. They appear to be so brave and confident. Yet before they got to that point, there were hundreds of little private steps they had taken that led to the act of courage. Many times they were probably trembling and afraid, yet they took the necessary steps, and one day they took the leap to make a major step. This is the triumph of the soul. They created the world they wanted.

Henry David Thoreau said the following:

I learned this, at least, by my experiment: that if one advances confidently in the direction of one's dreams, and endeavors to live the life which one has imagined, one will meet with a success unexpected in common hours. If we set a course of action for ourselves, we will not only be working toward a goal or milestone that we have set for ourselves, we will also find many treasures on the way of reaching that goal.

One of my clients wanted to change her career and began to plan to make that happen. She saw herself as an artist, someday living in a warm climate. Her plans included going back to school to work on her art. While in school, she met someone who became her life partner. He was from Hawaii, and when she finished school, they moved to his homeland, where she opened an art store and began producing her own art for the store as well as displaying the works of other artists. Not only did she meet her stated goals of becoming an artist and living in a warm climate, she also found a life partner and started a business. These latter two outcomes were not in her stated goals.

It's important to keep an open mind when undertaking a journey of change. We may want everything to go just as we scheduled it. Learning to appreciate the unexpected is part of the journey. Each time something extra happens and it turns out well, we become more courageous. Over time, we begin to live a life of courage.

Additional Reading

Pressfield, Steven. *The War of Art: Break Through the Block and Win Your Inner Creative Battles.* New York: Grand Central Publishing, 2003.

Strickland, Bill. *Make the Impossible Possible: One Man's Crusade to Inspire Others to Dream Bigger and Achieve the Extraordinary.* New York: Broadway Books, 2007.

Wegscheider-Cruse, Sharon. *Choice Making: For Spirituality Seekers, Co-Dependents, and Adult Children.* Deerfield Beach, FL: HCI, 1986.

Zander, Rosamund Stone, and Benjamin Zander. *The Art of Possibility: Transforming Professional and Personal Life.* New York: Penguin, 2002.

Workshops

Living Centered Program
Onsite Workshops
Cumberland Furnace, TN
www.onsiteworkshops.com
1-800-341-7432

forty-two

Acceptance

*We are most deeply asleep at the switch when
we fancy we control any switches at all.*

—ANNIE DILLARD

WE ARE TOLD OVER and over that we must accept what is happening. Very often, we want to cry out, "No, I will not accept!" There must be something we can do. We struggle as long as we can and try as many things as we can think of to resist accepting what is our reality.

Nevertheless, in the end we must accept what is real and what is happening. Before we can change anything in our lives and move on, we must accept what is. It is in the surrender to what is that what could be is born. When we accept, we find release and relief. It is as though the struggle were over.

We can stop struggling when we look in the mirror and finally say the following:

This is what I weigh.
This is who I am.

These are the mistakes I have made.
This is what I have to work with.
This is how I feel.
This is what is happening.
This is my real life.

When we can do that and can accept all of who we are, we feel a sense of rightness and some relief. Our energy returns and then we are ready to move on. Acceptance is the surrendering to what is. We accept our relationship to others, our present career, the conflicts with people we know, the self-image problems we face, our addictions, our financial status, and our health. Once we accept these things, we can move on. Without acceptance, we simply feel stuck.

Once we let go of struggle, we can look at options. We will indeed find that life is so much easier when we ride the horse in the direction it's going. We begin to trust the natural flow of our experiences instead of trying to control people and outcomes. We trust that life has some lessons to teach us from time to time. Life will teach us that those lessons might hurt, but we can learn from those lessons if we pay attention to their meaning.

Losses can become lessons. Many children who have grown up in painful families become resilient and learn about self-care early in life. When you go through a difficult divorce, you often find inner resources that were lying dormant. People who have faced life-threatening illness come through that time with a commitment to their health that will give them many healthy years. Working for a controlling and unappreciative boss or company has propelled many an employee into a position of entrepreneurship.

We will often not know what the lesson is until some time has passed. We can decide not to expect that something will happen today. We can accept that some things take time. Instead of waiting until things are perfect, we can work with what we have today. Today we look around, today we respond to what happens now, today we experiment with new behaviors. We don't wait for perfection to see an opportunity. We accept where we are and go on from there. Procrastination and perfection has robbed us of opportunity. There is another way to live. It's nonresistance. *Nonresistance* simply means that we stop trying to make something happen. We simply accept what is.

We don't always understand why things happen the way they do, but it helps to accept with faith and resignation that we can go forward and that the path will be laid out in front of us. Acceptance of our past and acceptance of the current conditions in our lives, the situations we cannot change, will bring some relief and peace. It is very tiresome to wish that circumstances would be different. When we accept, we harness energy that can help us to think clearly and take steps to do what can be done.

When someone in my family was critically ill, some family members tried in vain to understand why these circumstances were happening to them. They thought that it wasn't fair and that the universe was against them. They became stuck in the way they perceived a tough situation as futile.

Fortunately, other family members felt shock, shed their tears, and set about doing what had to be done. Some offered physical care, some paid bills, and others spent time looking for possibilities and hope. Acceptance began to smooth the ripples and the chaos that was so discouraging for everyone. The group that stepped in, however, was like the willow in the wind. Those people bent and did not break. The way was not easy, but they eased the way.

Each day can be a new beginning. We can choose to look ahead with hope. When we are facing circumstances that make us feel powerless, we can reach out to our Higher Power and to each other for help and guidance. Author Anne Wilson Schaef tells us that courage is closely tied to acceptance. She says, "When we face our fears and let ourselves know our connection to the power that is in us and beyond us, we learn courage." Courage is what we need as we accept our world today. Our work is cut out for us.

There are still situations of sexism, racism, and ageism in our culture, and each of us has hurdles in his or her personal life. Children have needs, parents have needs, and there is illness and loss with which to contend. There is war on a small scale and war on a big scale. All these issues rail against the human spirit. There is much we are called upon to accept.

Those who accept and face the reality of adversity are the same people who find courage to change the things they can. On the day your courage goes to work, hope is rekindled personally and in the world. We are challenged, and we may fall from time to time, but we will also keep going.

A diamond is one of the most precious stones. It is forged by both pressure and time. Under less pressure, diamonds are simply crystal. With even less pressure, diamonds are coal. With even less pressure, they are just plain dirt. People, like diamonds, can respond to life's most intense pressures fully and with courage.

Women have a way of not being defeated. When a woman cares for someone she loves, she is very powerful. Once she accepts her circumstances, she finds the courage to act. The best of a human being is finding that spirit.

Acceptance leads to courage, and courage leads to change. Change is like the mighty wave in the ocean. It cannot be held back, so it is best that we make our peace with it. When we are confronted with change, it can be frightening, for we need to navigate unfamiliar territory. Sometimes our old maps do not work for our current journey. That is why it doesn't matter if the change is positive or negative.

Any change generates stress simply because it is unfamiliar territory. We have to adjust to new situations, new people, new expectations, and new measures of comfort.

Some of the stressful changes in our lives are career decisions, leaving home and parents, marriage, babies being born, children growing up, children leaving home, divorce, and retirement. Those are just the natural times of stress. They do not include job changes, trouble with alcohol and drugs, money issues, and illness. As you go through each of these stages, opportunities for finding inner strength and clarity present themselves. Changes in our lives can create the time and space in which to define and explore what we really want from life. What might have been an acceptance we had to face could turn out to be an opportunity in disguise.

Acceptance forces us to grapple with powerlessness. It is natural to want to believe that we can change circumstances. When Sophia, a new mother, was told that her child had been born with a disability, it was a shocking message. Sophia was an executive with a technology company; almost thirty people reported to her. She was a close partner with her husband, and she cared for a comfortable home. She had many friends and a social presence. She juggled many things in her life and was extremely organized.

In short, she was accomplished and could make things happen. Her initial shock turned to anger. Why couldn't she fix this situation? There must be someone to contact, some action that could be taken, some way to stop the pain and the feeling of helplessness and hopelessness.

Sophia could not accept the truth. She kept looking for some way to fix the situation. She developed sleeping problems, she became short-tempered and irritable with her family and friends, and, deep inside, she blamed herself and she blamed God. In her race to find a way to handle this painful situation, she felt increasingly powerless and hit bottom. She did not surrender; rather, she gave up. The difference between surrendering and giving up is acceptance and faith.

Finally, she began the grief process. She found her anger and expressed it, she found her tears and shed them. She bared her painful soul to people who cared about her. In the raw acceptance of the situation she began to heal. As Sophia healed, she reached out even more to others. She accepted the truth and found her authentic self. She became honest with her feelings. She began to accept that pain and problems are part of life. She learned that everyone has to face everyday realities and that painful suffering and overpowering joy touch most people.

Our brokenness can be healed as we give love and support to one another. Sophia learned that it is in our brokenness that we find our true humanity. It is often the beginning of our spiritual awakening. We previously might have believed that *surrender* is a word for losers and weaklings. Through pain and loss, we learn that accepting our brokenness and our humanity opens us to a wholeness and a compassion that we might not have had before.

When we acknowledge that we do not have control over many aspects of our lives, we come alive with the rich new experience of being a whole person. May we each learn the spiritual lessons contained in frustration and grief. As we learn acceptance, it's a whole new journey. At our deepest level, we have yearned for life to be easy, full, and connected. We want our dreams to come true, and we want to control our destiny. Yet as we look deep inside, we find that none of us has a perfect journey and that none of us is totally self-sufficient. We need one another.

Acceptance is the beginning of the journey. Courage is a milestone, and connection is the part of the journey that teaches us love of ourselves and then love of others. Consider the complexity of thought and simplicity of expression in the original, full Serenity

Prayer composed by theologian Reinhold Niebuhr:

> God, give us grace to accept with serenity
> the things that cannot be changed;
> courage to change the things that should be changed,
> and wisdom to distinguish the one from the other.

Today millions use the shortened version in their daily living. That version is:

> Trust God
> Clean House
> Help Others

Additional Reading

Basset, Lucinda. *From Panic to Power: Proven Techniques to Calm Your Anxieties, Conquer Your Fears, and Put You in Control of Your Life.* New York: Harper-Collins, 1996.

Workshops

Living Centered Program
Onsite Workshops
Cumberland Furnace, TN
www.onsiteworkshops.com
1-800-341-7432

forty-three

Navigating Life's Emotions Isn't Easy

> *It takes courage to push yourself to places that you have never been before—to test your limits, to break through barriers—and the day comes when the risk to remain tight inside the bud is more painful than the risk it takes to blossom.*
>
> —ANAÔS NIN

RECENTLY I WAS STRUCK by two events. One occurred when a dear friend found out about a serious accident that killed someone in her family. As she told me what had happened, she started to cry. As soon as she started crying she began to say, "I'm sorry, I can't help crying." My words to her were "Cry, it's what you need to do." I couldn't help but wonder why she was so embarrassed and uncomfortable with tears.

The other event was a conversation I had with a mother who had lost a child. She stated that she just had to be strong and not feel it. She said, "I just swallow my feelings and pray that God will take the pain away." She kept her feelings medicated with nicotine. In her refusal to express her natural grief, she was setting herself up for future problems. She revealed that she was having lots of physical problems herself.

Both of these people were struggling with how to express their natural emotions. For much of my life, when people asked me how I was feeling, the range of my emotions consisted of hurt, upset, frustrated, happy, silly, excited, tired, discouraged, and afraid. It was too hard to admit that there was also anger.

Little did I know that there were many emotions bubbling up for me but that my awareness of them and my ability to verbalize them was pretty limited. Anne Morrow Lindbergh once said, "It is terribly amazing how many climates of feelings one can go through in a day." My many other feelings included the following:

lonely	helpless	grieved
overwhelmed	distant	disheartened
hopeful	joyful	encouraged
grateful	confident	inspired
proud	enraged	bitter
pessimistic	resentful	disgusted
exhausted	lethargic	indefinite
weary	sleepy	scared
terrified	nervous	panicky
anxious	worried	troubled
uncomfortable	withdrawn	embarrassed
calm	content	absorbed
serene	loving	satisfied
relaxed	affectionate	tender
appreciative	compassionate	amorous
trusting	stimulated	energetic
adventurous	playful	furious

Increasingly, many people are beginning to believe that emotions are our sixth sense. They tell us what is happening. They tell us the truth of the situation. Psychologist Joseph Bailey says, "Trust in the invisible force of feelings. They know more than your brain could ever know about making your dreams come true."

There is a difference between feeling our way through life fully alive and vibrant and just getting through life on automatic pilot. Being fully aware of our feelings and able to name them fills us with energy and confidence. We become actors on the stage of life. When we fear our feelings or give them less importance, we are simply reactors, responding to people and situations with a very limited ability to connect with them.

Some people say that they don't want to invest sharing their feelings with another because it opens the door to getting hurt. Catholic writer Evelyn Underhill says, "The pain of losing a loved one is the price we pay for having had that love." Building a coat of armor around our true feelings may feel protective, but the problem with this armor is that it also blocks joy, excitement, happiness, curiosity, and love. Our truth includes all that we feel, not just the feelings that are pleasant and that we want to have.

To avoid feeling, some people medicate themselves. Some of the greatest killers of feelings are cigarettes, mood-altering drugs, excess alcohol, excess gambling, excess food, and excess sex. More seemingly acceptable ways of numbing emotion are caretaking, overworking, and overexercising. The more someone abuses these behaviors, the further away they move from their own self-knowledge and truth. It becomes very hard for them to make and maintain satisfying relationships. Intimacy becomes impossible.

Then there are those who believe that intellect is more important than emotions. The reality is that much of what our intellect perceives to be true is open to interpretation. There are certain facts and figures that are nondebatable, but much of what we call intellect is really a combination of intellect and emotion. That's what gives us common sense and wisdom.

The ability to be emotional is absolutely necessary for our general health and well-being. Dr. O. Carl Simonton says, "Cancer is a high price to pay to solve problems that could be solved instead by altering your rules so that you give yourself permission to pay attention to your needs."

Emotions do not lie. They tell the truth. You can't heal what you can't feel, and you can't feel what you medicate. You may not want to get in touch with your most difficult feelings—such as sadness, rage, hurt, guilt, fear, loneliness, or resentment—but one way or another, they will get in touch with you.

It's natural that we don't want to go looking for our true feelings. Sigmund Freud's great contribution to the field of psychotherapy was the recognition that consciousness holds only a small fraction of what we know and feel. Beneath consciousness lies a large cavern that contains many of our other feelings. The name of this cavern is the *unconscious,* and the mechanism that keeps our unwanted feelings there is called *repression.*

As a therapist I have learned that what we resist persists. The more we withdraw from and push away difficult issues, the more likely they are to go underground—into a state of repression in the unconscious—and then seep out or explode at another time.

It's what happens to soldiers in combat. They are in so much pain and fear on the battlefield that they psychologically dissociate and later have a flat, emotionless memory or no memory at all. Then, with no warning, they may explode in a state of rage and despair or even erupt into violence.

Repression can happen anytime one is in intense pain or fear. It can be a result of living in an alcoholic home, being abused, or being in an accident. It's the way our unconscious self protects us. At some level, we know that something has happened, but we can't remember clearly. This tension is very exhausting. We try to stay away from relaxation and quiet times because the tension only becomes greater then. So we medicate, stay busy, and avoid.

The way out of repression is expression: opening ourselves up to all our feelings whenever and with whomever we feel safe. There are ways to begin to express our old feelings.

Choose someone safe with whom to share your feelings. If you sense that the feelings you have kept inside are deep and serious, you will need to have this person be a therapist. If you know that you have kept a great deal to yourself but do not sense a deep pain, sharing with a trustworthy friend might be a good start.

Ask yourself the following questions, and be honest with yourself:

- What do I almost know?
- What do I feel?
- Do I feel I have been hiding from myself and others?
- What are the secrets in my life?
- What are the emotional rules by which I live?
- How would I like my life to be different?

You can tell when you are sharing a true feeling. You say, "I feel . . . " and then you state the feeling. When you say, "I feel that . . . ," you are slipping into an opinion, and it's not a true feeling.

For instance, "I feel hurt" is the simple and true expression of a feeling. "I feel that you hurt me" is an intellectualization that assigns blame.

True feelings connect; blame pushes away. When we take the risk to share our true feelings, we find our authentic selves. When we tell our truth, we feel a sense of relief, and it becomes easier to connect with others. It is an empowering process.

Additional Reading

Dayton, Tian. *Emotional Sobriety: From Relationship Trauma to Resilience and Balance.* Deerfield Beach, FL: HCI, 2007.

Grabhorn, Lynn. *Excuse Me, Your Life Is Waiting: The Astonishing Power of Feelings.* Charlottesville, VA: Hampton Roads Publishing, 2003.

Williams, Mark, John Teasdale, Zindel Segaland, and Jon Kabat-Zinn. *The Mindful Way Through Depression: Freeing Yourself from Chronic Unhappiness.* New York: Guilford Press, 2007.

Workshops

Learning to Love Yourself
Onsite Workshops
Cumberland Furnace, TN
www.onsiteworkshops.com
1-800-341-7432

forty-four

Twelve Steps for Anyone:
A Way of Life

> *"If we share with caring and love, we will create*
> *abundance and joy for each other.*
>
> —DEEPAK CHOPRA, M.D.

IN THIS ERA OF major interest in recovery from addictions, knowing about the twelve steps is becoming part of our culture. The twelve steps were developed by two men, Dr. Bob Smith and Bill Wilson, in the 1930s. For many years, alcoholics used the twelve steps with great success. The steps helped them to stay sober and, just as important, to find a way of life that was meaningful and free. There are millions of people who now live the twelve-step way of life.

Because of this great success, many other groups have adopted and changed the wording to meet their needs. There are twelve steps for people with eating disorders, nicotine addiction, caretaking compulsions, gambling afflictions, sexual compulsivity, and so on. It is clear that there is a great deal to be learned by following the twelve steps.

One night, in one of my groups, a client came in and said, "Thanks for telling me about the twelve steps. I have read them all and they are good. Now what?" He had no clue about how to use the twelve steps. They are meant to be read, understood, and then applied to every area of one's life. It's the constant application to life that is the challenge and the hope. Each day offers us countless opportunities to apply the twelve steps.

The reason there are groups that meet on a regular basis is that it's difficult to keep applying these wise and simple rules on one's own. The groups provide ongoing support and guidance for using these steps. I remember asking someone who has used the steps for more than thirty-five years, "Why do you keep using the steps? You haven't had a drink in thirty-five years!" His reply was that the twelve steps are a reminder to live in a way that makes having a drink unnecessary. He goes to groups for support in that decision, and when he is doing well, he goes to help someone else. That sharing of the steps is step 12.

The twelve steps are helpful for anyone to use, and many diverse groups have adapted them. Here is one adaptation of the original twelve steps:

1. We acknowledge and accept that we are powerless in controlling the lives of others and that trying to control others makes our lives difficult and unmanageable.
2. We have come to believe that a power greater than ourselves—such as God, Buddha, a Spirit, a group, nature, or goodness—can restore enough order and hope in our lives to move us to a sense of inner peace.
3. We make a decision to live our lives to the best of our ability and accept that taking responsibility for ourselves is the only way inner peace will come.
4. We look at our own mental, emotional, spiritual, physical, and political assets and liabilities. We look at what we have, how we use it, and how we can heal ourselves and hopefully heal others.
5. We take a look at ourselves and see if there are any ways we are

causing anyone else pain or hurt by our misguided control.

6. We offer to our Higher Power our mistakes, our attempts to control others, and our willingness to change when necessary. We look at our rigidity and our judgments.

7. We ask for help when we need it and offer help to others when we can.

8. We choose to change in any area of life that we ought to change.

9. We make a list of people to whom we want to make amends and then do so, except in areas where doing so would cause further pain.

10. We ask for feedback from others to be sure we see ourselves in a true way.

11. We take in new information by reading, listening, and sharing. We expose ourselves to people who are different from ourselves.

12. Having experienced the power of this kind of growth, we find our spirits awakened to a new sense of well-being. We recognize that we are becoming who we are in this lifetime task of change. We accept that it is done "one day at a time."

Variations of the twelve steps have helped millions of people to find a sense of inner peace and hope. The steps are easy to read and understand, and it is very challenging to try to live by their wisdom. Those who have been able to do so have found great healing.

Once, when I was going through many changes in my life, someone wisely told me to pay attention to the shortcut of the twelve steps. The shortcut goes like this:

• Steps 1–3: Trust God.
• Steps 4–10: Clean house.
• Steps 11–12: Help others.

Trust God. My life had been full of twists and turns, yet it seemed that I could continue to make it. Wonderful things had happened to me. Trusting God was easy for me to do.

Clean house. Oh my—this was my stumbling block. Cleaning house was the most difficult part of the plan. My physical house was not really bad, yet there were things going on in my life that were not the best for all concerned. Rationalization was part of my life. There were things I fudged about, and taking what I thought I needed and deserved was part of my lifestyle; so too were minimizing the importance of certain situations and of allowing free thinking.

Thus, when I thought about cleaning my emotional house, it was clear. I needed to make myself as honest and as direct as I possibly could. This meant many changes in my daily life. I made those changes and experienced great loss and isolation. However, that time of my life was short-lived, and the long-term gains became much more important. It took me a year, but my life changed dramatically when I worked those steps.

Help others. My personal life and my career were all about helping others. That is where my passion was. It fit my values; it was where my heart felt full. Helping others was the easiest part of my journey.

Learning about the 12 Steps is easy. Learning to put them into practice is much more difficult. Yet it is a wonderful and comforting way to live.

Additional Reading

Eliot, Eve. *Insatiable: The Compelling Story of Four Teens, Food, and Its Power.* Deerfield Beach, FL: HCI, 2001.

Heineman, Mary. *Losing Your Shirt: Recovery for Compulsive Gamblers and Their Families.* Center City, MN: Hazelden, 2001.

Schaeffer, Brenda. *Is It Love or Is It Addiction?* Center City, MN: Hazelden, 1997.

Sheppard, Kay. *Food Addiction: The Body Knows.* Deerfield Beach, FL: HCI, 1993.

Weiss, Douglas. *Beyond the Bedroom: Healing for Adult Children of Sex Addicts.* Deerfield Beach, FL: HCI, 2005.

Resources

Look for support groups in your local area.

Alcoholics Anonymous (AA)
www.aa.org

Adult Children of Alcoholics (ACOA)
www.adultchildren.org

Narcotics Anonymous (NA)
www.na.org

Nicotine Anonymous (NicA)
www.nicotine-anonymous.org

Debtors Anonymous (DA)
www.debtorsanonymous.org

Gamblers Anonymous (GA)
www.gamblersanonymous.org

Overeaters Anonymous (OA)
www.oa.org

Sexaholics Anonymous
www.sa.org

Part eight:

WELLNESS (STAYING WELL)

She who has health has hope, and she
who has hope has everything.

—*Anne Morrow Lindbergh*

forty-five

Stress Is Part of Each Day: How Do I Handle It?

> *If women were convinced that a day off or an hour*
> *of solitude was a reasonable ambition, they would find*
> *a way of attaining it. As it is, they feel so unjustified in*
> *their demand that they rarely make the attempt.*
>
> —ANNE MORROW LINDBERGH

WE ALL HEAR PEOPLE SAY, "I'm so stressed out." There is this and that and more of this and that. Those who feel stressed are truly having a hard time coping with time, pressure, expectations, and obligations. Any suggestion of change is met with resistance and the message "You don't understand."

When I was working as a counselor, a speaker, the president of a company, and an author, I was also a mother of three and a wife. Then there were my friends and a load of community work.

Many of my friends and relatives would tell me of their concern that I was overextended, subject to colds and flu, and clearly under a great deal of stress. When I heard these messages, it just added more stress to my life, because now people were telling me to do something about my stress. I thought they just didn't understand my situation. I continued trying to hold many things together, but I was brought up short, and when I acquired two serious illnesses I saw the folly of my denial.

I realized then that stress is a killer. Actually, it's not the stress that is the killer, it's the reaction to life that causes stress that is the killer. I am the only one who can change my life. Here is an illustration of the effects of long-term stress.

Hold a bag of apples (or ask someone else to do this) and guess how heavy it is, rating it from 1 (lightest) and 10 (heaviest). Most people say that it's about a 4. The weight doesn't really matter, and holding it for a minute is no big deal.

Now hold it for ten minutes. Stress increases, and the arm feels the strain. Now hold it for an hour. Stress increases again, and the arm hurts. If you hold it for the rest of the day, it becomes pretty uncomfortable. In each case, it's the same weight, but the longer it's held, the heavier it becomes.

That is the way it is with stress. If we carry our burdens too long, they take their toll. From time to time, if we put the apples down, we can relieve the stress and hold them again. Not resting from the holding will eventually cause pain and struggle.

We all have stress. We can all make decisions about when and how to put down the burden of stress, but those decisions come with a risk. When I put down my burden of a schedule that was simply too full, there were consequences. People were disappointed in me when I was not available. I worked less, so I made less money, which changed my lifestyle. There was less money and more time. My time became a commodity that brought me great satisfaction and happiness. When I adjusted my lifestyle to purchase fewer things and accept satisfaction more often, it made room for many people to connect with me in my life. Connecting was a greater joy to me than the ability to accumulate. My lesson learned: Life is short—enjoy it!

In my life, I have always wanted to achieve, do well, and come in first. The day that someone reminded me that it is the second mouse that gets the cheese, I let up on my expectations for myself. When one of my daughters was in high school, she was almost a straight B student. She volunteered at a nursing home, played the viola in the band, had good friends, and loved to go camping.

When I asked her once if she would like to study a bit more and move up to being an A student, her response was "It's not worth the stress. Right now I really like my life. I do the things I want to do, and being a B student is good enough for me." This is the daughter who went on to become a registered nurse, a psychologist, a happily married woman, and a great mother of two.

Simple living is a concept that is catching on. It means getting away from a hurried, multitasking lifestyle. It's about making connections, making decisions, and giving up buying, accumulating, and adding more things that only produce stress. One of the reasons we are so busy is that we have to work to pay for all the stuff we think we want. However, most people in this country are drowning in stuff. Satisfaction is an underappreciated virtue. Take back your freedom. Reclaim your time. Make decisions that simplify your life.

Most important, find balance in your life. Our culture is designed to use you up, burn you out, and then discard you. Fight back and reclaim time and energy. It's about you, not about the culture. What are you willing to give up to have more time, connection, and energy in your life? We all have twenty-four hours a day. How are you using them?

I remember a workshop at which the leader had a pile of books sitting on the floor. She asked me to hold a book for each expectation I had for myself and for each person with whom I wanted to spend time. I ended up trying to hold about sixteen books. I was hot and uncomfortable, my energy was gone, and I felt stupid. She showed me graphically how ridiculous it is to be all things to all people and all situations. That day started "cleaning house."

My choices are not your choices. Your choices are not someone else's choices. You need to make your own choices and live with your own consequences. My challenge to you is to find your passion, follow your bliss, leave behind the nonessentials, and clean out toxic people and situations. Take time to clear your schedule, say no frequently, reassess family demands, clear your brain, and carry on. Your stress level will drop dramatically.

As you do this, turn off your cell phone and take messages at home. Return all your calls once a day at the time you choose. Answer your e-mail once a day at a time you choose. Stop being available. Take charge of your life.

Balance is a wonderful energy producer. If you have a chosen balance in your life, your energy, your spirit, your passion, and your creativity will flourish, and you will know a much greater level of happiness.

Additional Reading

Breininger, Dorothy K., and Debby S. Bitticks. *Time Efficiency Makeover: Own Your Time and Your Life by Conquering Procrastination.* Deerfield Beach, FL: HCI, 2005.

Kabat-Zinn, John. *Full Catastrophe Living: Using the Wisdom of Your Body and Mind to Face Stress, Pain, and Illness.* New York: Delta, 1990.

Klauser, Henriette Anne. *Write It Down, Make It Happen: Knowing What You Want—and Getting It.* New York: Touchstone, 2001.

Smallin, Donna. *7 Simple Steps to Unclutter Your Life.* North Adams, MA: Storey Publishing, 2000.

Wegscheider-Cruse, Sharon. *Learning to Balance Your Life: 6 Powers to Restore Your Energy and Spirit.* Deerfield Beach, FL: HCI, 2005.

forty-six

Living Alone:
Staying Healthy and Safe

When you are alone, you are all on your own.

—Leonardo da Vinci

One of the greatest fears among baby boomers and older single women is health issues. Not only are there many concerns about insurance and medical care, there are fears about who will be there when they need help. Women are used to being the caretakers, the center around which many homes operate. They are the stalwart core of the household, and too little has been written about what happens when they are in need. Single women, single mothers, and widows need to address three main issues:

1. What can I do to remain as healthy as possible for as long as possible?
2. What signals do I need to notice when something is wrong?
3. How can I help myself?

Addressing the concerns outlined below will help you to remain healthy.

Daily Exercise

If you exercise regularly, your overall risk of heart attack is about half that of people who are sedentary and out of shape.

Exercise does the following for you:

- Increases the diameter of your coronary arteries
- Decreases the level of cholesterol in your blood
- Helps to control your blood sugar
- Helps to control your weight
- Increases your immune system activity
- Reduces anxiety and depression

Start out slowly and gradually add more exercise each day. Include a variety of activities, such as walking, aerobics, weight training, swimming, and biking in your routine. Do not overdo, especially in the beginning of your workouts. For your own protection, do the following:

- Exercise regularly, but don't do too much at one time.
- Warm up and cool down.
- Take the talk test—you should be able to talk while exercising.
- Wait two hours after a large meal to exercise.
- Tailor activity to weather conditions; go lightly on hot, humid days.
- Listen to your body.

Sensible Eating

There are countless books on nutrition and health, so it's not necessary to cover nutrition here. Stick with fruits, vegetables, whole grains, beans, and lean meat and fish. Watch out for too much fat, cream, white starch, and salt. It's really just that simple. Find what works for you.

I've found that sticking to three meals a day with no snacking works for me. Breakfast is necessary because it starts my furnace running. Whether it's scrambled eggs, toast and peanut butter, cold pizza, or last night's leftovers, a little food starts my day right.

My other self-care trick is that having a tiny bit of a really good food—such as dark chocolate, a creamy sauce (like hollandaise sauce), or filet mignon—is as good as having a full serving. A tiny bit stops the craving and obsessing.

Another practice that works for me is to eat only things I really love. I don't eat just to eat, or because it's a certain time, or because I'm offered something at a dinner party. I eat only what I love. When I think about what to eat, rarely do I pay attention to what I need on a daily basis. If I get what I need on a weekly basis, then an egg sandwich for supper or a cold casserole for breakfast works fine for me.

What helps me most is keeping what I consider to be bad foods or unhealthy foods out of the house and having plenty of good and healthy foods and snacks in the house at all times.

Stress Management

Stress is a major factor in the development of cardiovascular disease and obesity. Stress is what you feel when the demands on your life exceed your ability to meet those demands. Your heart beats faster, your breathing quickens, and your blood pressure rises. You're also more susceptible to angina, a type of chest pain, and heart rhythm irregularities.

In some people, these reactions can be so dramatic that increases in blood pressure and heart rate are extreme. If stress persists, increased blood clotting as a result of the stress response can put you at risk of a heart attack or stroke.

If you have symptoms of excess stress, try the following:

- Change whatever factors you can. You may not be able to walk away from a stressful job or home, but you can develop new responses to defuse anger or conflict. Delegate what you can and learn to say no.
- Relax when you can. Use guided imagery, meditation, muscle relaxation, and deep breathing. Spend an hour a day reading something that is relaxing.
- Take up some new hobbies and activities, such as walking or listening to music, and quit some old activities that have lost their luster. Just because we have belonged to a certain club or enjoyed a certain pastime doesn't mean that we have to do it forever.

Regular Medical Checkups

The following medical checkups can help to catch problems early:

- Blood pressure test. Be screened at least once, preferably twice, a year to make sure your blood pressure is in normal range.
- Cholesterol test. By age forty-five, have this done annually.
- Mammogram. Women should have one every year. A good way to remember is to schedule it the week of your birthday.
- Pap test. By age twenty-one, women should have this done annually.
- Pelvic exam. Women should have this done annually.
- Colon and rectal screening. Do this every five years—more often if there is colon cancer in your family.
- Bone density measurement. Annual screenings are recommended for women over sixty years old.
- Dental checkup. Have one every six months.
- Eye exam. This is recommended every three years for people ages twenty to thirty-nine, every two years for people ages forty to sixty-four, and annually after age sixty-five.

- Fasting blood sugar level. This should be checked every year, or every six months if there is diabetes in your family.
- Skin exam. This is recommended once a year.

In addition to having regular tests, you should also know how to recognize when you're experiencing a heart attack or a stroke.

How to Recognize a Heart Attack. Women often do not get the arm pain that is associated with heart attacks. They are more likely to have intense pain in the jaw. Nausea and intense sweating are also common symptoms.

Let's say you are driving home after work and you are tired, upset, and frustrated. Then you have pain in your jaw. Head for the emergency room or stop and call 911. It could be a heart attack. You have only a very short time before you will lose consciousness. However, try to cough, and keep coughing as deeply as possible. This brings oxygen into the lungs and will keep your blood circulating until help arrives. It's better to make an unnecessary call than to lose consciousness and let the damage happen.

How to Recognize a Stroke. If a stroke victim can get help within three hours, most often the damage of the stroke can be reversed. Too often, however, we do not recognize the symptoms. Here is how to help someone:

1. Ask the individual to smile.
2. Ask him or her to raise both arms.
3. Ask him or her to say a simple sentence. If the sentence is not coherent, it could be the sign of a stroke.

If there is trouble with any of these three things, then the person is probably having a stroke. Call for help immediately.

Single women should do the following:

- Have your doctor's phone number by each phone and programmed into your cell phones. Do the same with hospital numbers.
- Prearrange with at least two people whom you can call any time of the day or night.
- Have all your necessary papers in one place in your home, and make sure that the above two people know about it.

Living alone does not have to mean that you are isolated. Be sure that your phone is always handy. If you use only a cell phone, be sure that it is always charged. Give someone you trust the key to your home and make an arrangement that there is someone in your life who will check on you at regular times if you have not been in contact.

A friend of mine has one shade on her window that is a different color. She pulls it down each night and has an agreement with a friend that if that shade is not up in the morning, the friend will use the key and come in to check on her.

It's important to find ways to stay connected and not become isolated. Be sure to wear medical bracelets that contain your important data, and keep a list of medications you take taped to a kitchen cupboard and in your purse.

These precautions are not just for older women. One of my friends is very young and a severe diabetic. Another is young and has severe asthma attacks. It is each person's responsibility to be prepared for emergencies.

Additional Reading

Iknoian, Therese. *Fitness Walking*. Champaign, IL: Human Kinetics Publishers, 2005.

Margolis, Simeon, ed. *The Johns Hopkins Complete Home Guide to Symptoms and Remedies*. New York: Black Dog & Leventhal Publishers, 2004.

Mayo Clinic. *Mayo Clinic Family Health Book,* 3rd ed. New York: HarperCollins, 2003.

Siegel, Bernie. *Peace, Love, and Healing: Bodymind Communication and the Path to Self-Healing*. New York: Harper, 1990.

Vaillant, George. *Aging Well: Surprising Guideposts to a Happier Life*. Boston: Little, Brown and Company, 2003.

Weil, Andrew T. *Health and Healing: The Philosophy of Integrative Medicine and Optimum Health*. Boston: Mariner Books, 2004.

forty-seven

How Can I *Really* Enjoy Daily Exercise?

Don't compromise yourself, you are all you've got.

—BETTY FORD

NEVER BEFORE HAVE WE had as many gyms, home equipment rooms, aerobics classes, community programs, and other ways to exercise. In 2007, Americans spent more than $17 billion on health club memberships. Working out seems to reach its peak in January and February, then slack off somewhat until the next January and February when the new year triggers a resolution to become serious about exercising.

What changed in my life was not the format of workout programs. My life changed when I found an exercise that I really enjoyed and looked forward to doing. I was never the same after I visited a spa years ago and learned to love to walk. What I appreciated about that particular spa was that it gave me motivation and a way to really enjoy and look forward to walking.

That initial experience was about fifteen years ago, and my love for walking has only grown. My preference for walking is outdoors. I love the air and all the benefits that outside walking affords. When I can't be outside, I have found a way to love walking indoors.

I've also learned how to make the most of my walks, which enhances my pleasure and makes every walk different.

The first thing I learned at the spa was to make walking a special event. Over time, I have collected favorite clothes that I use only for walking. When I put them on, my focus changes from what else is going on in my life and I am put into a different mood—one of hope, inspiration, and well-being. I have a good feeling about myself.

The next important ingredient for my walks is really good music. I have gone from a small radio to tapes to the iPod. My favorite music is on my iPod, and I really look forward to singing along and keeping pace with my music. On my walking iPod, I have all my favorite upbeat and fast songs. It's easy to set my walking pace when the beat works with me. I save my meditation and ballad music for other times. My walking music has to have the beat. With it I can do a fifteen-minute mile, and most days I try to do two or three miles.

Most of my walks involve music, but silence is also my friend. There are times when my emotional and physical self is crying out for relief and relaxation. On those days, I prefer silence. On those days, I listen to the sounds of nature, I look at the mountains, and I hear my feet pounding on the sidewalk. My thoughts are random and fleeting. Sometimes I will suddenly find that two miles are already behind me and that calming and focusing is happening.

Walks can be meditation times. When my creativity seems stuck and new thoughts and ideas just aren't happening for me, my walks become my meditation times. There might be a decision to make, a problem to solve, or a choice to be made. Walking stirs something in my spirit on a regular basis and is a source for much of the creative work I do.

My special walks include my partner. There is never enough time for us to share, so walking is a wonderful, focused time for us to be with each other. We love sharing this time together, whether we are using it for meditation, solving problems, making plans, or rehashing a party we just had.

Walking has wonderful physical benefits. The consistent pace is good for the heart rate, for the blood sugar level, and for the burning of calories. Studies have shown that it doesn't really matter whether you walk for an hour at a time, take two half-hour walks, or take a series of ten-minute walks. Everyone can make time. It doesn't matter whether you take your walk before breakfast, on your lunch hour, while waiting for an airplane, or going through a shopping center. You can keep a pair of walking shoes in a shoulder bag with you at all times.

One of my extra ways to build mileage is to park farther away from my destination or to meet a friend for a walk instead of coffee. On days when the weather is bad, I love to do a two- or four-mile walk with Leslie Sansone on tape. Walking is good for me in so many ways that bring me pleasure that it has become an important part of my life.

All exercise is good for you, but walking is the least expensive and the most available, and it has so many benefits.

Additional Reading

American Heart Association. *The Healthy Heart Walking Book: The American Heart Association Walking Program.* New York: Macmillan, 1995.

Iknoian, Therese. *Fitness Walking.* Champaign, IL: Human Kinetics Publishers, 2005.

Peeke, Pamela. *Body for Life for Women: A Woman's Plan for Physical and Mental Transformation.* New York: Rodale Books, 2005.

Wegscheider-Cruse, Sharon. *Learning to Balance Your Life: 6 Powers to Restore Your Energy and Spirit.* Deerfield Beach, FL: HCI, 2005.

Resources

Walking tapes by Leslie Sansone

Dancing tapes by Richard Simmons

Miraval Resort (mind, body, spirit focus)
Tucson, Arizona
www.miravalresort.com

Red Mountain Resort & Spa
Ivins, Utah
www.redmountainspa.com

forty-eight

There Is Nothing Better Than a Good Night's Sleep

A quiet mind is the best hope for a restful sleep.

—JANE LUNDE

THERE ARE WONDERFUL NIGHTS when sleep is plentiful and we wake up refreshed, energetic, and ready to go. Then there are nights when tossing and turning continue into the wee hours and we can't seem to turn off our thoughts. Sometimes we fall asleep easily, only to wake up soon after, and then the tossing and turning starts. Going through our minds are all the things we have to do once the alarm rings and thoughts of how tired we are going to be the next day.

As the time goes by, the tension builds and the chances of getting restful sleep diminish. For a public speaker, it's devastating when that night happens to be the night before an important event.

Studies have shown that up to 50 percent of adults experience some type of insomnia. It is very often connected to medications, and for women it is often part of menopause.

Insomnia has many variations: falling asleep quickly and then waking up, not being able to get to sleep in the first place, or sleeping lightly and waking up often. It can be caused by stress, anxiety, depression, poor eating habits, physical pain, or aging. Caffeine—whether from coffee, tea, sodas, or chocolate—is also a problem for many people. Sometimes it's caused by people trying too hard to fall asleep. Sleeping is a natural process and can't be forced.

Many experts have warned about what doesn't work and what doesn't help in the long run. Using alcohol can help you to fall asleep, but usually when the effects of the alcohol wear off, you wake up and cannot get back to sleep. This is known as the 3:00 AM wake-up call.

Nonaddictive sleeping pills can be a short-term aid for intense insomnia, but used on a regular basis, they come with problems of their own. Even infrequent use comes with possible complications. One of these complications is binge eating, and another is driving while asleep. In both cases, you do not remember what has happened. Use of these medications on a regular basis can lead to dependency and increase the problem of insomnia.

Sleep deprivation has been known to contribute to certain illnesses, a sense of irritability that is harmful to relationships, accidents, and depression. If you have regular trouble getting to sleep, this should be investigated by a doctor. If you have infrequent but bothersome bouts of insomnia, you might want to try some of the following behavioral changes:

1. *Refrain from any caffeine for at least six hours before going to bed.* This includes caffeinated coffee, tea, sodas, and any products with chocolate, especially dark chocolate.
2. *Limit alcohol use before bedtime.* A glass of wine with dinner might be okay, but stay away from after-dinner drinking of any kind.
3. *Do not eat a large meal for at least three hours before bedtime.* It's best to have your dinner early and then a small snack before

bedtime. Milk, cereal, and toast make good snacks just before bedtime.

4. *Prepare the sleeping room.* It's best not to use the room for anything except sleep and sex. Do not have a computer in the bedroom. It suggests work and/or responsibility and can remind you of all that you have to be doing. There are different points of view about television. Some sleep experts believe that television can be too stimulating, whereas others think that it is relaxing. You should decide for yourself.

5. *Use colors that are relaxing.* Beige, pale green, light blue, lilac or lavender, gray, and cream are colors that most people find relaxing. Stay away from red, orange, deep purple, or loud designs that stimulate the eyes.

6. *Be very careful about light.* Keep the room as dark as possible. An investment in room-darkening shades is a good idea. The room should be able to be closed off to maximize darkness. For some, even the small lights on a smoke alarm, a glow-in-the-dark clock radio, and a TV are too much. If you have these lights, it's best to cover them with a small black cloth.

7. *Keep the temperature moderate.* Keeping the room at 65–67 degrees will ensure enough warmth for you to be comfortable when your body heat is being conserved by the bedcovers. The coolness on your face and arms will be restful.

8. *Decorate the room with meaningful photos, artwork, treasured items, pillows, and flowers.* The more beautiful, safe, and welcome the room, the more restful the time spent there will be.

9. *Make good decisions about what you watch on TV before going to bed.* Watching something highly stimulating or controversial might keep you up thinking about the program.

10. *Do not exercise for four hours before bedtime.* The stimulation from exercise has to wear off before sleeping will be easy.

11. *If you meditate or pray, this is a good time to engage in these activities.* Pay attention to your breathing. Listening to quieting relaxation tapes or CDs will help your body to slow down and start feeling sleepy. Your mind will start to wander, and you will have a good chance of falling asleep. Studies show that people who meditate and pray tend to move from light sleep to deep sleep quite easily.

Sometimes there is more than just insomnia going on; there could be a medical or an emotional problem that has to be investigated. If none of the above remedies help, it might be time to get a medical checkup. If nothing is physically wrong, the next step would be to see a psychologist.

Additional Reading

Ambrogetti, Antonio. *Sleeping Soundly.* Crows Nest, New South Wales, Australia: Allen & Unwin, 2001.

Hauri, Peter, and Shirley Linde. *No More Sleepless Nights.* Hoboken, NJ: John Wiley & Sons, 1996.

Heller, Barbara L. *How to Sleep Soundly Tonight: 250 Simple and Natural Ways to Prevent Sleeplessness.* North Adams, MA: Storey Publishing, 2001.

Kryger, Meir H. *A Woman's Guide to Sleep Disorders.* New York: McGraw-Hill, 2004.

PART NINE:

SPIRITUALITY

The day will come when after harnessing
the winds, the tides, and gravitation, we shall
harness for God the energies of love.
Then, for the second time in the history of
the world, a man will have discovered fire.

—*Teilhard de Chardin*

forty-nine

Wise Women, Gutsy Women, Sages, and Mentors

*It's good to be a seeker, but sooner or later, you have to
be a finder. And then it's well to give what you have
found, a gift unto the world for whoever will accept it.*

—RICHARD BACH

WISE WOMEN ARE WOMEN who have combined their knowledge and
experience in a way that brings about wisdom. They have mastered
their internal worlds and made their wisdom manifested in their
outer worlds. Some are very young and some are very old; all ages are
represented by wise women. Their mothers have given birth to these
women through physical pain, but these women have lived in a way
that has birthed their own emotional and spiritual lives.

These are women who have found their power and a balance of
mind, body, and spirit. They know that when our thoughts, health,
and values are in harmony, the universal energy that is available to all
of us is present. When this energy is released, so is power.

Power is an interesting word and is often misunderstood. Power
is not about control over others; it is not dictatorial, nor is it unkind
or judgmental. Power is energy that comes from within and that

unleashes confidence, competency, and compassion. It moves us to commitment and contribution. The five Cs are the basis for our spiritual essence:

- Commitment
- Competency
- Confidence
- Compassion
- Contribution

Powerful women are simply women full of power. When women are at full power, we are able to do the following:

1. Think clearly, not being overwhelmed or scattered
2. Work out ideas, not feeling stuck or confused
3. Make decisions, not procrastinating or waivering
4. Make things happen, realizing that "someday" is now
5. Influence events by being a leader rather than a follower
6. Win the respect of others rather than demanding it
7. Take charge of a situation rather than waiting needlessly
8. Have a vision and carry it out rather than always accepting circumstances
9. Be a force that unifies rather than destroys
10. Experience mastery rather than remaining a seeker

Through empowerment, women are able to experience their own choices and freedom in life. Whether they work outside the home or choose to be a stay-at-home mother and wife or a stay-at-home employee, they are able to connect with other women and feel as though they have some power in their choice of lifestyle.

This power comes from within. We can call it a soul, a spirit, or an inner guide. Whatever we call it, it's the inner voice that helps us to discover who we really are, what our purpose on Earth is, and what kind of journey we want to take at this moment in our lives.

It takes a great deal of courage to be a woman today. The world is full of conflict, brutality, and danger. We live in a culture of sexism, racism, disease, ageism, and other attacks on the human spirit. Yet women have great courage. Women have a strength that amazes men. Here are ten of the most amazing things about mothers:

1. They carry babies in their bodies.
2. They give birth.
3. They care for their children like a mother bear cares for her cub.
4. They stay awake or only sleep lightly when someone they love is on the road; they want to know when that someone arrives safely.
5. They are caretakers in the best sense of the word.
6. They walk the extra mile to get their children to school or to the best day care center.
7. When they can't find money for something they want, they find money for what their children need.
8. They continue to learn because they know that knowledge is power.
9. When they suffer great sorrow because they have lost someone in the family, they keep going because someone else in the family needs them.
10. Just when they think that their children are grown and they can take a breather from concern and worry, grandchildren arrive, and they start all over again.

Women have much to share and to give. A woman's beauty is not in the clothes she wears, the body she inhabits, or the way she looks. Her beauty is in her eyes, in her heart, and in her hardworking hands that have the ability to soothe. Her beauty is in her soul and her caring. It's in her passion and kindness.

As women, we are not born all at once, but rather bit by bit. The body is born first, the spirit later. Our mothers were racked by the pains of our physical birth. We, as powerful, gusty, and courageous women, suffer the long and more difficult pains of our spiritual growth.

It takes courage to have a child. Your heart is with your child forever. It takes courage to rear a child, to answer that child's cries, and to feel that child's anguish and pain.

It takes courage to be a lover. It's a gutsy proposition to enter a partnership, to share intimacy in body, mind, and spirit. It's a risk to commingle your identity with someone else's identity. To be willing and able to share honestly and with integrity while having fun, experiencing sorrow, accepting differences, and working toward similarities is a challenge. It takes courage.

Women throughout the ages have known about the power of friendship. They gather in groups in a way that is different from how men gather. Women come together to share from their hearts and souls. They talk about the way they feel and what they think, and they share with a compassion and a depth that is tempered only by the level of safety in the group.

There cannot be too many glorious women, too many queens, and too many goddesses. We, as women, need to give ourselves permission to have a full and passionate life. Woman with similar stresses can and do support one another. We can be eccentric and still be perceived as wonderful. We can step out of the boxes into which women have sometimes been put. With support, we can create our own ability to follow our passions and decisions. It used to be that women made coffee and men made decisions. Now men have learned to make coffee and women have learned to make decisions.

In friendship, we touch the stars by standing on the shoulders of the giants who have gone before us. We all have had role models and mentors. Once we get where we want to go, we need to hold out our hands to those who come after us. A wise woman and one of my mentors said, "We must have a transfer of *wisdom* between women, not just knowledge." Experience and verbal sharing is the vehicle for passing on wisdom.

Throughout history, women have been nurturers. It is natural for women to give, but when they go to extremes, they sometimes do not replenish themselves. They often sacrifice too much. When this happens, there is usually an interruption in their lives. The call can come in the form of a crisis, an accident, or an illness. This interruption becomes a wake-up call.

Constant overdoing for others robs us of our power and our health. If we are having frequent illnesses, depression, feelings of being overwhelmed, accidents, or excessive weight gain, we should not be in a hurry to fix or heal until we have learned the lesson that the illness, the accident, the weight gain, or the depression is teaching.

Learning how to work with a mentor has been a gift and a challenge. I try to have a mentor all the time. Some of my most cherished mentors and role models have died and have been hard to replace. However, I work on it, and there is always someone who can teach me something. I have mentors in every age group.

The word *mentor* has traditionally meant that one person looks to another person to be a teacher, a leader, and a fountain of wisdom and information. Traditionally, one person would be a protègè: someone whose welfare, training, or career is promoted by the more experienced, influential person. Information flow was mostly one-way. This is a meaningful type of mentorship.

Another type of mentor is the sharing mentor. In this case, one has a variety of mentors and asks for only one thing from each one. A mentor is not necessarily someone who is at a higher level, whatever that may mean, but simply at a different level.

The pool of mentors can be quite large and is much more recip-rocal. To me, it means many masters and no gurus. Friends, cowork-ers, or family members might become mentors to one another. It simply means that someone has a knowledge or a skill that you would like to develop. The more we grow and share, the more likely we are to find women with a spirit of generosity. You can have many mentors and be one yourself—all at the same time.

The knowledge and wisdom that sages and mentors pass on can help us to identify what we truly value and want for ourselves. They can help us to identify our priorities. They can teach us to ask ques-tions to which only we have the answer.

Another way to practice recognizing and naming priorities is to take a look at your life and ask yourself three simple questions, each of which generates more questions. The answers can have profound impacts on your priorities and choices.

If you knew that you only had three years to live, how would you spend those three years? This generates the following questions:

1. Who would you spend time with, and how much time?
2. What unfinished business would you take care of?
3. What would you like to tell someone that you haven't told him or her?
4. Where would you like to go?
5. How would you like to live?
6. What would your days be like?
7. What would your evenings be like?
8. What would you eliminate from your life?
9. Whom would you eliminate from your life?
10. What would you want people to know about you?
11. What would you tell those you love about yourself?

If you only had two years to live, how would you answer the above questions?

If you only had one year to live, how would you answer the above questions?

Any of us, at any time, could be experiencing his or her last day. Are you ready?

When you start living with clear priorities, when you truly accept that each day could be your last, you open a door to joy in all you do. Joy is a great celebration. The great philosopher Thomas Merton says, "Pray, but move your feet and do all you can to bring joy into your life."

Joy consists of having a great excitement in life. Leo Booth, a dear friend of mine, says that he loves burned-out people. He says they are great people precisely *because* they are burned out. He adds, "Only people with great passion burn out. Mediocre people do not burn out because they have never been on fire."

Throughout the ages, we have been blessed by gutsy, courageous, wise women who have put their knowledge and experience together, found wisdom, and shared their wisdom with us. Here are some wise words from wise women that have meant a lot to me:

- Thank God we don't get everything we ask for. Sometimes God has better plans for us.
- We have to give up some of the old to make space for something new.
- I have learned that life is tough—but I am tougher.
- Happiness is something to do, someone to love, and something to hope for.
- We will keep getting in situations with the same problems until we heal those problems in our life. That is the tenacity of the human spirit.

- Each person is born with a reason for being. Life is a quest to discover that purpose.
- People say that time heals. This is not true. Love and courage, not time, heal wounds.
- Doing the same thing over and over the same way with the same person and expecting a different result is a form of insanity.
- When death finds you, hope that it finds you alive. Live until you die.
- In the final analysis, it is the knowledge that we are free to choose among alternatives that makes us powerful.

The list is endless, and each time we incorporate an important saying into our belief system and choose a behavior to support our belief, we become a little more powerful.

Additional Reading

Bolen, Jean Shinoda. *Crossing to Avalon: A Woman's Midlife Quest for the Sacred Feminine.* New York: HarperOne, 1995.

Cameron, Julia. *The Artist's Way.* New York: J. P. Tarcher, 2002.

Lerner-Robbins, Helene. *Our Power as Women: Wisdom and Strategies of Highly Successful Women.* Berkeley, CA: Conari Press, 1996.

Martin, Katherine. *Women of Courage: Inspiring Stories from the Women Who Lived Them.* Novato, CA: New World Library, 1999.

Martin, Katherine. *Women of Spirit: Stories of Courage from the Women Who Lived Them.* Novato, CA: New World Library, 2001.

McMeekin, Gail. *The 12 Secrets of Highly Creative Women: A Portable Mentor.* San Francisco: Red Wheel/Weiser, 2000.

fifty

Is There Any Reason to Have Faith in the Future?

> *It is only possible to live happily ever after on a day-to-day basis.*
>
> —MARGARET BONNANO

MY FAVORITE UNCLE used to walk around with a smile on his face, saying, "It's a good life." Some of his days were up, and some were down, but the saying remained the same. Many years later, what I remember about this now deceased uncle was his beautiful optimism. He had many situations in his life that could have diminished his optimism, but he never let that happen.

Now, even though he is gone, that beautiful memory lingers in my mind and in the minds of several people in our family. That is a true and appreciated legacy. In a way, his influence has become immortal. Some of it must have rubbed off on me, because my life feels good, and for that I am grateful.

I know that the world is a scary and an upsetting place. Every day we face the realities of our times: terrorism, pollution, domestic violence, war, alcohol and drug abuse, global warming, criminals, and economic stress. Oh, for the olden days when all we had were world wars, famine, epidemics, depression, and hard times.

Perhaps the truth is that life has always been subject to danger and serious problems, yet the human race has endured and evolved. In spite of all the ways it could have been wiped out, it has lasted. People survive; they conquer adversity and they thrive. Each day we can choose how to survive, what to conquer, and how we want to thrive.

Each morning as I get ready to meet the day, I think about a few things I am grateful for and how they impact my life. Sometimes they are serious, sometimes they're just fun, and sometimes they make me feel very grateful. There are always the obvious ones: good health, great friends, a wonderful family, and a deep faith; these are in my mind constantly and are part of my morning routine. Today I felt grateful for the following dozen things:

1. *Books.* What would I do without my books? They have taken me to distant lands; taught me about decorating, history, culture, feminism, and money; and enriched my career. They have delighted me with romance and humor and have jump-started my dreams.

2. *Starbucks.* On a cold day, a hot decaf mocha with skim milk warms me throughout, all the way from my tummy to my soul. All is right with the world when I sip that mocha given to me by a cheery young person. It works the same way on a hot day, when I have the same drink with ice.

3. *TiVo.* Television is still an important part of my life. I use it to keep current on the news, and I TiVo my favorite shows and watch them when it's convenient. It's like having a few friends to know that some of my favorite people will be in my life on a regular basis. It's sort of like a one-way friendship. The shows give me news, comfort, humor, and pleasure when it's time for me to pick one of them to watch.

4. *Diversity.* Finally, our culture is growing and accepting and supporting people's differences. We are developing an understanding of people's different sexual orientations and different races; we are taking more interest in older people and are working with people who have disabilities. I am hopeful that we will continue to learn all we can about one another and about each person's needs and special value. People today seem more accepting when values clash, and they are able to tolerate one another's differences. This gives me hope for the future.

5. *The recognition of fundamentalism as fanaticism.* Obviously, there are still people who feel justified hurting other people in the name of their political and religious values, but those numbers are diminishing. Rude and cynical comments are being recognized for what they are. Tolerance, understanding, and goodness are slowly gaining ground.

6. *Movies.* Movies have taken me to most countries, inside institutions and politics, right to the middle of family life, close to the animal world, and into history. I have been involved in complex mysteries, on medical journeys, and in space. I have lived in the old west, through the world wars, and in prehistoric times. How could I have visited these areas and eras without movies? They have enriched my life beyond measure.

7. *Airplanes.* My work and my public speaking have taken me to every state in the United States and to many countries. To have traveled this much by any other means of transportation would have been impossible. After I actually went around the world by ship, a journey of three months, my awareness of the speed and efficiency of air travel was heightened. Shipboard life was incredibly wonderful, but airplanes make so much possible in a much shorter period. My life would have been very different without air travel.

8. *New Zealand.* Walking the streets of Christchurch, New Zealand, made me feel the most hopeful I have ever felt about our planet. Flowers, gardens, beauty, clean water, friendly people, a clean environment, great food, reasonable prices, and little pollution were all around me. My thought was "Maybe this is what heaven is like." It was unforgettable. For a long time I said, "If my family and friends would move there, I would move tomorrow." When I left New Zealand, I felt hope for New Zealanders, and for the world that some unspoiled places are still with us. This left me permanently inspired. It left me wanting and willing to work for a little more New Zealand in my surroundings.

9. *Good friends.* Being open to new friends as well as cherishing old friends has given me a full and rich life. At one time, I could barely maintain the friendships I had, let alone try to make new friendships. Yet I found out that making new friends is a little like being a mother. A mother can always find more room in her heart for a new baby. Similarly, we can always find time for a new friend. We simply have to become a little more clever. Maybe we can have potlucks, or maybe we can find different ways to be with friends. One friend goes to the movies with me, another on vacations with me, another goes shopping, another is a phone or e-mail friend, and another is the one I can call in the middle of the night.

One of my newest friends has become one of my best friends. I would be sad if I hadn't made the time to get to know her. There is so much goodness in the human soul, and connecting with as many friends as possible is important to me. Whether I am happy, sad, excited, energetic, or stressed out, a visit with a good friend makes me feel better.

10. *Salt lamps.* My daughter gave me a salt lamp a couple of years

ago. It's made of pure salt and gives off a bit of a glow. Putting it in my office made a difference; it was both inspiring and relaxing. It reminded me of the permanency of salt and of the creativity of the person who made it into a lamp, and it offers me comfort. The advertising says that rock salt is now increasingly being used as a therapeutic source, and research has discovered its beneficial effects on the mind, body, and spirit. Salt is a naturally occurring mineral and a rich source of negative ions. It has three fundamental functions: preserving, cleansing, and healing. I, a healer, know that healing is happening in my house. My partner, the scientist, says, "They're pretty." Who knows for sure?

Besides the salt lamp in my office, I have two others, in my living room and my den. They burn 24/7. When I wake up in the middle of the night and come into one of those rooms, the glow feels safe and comforting.

11. *Faith.* At a hard time in my life, someone gave me a sign that said. "I am not afraid of tomorrow, for I have seen yesterday and I love today." All of us have had adversity in our lives, yet I am writing this book and you are reading it. That gives me great hope that we all want to give our best and connect with others who give their best. Together, maybe we can help make this world a better place.

12. *Pizza.* A thin-crust, hot bubbly pizza on a cold windy night, eaten in front of the fireplace with a good rented movie playing, is a great pleasure. However, the humble pizza is much more than that. It ties couples together with a bottle of wine as they unwind from a busy day. It's the standard take-out fare when teams of people are working on a project. There has been much written about the White House pizza runs. It ties grandparents together with their grandchildren when the

grandparents are too tired to cook. When our grandchildren are at our house, we order several large ones and put them in plastic bags, and the grandkids think we are cool because we provide cold pizza for breakfast. Pizza and wine, pizza and beer, pizza and hot cheese bread, pizza and chicken wings— pizza goes with everything.

These are the dozen reasons that I feel great about my world today. Tomorrow I will find another dozen, and the next day a dozen more. There is a choice every day. The choice of being depressed and discouraged is not for me. I have faith in the future.

Take time to sit down and list your own twelve reasons to have faith in the future.

fifty-one

The Difference Between Religion and Spirituality

Explore daily the will of God.

—CARL JUNG

RELIGION IS A BELIEF SYSTEM and the worshiping of God in a specific organized fashion. Religious beliefs are built on certain philosophies and codes.

Spirituality pertains to the soul. It is the energy of the spirit and brings about a sacred connection to yourself, to other people, and to the world. It is to live with the spirit of love and caring. Being spiritual is a never-ending commitment to what is good in this life and an openness to the situations and possibilities that present themselves.

To be religious, one has to follow the code or commandments that are spelled out in each religion. To be spiritual is to continually seek ways to bring goodness and kindness into our lives, our families, our connections, and the world.

Religion tends to be exclusive and includes only those who adopt a certain set of principles. Spirituality tends to be more inclusive. These are two somewhat different journeys. You can be spiritual without being religious, and you can be religious without being spiritual.

There is a great deal of information available on different religions. You will find houses of worship, books, and groups that will teach about the many different religions. The rest of this chapter, however, will address the elusive subject of spirituality.

The journey inward is not just for clergy, saints, and mystical people. Each of us has a part to play in this life; we are cocreators with some force in shaping our destiny. What is this source of energy? The classic movie *Star Wars* referred to the Force. The book *The Secret* by Rhonda Byrne hints at the power of goodness. Millions of alcoholics and other recovering and transforming people refer to a Higher Power as their inspiration. It may be that each of us is a cluster of energy cells, empowered to cocreate, to work with a Source or Higher Power to make meaning out of a world in need of love, support, change, and spiritual transformation.

From time to time, we all experience complete and total helplessness, and we are reminded of our powerlessness. A relationship ends, an illness strikes, an accident happens. Yet we survive. We do so because our strength and connection with a source pulls us through, reminding us that we are not alone. It is a reminder of our faith and our spirituality. Our faith is the thread we hang on to when our lives are falling apart.

Each of us, in his or her own way, knows what it is like at those moments when someone says, "I am here for you," "I understand," or "I care about you." When we hear those words, it's like coming out of a fog. For a moment, we know that we will survive and that someone will be with us through the journey of survival.

That is the Spirit, our Higher Power, the Source. It's like the wind blowing through us, taking away the pretense, games, and phoniness in life. We feel vulnerable and real. We feel connection. Dag Hammarskjöld, one of my masters, wrote, "The longest journey is the journey inward, for he who has chosen his destiny has started upon his quest for the source of his being."

The life of spirituality is not for the weakhearted. It involves venturing into unfamiliar territory. It is for those who cannot bear to live another moment in the world of racism, sexism, domination, and arrogance. It leads us to choose friends, family, and situations that are infused with acceptance, kindness, and a committed desire to bring fairness and justice to all people. It does not allow for judgment, cruelty, or selfishness. It forces us to be gentle and giving in all areas of our lives.

We are each like a note of music. One's understanding of one's personal journey provides a clear note of music. Then when your note and my note come together, they make a kind of music. There is harmony; we can live in harmony with ourselves and one another.

This is the chorus of all who are spiritual. We become cocreators with the universe, and that's the only dance there is. We become enlightened. Enlightenment is the result of seeking meaning in one's life. Enlightened people have a twofold existence. They conscientiously perform their work in the world, and they live immersed in spiritual inner peace.

We hear people talk about the bad shape the world is in, the young people with few values, the old disgruntled and disillusioned people, the danger behind every bush, the corrupt business and politics that aren't working. Too many people are unhappy and dissatisfied with their lives.

Perhaps it's not all the outside pressures and situations that are causing such inner strife, however. It may be that the soul is restless and will keep us disgruntled and restless until we are fulfilled. The journey inward to find fulfillment may be the biggest trip anyone can take. For many people, the path to fulfillment and serenity can be found simply by choosing to be fair and kind in all their dealings. Caring about the right things becomes a kind of spirituality in itself.

Many people ask, "How do I know if I am on a spiritual path or journey?" One of the ways to tell is to see how your life is going. You know you are on the right path when you align yourself with your Source. Things shouldn't consistently be hard. They should flow. Things will be easier and you will find that they come together when you are on the right path. If there is too much consistent struggle, you just might be on the wrong track.

Inner peace is yours for the asking. Do not waste time over past hurts and disappointment, and let go of resentments. Stay away from toxic people and toxic situations. That means staying away from people and situations that make you feel bad. You don't need them in your life. Pay attention to people who make you feel good. Cherish these people and learn from them. The restless place inside you will start to lead you to people and places that enrich you. Make the necessary changes. Your soul and your space inside will fill up with purpose and meaning.

There are so many ways to learn about spirituality. Here are some ideas:

- Jewish tradition says that when a person is singing but cannot lift his voice, if another person comes and sings along, the first one will be able to lift his voice. That is the secret of the bond between spirits.
- The psychologist William James said, "We and God have business with each other through the spirit, and in opening ourselves to God and each other, our deepest destiny is fulfilled."
- The Talmud says, "Man will hereafter be called to account for depriving himself of all the good things the world has to offer."
- Jesus Christ said, "The Kingdom of God is within you."

There have been countless sermons and rituals and people making sacrifices. Yet they are meaningless gestures and hollow noise if we do not make an attempt to understand and care about one another. This is especially true for people who are different from us.

You have probably heard people talk about the God-hole. This is the vague internal restlessness that many people feel. Never fear! That hole can be filled with satisfaction, inner peace, and joy. If you keep striving to understand your life, keep loving those in your path, and continue to be open to new experiences, there will be no spiritual stagnation.

Pay attention to all the lessons you are learning, and keep caring about others. The restless space inside will fill as you continue your journey. This space is there until each of us fills it with a calling and a purpose.

A calling is a deep sense that your very being is being called to do something. That feeling of being called comes to me when I feel ready to write a book, schedule a family reunion, take a special trip, pursue a dream, or do something special for someone else. It is something specific that is demanding our attention. These are spiritual stirrings and give us a clue about something we need to do. It is as though this moment is the perfect teacher at this time.

You owe it to yourself to find pockets of tranquility in your busy world. Make a quiet space in your home, be it a room or a corner. Furnish it with a good chair, favorite books, candles, rocks, or flowers. In my corner, I take a pad of yellow sticky notes and write down names of people I want to wish well and pray for, then I place them on the table near my chair. Spending a bit of time in this sacred place brings great serenity.

Find something to smile about each day and say a small prayer. My frequent prayer is the following:

> God grant me the serenity to accept the things I cannot change, the courage to change the things I can. And the wisdom to know the difference.

Today I offer myself to you, dear God in everything I think, say, or do.

Please take care of my partner, my children, their partners, and my grandchildren.

Then I add a special prayer for all the family and friends who need comfort.

This time of being calm and peaceful, free from disturbance or agitation, brings me serenity, tranquility, and a sense of deep spirituality. To me, that's all there is.

Visit several churches, synagogues, or other places of worship to see what you feel connected to and what brings you peace and comfort.

fifty-two

What Does *Spiritual Transformation* Mean?

> *I am only one, but still I am one.*
> *I cannot do everything, but still I can do something.*
> *I will not refuse to do something I can.*
>
> —HELEN KELLER

> *We pave the way for those who will come after us.*
>
> —HELENE LERNER-ROBBINS

TRANSFORMATION IS A SPECIAL WORD. It is different from *change.* Change is external; it has to do with outside behavior. Transformation occurs inside; it has to do with a shift in our consciousness. It always has the following components:

1. We hold a basic belief.
2. We receive some new information.
3. We feel conflict between the new information and the belief.
4. We enter a time of struggle.
5. We come out of the struggle with new decisions, new directions, and new energy.

6. We take action.
7. We integrate the new belief with our basic belief.
8. We now have more beliefs, and they are part of us.

The journey through transformation starts when we are experiencing some sort of chaos and are facing an important problem. Something in life is not working, and we are struggling. It might have to do with family life, work, relationships, health, politics, or beliefs. We feel a sense of loneliness that others might not understand. We may also feel overwhelmed. Actually, these moments are really opportunities in disguise. My mentor Virginia Satir used to tell me, "Sharon, in every situation, there is an opportunity and a handicap."

Most of us want to run away from struggle or possible pain. Yet pain has much to teach us. There is something very profound in a painful experience that will teach us something. Just stay with the experience and learn something from it. Do not run away. Pema Chödrön, an American-born Buddhist nun who is one of the most influential voices in contemporary spirituality, tells us, "This very moment is the perfect teacher."

One thing I've learned to ask, especially in difficult situations, is this: "What is here to teach me?" When we are in struggle or pain, it is important to open up, not shut down. Once we admit our struggles, we can become aware of our possibilities.

The next stage of transformation is commitment. As we grope our way through our overwhelming thoughts and feelings, we have a new opportunity to commit ourselves to whatever the universe has in store for us. We are willing to face whatever anger, fear, and uncertainty our circumstances may bring. We decide to stop being stuck and find a new way to move on. We begin to look around for possibility.

The next stage of transformation is becoming faithful to ourselves. We decide to trust our inner selves, our guts, and our intuition, and go forward. One of my very favorite mentors, theologian Anthony Padavano, says that there is a great deal of difference among loss, change, and transformation. Loss is a step backward, change is an opportunity, and transformation is a step forward. All involve the fact that someone has to give up something.

Loss is natural. We lose our youth, some friends, some dreams, and eventually our loved ones. We cannot hold on to all that we have encountered in our lives.

Change is also natural. We change from an infant to a child, from a child to an adult, and from an adult to an elderly person. Every change requires a redefinition of ourselves. We can go inside and pull out our best resources for this journey. We are always surrendering. There is always a bit of pain when we change or lose something.

Transformation, however, involves a conscious and bold decision to change. It has nothing to do with time or age. It has everything to do with having values and yearnings on which we must act. We embrace life, we look for meaning, and when we find something meaningful, we embrace it and redefine ourselves one more time.

We might change jobs, end a relationship, begin a relationship, heal a hurt, support someone, give part of ourselves to help someone else, move to a new location, find a new interest, or forgive someone. Who knows what we might be asked to do? It could be risky, scary, and different. Nevertheless, we do it because we know we need to do it.

We become faithful to ourselves. Rolling up our sleeves and paying attention to our lives is more likely to help us find serenity, peace, and wisdom than any workshop, book, or guru. We become our authentic selves when we go deep inside and find our passion and our bliss.

Some of the following words are from my mentor Anthony Padavano. The truly faithful person is not the one who does what he or she has been told to do, but the one who does what he or she must do. The truly faithful person is not the one who remains committed to his or her first commitments, but rather the one who remains committed to life energy at all cost.

Listening to this calling is not always easy, and there are often losses and grief. When we experience hurt and abandonment, we learn about insecurity. This reality often coaxes us into a life of mediocrity. This is precisely when a person of faith says, "No, I will set the past aside and follow my dreams." The stakes are high, but the victory belongs to the brave.

Transforming people believe the following:

- We all need to make this world a better place.
- Experience life with focus; do not just drift through it.
- Information without action leads to frustration and depression.
- Life is a wonderful, exciting journey.
- When we are extremely busy and scattered, it is hard to know ourselves or to be close to anyone else.
- When we go after what we want with goodness and intensity, we get most of what we want. Transformation to wholeness comes from the inside out.
- Transformation takes place when knowledge and experience meet.
- When we have undergone a transformation, we experience the world in a different way.
- Instead of waiting for someone to send you flowers, plant a garden.
- Making choices and transforming is not for the weak.
- If we do not make choices, we become drained with indecision and unable to enjoy all the good things in life.
- With true friends, giving and taking comes naturally and without pressure.

Maya Angelou says, "When you know better, you do better."

When you decide that transformation is important to you, new behaviors become easier. Those behaviors include the following:

1. Resisting conformity instead of conforming to what others want
2. Inventing new lifestyles instead of acting like victims
3. Becoming leaders instead of followers
4. Defining goals instead of drifting from one thing to another
5. Responding to oneself instead of reacting to others
6. Living in the present instead of the past or the future
7. Accepting pain as part of life instead of avoiding possible pain
8. Finding balance instead of being fragmented or overwhelmed
9. Becoming direct and simple instead of complicated
10. Making decisions instead of being indecisive and confused
11. Feeling a sense of freedom instead of being stuck
12. Feeling one's inner power instead of feeling powerless

Transformation is such an exciting and delectable experience that it is like a smorgasbord of possibilities and options. You know what happens if you eat too much at the great-looking smorgasbord. We can become gluttons in our eagerness to sample all the options. That is especially true if we are hungry for spirituality—or worse yet, famished. Then we find it hard to resist the temptation of the feast.

Mystics and sages warn about the spiritual glutton, the transformation junkie, and the never-ending search for the right guru. Even as you keep your head in the clouds, keep your hands reaching out and both feet planted firmly on the ground.

Transforming people pay their bills, do their grocery shopping, arrange family reunions, care for children, and often have quiet evenings at home. Transforming people go for medical checkups, have their eyes examined, disagree with their spouses, and take care of their pets.

Transforming people live in the world as well as in a joyful and peaceful state, knowing why they do so. They are ordinary people who find meaning in an extraordinary approach to life.

The spiritual quest is such an individual journey that it is difficult to recommend books as guides for it. Each person comes with a history, a tradition, and a belief system that is extremely personal. I have decided to list the books that have helped me on my journey and then encourage you to search for books that will be important and meaningful to you. The books listed below are some of my favorites, and I offer them to you for the purpose of sharing.

Additional Reading

Cerutti, Edwina. *Olga Worrall: Mystic with the Healing Hands.* New York: Harper & Row, 1975.

Cole-Whittaker, Terry. *Love and Power in a World Without Limits: A Woman's Guide to the Goddess Within.* New York: HarperCollins, 1989.

Dalai Lama, The. *The Compassionate Life.* Somerville, MA: Wisdom Publications, 2003.

Kasl, Charlotte Davis. *Finding Joy: 101 Ways to Free Your Spirit and Dance with Life.* New York: Harper, 1994.

Moore, Thomas. *Care of the Soul: A Guide for Cultivating Depth and Sacredness in Everyday Life.* New York: Harper, 1994.

Russell A. J. *God Calling: The Power of Love and Joy That Restores Faith and Serenity in Our Troubled World.* New York: Jove Books, 2006.

PART TEN:

MAKING THE WORLD A BETTER PLACE

People have made at least a start on
discovering the meaning of human life
when they plant shade trees under which
they know full well they will never sit.

—*D. Elton Trueblood*

fifty-three

Bringing Peace to Our World

We can say "Yes" to life even at its darkest moments
if we see it as part of the greater reality.

—MARY NORTON GORDON

RECENTLY I SAW A POSTER that said, "Peace begins with me." If people were brought up in peaceful families, they would learn how to be peaceful individuals, and we would all live in a peaceful world. Some families do have harmony, safety, and inner peace, but many families do not. We live in a culture that is broken and shattered in countless ways.

Our challenge as women at this time in history is to disrupt the old processes that have brought us to this crisis. We can learn to treasure and accept the miracle that each of us is, then learn to accept that miracle in others. We need to end isolation and do our part to bring about a critical mass that fosters inner peace, family peace, community peace, and ultimately world peace.

 Over the years, I have received many letters and e-mails from women of all ages who want to connect through my books. Some live as far away as New Zealand, Europe, Australia, Guatemala, South America, Ireland, and Scotland. It is from their communications to me that the idea for this book was born.

Paul Pearsall, in his book, *The Heart's Code,* tells us that the heart has a powerful energy. He reminds us that as we venture into space, create global communication, and invent all sorts of technical tools, we run the risk of losing our hearts. Nevertheless, in the many ways that women gather and connect, we can increase the power of heart energy.

Calling All Women: From Competition to Connection has been written to give you a jump-start on seeing things from another perspective and having a heart-to-heart communication. I hope that the information I have shared will soothe your heart and your soul. My life has been blessed with people with whom I can have heart-to-heart connections.

There are a few premises that I have made in this book. They are the following:

- Women have strong heart and soul connections.
- Women would rather support one another than compete with one another.
- Women know compassion, trust, adequacy, and loyalty in themselves and recognize it in others.
- Women have the power to change and improve their lives at every stage of life.
- Women find answers to problems because they look for and are open to solutions.
- Women know the value of mentors and teachers and are not threatened by advice.

In her masterful book *The Artist's Way,* Julie Cameron suggests that we form "creative clusters." She believes in a peer-run collective process. She speaks of sacred circles, of being midwives to each other, and of success occurring in clusters. She tells us that twelve-step groups seem to work well for people who are recovering *from* something and that creative clusters show us how to move *toward* something. That something could be doing our part to heal broken people, families, and cultures.

Another wonderful mentor for me, through her words, is Dr. Jean Shinoda Bolen. She writes extensively about women's circles. She believes that through friendship, networking, and the Internet, women in circles can create a movement of ideas, support, and action. These groups would cross national, racial, and religious boundaries.

It is my belief that when a woman is connected to her spiritual core and has a set of beliefs that she is willing to live for, she becomes active in ensuring the spiritual, psychological, emotional, and intellectual health and well-being of all people. She finds and uses her voice to speak her truth. She is aware that she is only one person, but she is a whole person and she can join with other whole women, and each voice will add more to the first. Together they can create support and strength that will lead to hope and change.

Being a woman is not always easy, but it is always rewarding. As women find their voices and activate their passion, great things can happen. A grassroots movement of inspired women listening and supporting one another can bring peace to this fractured and broken world. This is what a heart-to-heart connection is all about.

Additional Readings

Bolen, Jean Shinoda. *The Millionth Circle: How to Change Ourselves and the World—the Essential Guide to Women's Circles.* Berkeley, CA: Conari Press, 1999.

_____. *Urgent Message from Mother: Gather the Women, Save the World.* Berkeley, CA: Conari Press, 2008.

Cameron, Julia. *The Artist's Way.* New York: J. P. Tarcher, 2002.

Pearsall, Paul. *The Heart's Code: Tapping the Wisdom and Power of Our Heart Energy.* New York: Broadway Books, 1999.

fifty-four

Heart-to-Heart Connection Groups

*The opportunity for connection presents itself
every time you meet a human being.*

—JANE WYMAN

MY LIFE HAS BEEN so enriched by the circles of women in which I
have participated. These circles have been in my life at every age and
stage and have included the following:

- Little girls
- High school friends
- Daughters of alcoholics
- Young mothers
- Spiritual retreat participants
- Tap dancers
- Grandmothers
- "Same time next year" friends
- Spa retreat friends
- Those who gather to support each other's losses
- Those who gather to share in loving kindness

Each circle gave to me and I gave to it. Together we take action to make this world a better place. Many of the circles continue in my life, and I am certain that there will be others. I offer you the suggestion to celebrate your womanhood in circles that you are already part of and to form your own heart-to-heart connection group.

A heart-to-heart connection group is invested in the support and strength of its members. The support and strength that the members need will vary. Each group and each meeting will determine the content of the meeting.

There are no leaders and very little structure. These meetings can take place in members' homes, the workplace, churches, synagogues, or any place you choose. The group decides how often to meet and where. What is important is that each woman is committed to giving and receiving.

During each sharing session, the following pattern is introduced to aid discussion:

- What is on my mind today?
- What I need from the group is . . .
- What can I give the group is . . .
- What I am grateful for today is . . .
- What I can offer the world to make it a better place today is . . .

Then sharing takes place. If the members wish to do so, they can close each meeting with the following prayer:

> May I know that all that concerns me and that I fear is powerless to hurt me.
> May I know there is a Higher Power and that peace is possible.
> May I be a link in the chain of love and support.

I truly hope that this book has encouraged and inspired you. Seize the moment and make every minute count. Live life fully.

To receive a free monthly newsletter, contact
www.sharonwcruse.com

To reach Sharon, contact either the website or
sharonwcruse@gmail.com